VIEW FROM

VIEW FROM A LOW BOUGH

BARRIE CROWLEY

ALLEN & UNWIN

Copyright © Barrie Crowley 1997

All rights reserved. No part of this book may be reproduced or transmitted in any form or by any means, electronic or mechanical, including photocopying, recording or by any information storage and retrieval system, without prior permission in writing from the publisher.

First published in 1997
This edition 1997
Allen & Unwin
9 Atchison Street
St Leonards NSW 2065
Australia
Phone: (61 2) 9901 4088
Fax: (61 2) 9906 2218
E-mail: frontdesk@allen-unwin.com.au
Web: http://www.allen-unwin.com.au

National Library of Australia
Cataloguing-in-Publication entry:

Crowley, Barrie, 1949– .
 View from a low bough.

 ISBN 1 86448 779 8.

 1. Crowley, Barrie, 1949– . 2. Vietnamese Conflict, 1961–1975
 —Personal narratives, Australian. 3. Soldiers—Australia—Biography.
 I. Title.

959.7043394

Set in 12/12.5 pt Bembo and Garamond by DOCUPRO, Sydney
Printed and bound by Australian Print Group, Maryborough

Cover design by Liz Seymour

10 9 8 7 6 5 4 3 2 1

AUTHOR'S NOTE

One morning I was idly observing Shane Maxwell, a young man with whom I worked, trying to master a new inkjet printer so that he could demonstrate it to a client. He looked up at me.

'Barrie, when you were in Vietnam did you see much real action?'

'Yeah, a fair bit.'

'Do you have any dreams?'

'Yes . . . one.'

Hence this book.

PREFACE

YOU'RE THE CURIOUS TYPE, ARE YOU? Don't tell me you didn't read the book first. I'm a reader, and I've never been guilty of reading a preface before reading the book. What sane person would?

A preface is supposed to be an introduction, a lead-in to the book itself, but because hardly anyone ever reads it first it's usually the place to put cunning disclaimers against possible libel suits, or to crap on about how the book would never have been completed without Led Zeppelin's greatest hits constantly playing in the background. Libel's not of concern to me, and my choice of music's my own business.

I thought, by way of a change, I'd tell you a bit about myself, and a bit about the process that produced this book. If you're not a writer it may interest you.

One morning I sat on the back of a truck with Dave and Pete and some of the other blokes, watching the Dat go past for the last time, and I said: 'There's a story in all this, and one day I'm gunna write it!' Knowing looks were exchanged among those present, of course.

And that should have been an end to it. I merged into normal society, tried to fit in, failed. But that's nothing new.

I don't know that I would ever have gotten this book down except that a young man once asked me a question in just the right way, and I felt compelled to answer it, in a way he could understand.

I found it impossible to write reality by night and observe insanity by day, so I quit my job and learnt how to write. Somehow Sandy paid the bills. Somehow our children learnt to go without. We learnt to ignore the muttered slander from the narrow-minded idiots in our community. We learnt to live separate lives—me in the Pink Room most nights, typing out text I'd mulled over while keeping house during the day; Sandy and our children keeping their own company.

I learnt to live with the constant doubt that awoke me each morning, undermining me, and confronting me with: 'Where's your story? People won't want to read this! Get into the real world for Christ's sake!' The other reminders—the middle-of-the-night jolts—I'd learnt to accept as part of life's experience many years before.

To ensure that I wasn't simply cracking up I called in John Weiland to act as my reader. I've known John since I first got out of the Army. The only thing we have in common is that we liked each other from the moment we first met, and never found cause to change that view. Well, that and all the other contingencies which make up a friendship. I saw very little of John—he was seldom near my home—but I mailed him the chapters as they rolled off the printer.

He posted them back to me, with comments and questions scribbled in the margins: 'You're sending me to sleep.' 'Tighten up!' 'This passage bores the arse off me!' 'I know I asked for detail but . . .' Now and again I'd get 'Good description.' 'Tell me more about this event, there's a gap. It confuses the reader.'

Finally, his part done, he steered me to a publisher. The right one as it turned out—if integrity is still a virtue, that is. Ian Bowring is his name. Ian assured me he was interested, kept in contact, passed my draft around, seemed in no great rush to do much else. I fiddled with my manuscript. It beat painting walls and fixing leaking taps.

Then Ian called for the final manuscript, to be sent to an external editor, Devon Mills. I had no say in the appointment.

Devon did his job. He dragged me bodily out of my pulpit, and asked—no, demanded—that I be both more fluent and more economical in what I said. The heartless bastard ripped a diagonal line through pages that to me were more than worthy, unhesitatingly tore living people and events that I cared about from my dwindling stack of precious pages, intent on one goal only—delivering only the best to you. I acknowledge his contribution unequivocally.

It has been a long, crazy, often taxing journey, not entirely what I thought it would be. But if I've helped to create an environment in which you feel that you can tell your own story, in your own way, without worrying about offending the prevailing view, my guess is we've both taken a step forward.

Whichever way it goes, look out for me. I'll be looking out for you.

Barrie Crowley

Chapter 1

WHO LET YOU IN HERE? WHO ARE YOU? Who? Forget it! It's OK, you can stay, just slow down. Pull up a chair, smoke if you want. I do. How do you like it? My room. My Pink Room I call it. Pink carpet, pink curtains, pink chair—yours is anyway. Beige computer and work bench, blondwood desk with the map of the world dating back to when a bunch of countries were called the Belgian Congo. That might be an antique. We're going to go somewhere very like that place.

Pink Room is also a metaphor, but it's not important yet. Forget I said it. It's not exclusively my room, we all use it; I just get to use it most. The others have other things to do. So have I—the housework, the meals, the shopping, the washing, which everyone says aren't done well enough or often enough. Slovenly bastards—the kids at least. They reckon they're environmentally aware. Could have fooled me! Still, they have the attitude, I guess that's a start. My wife, Sandy, works to support us. I should be out there grafting too; we're just scraping by, measured against today's standards. Mind you, I'm not just sitting on my arse, I do flit in and out. But I'm trying to get something down, something important that happened in my youth. A book? Dead right. You're quick, but I'll adjust to that.

I'm not crazy. Once I was, crazy just like you, I know the difference now, and I'm sane. But it's a battle: kids at those dreadful ages whatever they might be; a wife who is very supportive but quite possibly doesn't like me as much sane. Being crazy pays better. But she is coming to terms with what I am as her studies progress and she earns her degree. Between the lot of them I'm hanging in there defiant. I know what I'm doing.

So let me tell you a story. There'll be a few laughs, some thrills, and where possible some uninterrupted views—plus a few political prompts and supporting observations along the way.

Having established where I'm coming from, I'm going back now to the day I went insane. And then back to the beginning. This is a story about the organisation of human society as I saw it at its worst. It took place in Vietnam, obviously, because that's where I saw it. People have seen worse, no doubt about that, but it bears looking at properly, in perspective. The perspective is mine, and is called a view from a low bough. So they can sue me, the cunts! It'll just make me rich, and benefit a few old friends too.

You don't like the use of the word cunt? Perhaps you don't know its meaning. It is the only word which perfectly describes a person who asks only 'What's in it for me?'. It has no gender, it is not a sex organ. Get used to the term. We're in the army now, we don't talk bullshit.

Seen it all before? No, you haven't. You've seen media coverage, read academic books, loony books, and watched movies made by wankers with bucks on their minds. Much of it is true, but it doesn't get you anywhere, doesn't give you anything you can hold on to—to take with you into the future. And it should! Because being what we are—a very unstable, stubborn, stupid species—war is always with us, even when we believe life is peaceful, ordered, ruled by leaders with compassionate vision. What's different about my story? Simple. You are coming with me.

Still here! Relentless bastard aren't you. Or maybe just bored with life. But I'm not here to entertain you, get that straight. You're here to see, then go away and think.

We're in another room, my barrack room in Australia. It's late July 1970. This room's grey, with blotchy drab grey vinyl tiles, the type that hospitals, post offices, high schools, you name it, used to have before we went private. Hard-wearing.

Blondwood two-door head-height wardrobes partially separate the room, giving some privacy to four army beds: grey-painted tubular steel, salmon-brown blankets with a green dragstripe down the guts. Don't sneer, it breaks the monotony. The windows are legal but lightless, also curtainless.

That'll do for the room. Hang on . . . a steel desk each, a steel chair. Want to see the shithouse? Nah. It's not that kind of book. Not yet.

I'm sitting on my bed in civvies and I'm packed. No regrets, I'm out! I've asked the cunts enough times. Three years flushed down the shithouse. Eighteen months' intensive training, thirteen months' active service in Vietnam, five months' toy soldiering at the end of it. If I want to stay in I have to adopt the public servant mentality—become an arse-kissing, time-serving robot. No thanks.

I'm sitting on my bed looking at the wall, waiting for Dave to turn up, when I go insane. It's a good room for doing that in. The occupant in the far bed's already well away. Bex fiend, married sort of, pisshead, brick-red face. Self-control coiled on a hairtrigger. I know who's fucking his wife. Bed next to him's vacant—little wonder. Bed next to me's usually vacant too. Occupied by a married man who'd also been over with us, but in another company again. He's holding his ground, but always looking to duck. Hope he holds out, he's a good type. Neither of them served in my company and I don't know them, don't have to. It's all the same story—just didn't share my particular pain; had enough of their own.

Sitting here, I'm going back to Vietnam. In my mind. Glad you're coming back with me. I won't misguide you, I know the way.

But first, a bit more about your guide. I went to fourteen possibly quite good schools in my youth. I only had eleven years in which to view them and they covered two States, Victoria and Western Australia. My Mum always said Dad had some Bedouin in him, but that was bullshit. He had a lot of fresh Pommy in him; I heard it at school. And he was sometimes gullible; I worked that out for myself. He was a brilliant man in many ways, but we're here to talk about me. I didn't have it as bad as my parents—most of my circle were Aussies. But have you ever been the new kid fourteen times? Try it, you won't like it. And, anyway, my friends' parents looked to me every time something got broken or nits hit the school. First-generation Australians I'm describing, direct descendants of Poms for the most part. It wasn't my fault I understood the questions at school, and got a few answers right.

I can't say I ever really felt included, not fully. And of course I wanted to be—who wouldn't? This country could be paradise. Vietnam was on, it was late '66 and a pretty popular little war at that time. I made a conscious decision to go, against only my natural inclinations, well suppressed. I didn't enlist till '67, too young at 17. You know how it is: you get a set in your mind at 17; at 18 you still haven't outgrown it. I wanted to earn my place in this country in absolute terms, so no one could kick me out.

What do I look like? You superficial bastard! OK. Ash blond hair; big 'knowledge' bump on the back of the head, vacant at this time. Slightly horsey face; I blame Dad for that. Weak jaw; fair-sized hooter turned up—it's sagged downward over time but it's still not my best feature. I blame these flaws on Mum, though they look good on her. Big blue eyes; these and the hair are my best features. I've still got 'em all but I wear glasses a lot now and the lights in the hair have died. Er . . . slim build, five foot six—but if you want to stay my friend don't call me a shortarse. I'd take it from friends but they've never said it.

Right, let's recall the voyage, and a few other events. The trip isn't that hard once you've got this far. Just be packed. Be back in camp by such and such an hour for rollcall. We reckon you're ready, tomorrow we go.

Two that I know of didn't. They hadn't died, or been judged unfit, and they were both from my old and future company. One was a Frenchman. Looked good; bit ugly for my taste but then I'm not a woman. When we got issued ill-assorted clothing and equipment we all looked like bags of shit. Not him! Looked like a Legionnaire leaning arrogantly against a captured tank. The epitome of a warrior. Had a fucking huge hooter, what some would describe as proud. It was the only feature of this cunt that warranted the description. What he wasn't going to do to those 'little yella slant-eyes . . .', you've met the type.

I first heard of Dien Bien Phu from him. The Frenchman didn't turn up of course, then or later on. No guts.

The other was a true disappointment. He was Maltese. The only gutless wonder of that nationality I've ever met. When I was a kid they took a fair bit of shit at school, but they went down fucking hard. This one was snaggle-toothed, shortish, stocky and bandy-legged. Pretty ugly and you didn't need to be a woman to judge that. Loved pistols. Belonged to a small-arms club and had a bagful of exotic handguns that let him blast his rocks off at set targets. Nobody liked him much—inoffensive enough, just not much to him. *Someone* must have liked him, though. He was married with a kid before enlisting as a Reg. He let his silly little dreamworld take over his waking hours, so when he snapped out of it he was a day away from the real thing. He missed the boat, but no hard feelings. He really shouldn't have gone in any case. Not up to it.

That's the first two over the rails, both Regs—that means regular soldiers, volunteers signed on for three- or six-year terms. At camp we milled around, we queued, we queried, we waited. Then we were all eventually summoned, bundled on to open trucks, and driven off down the road. With freshly hungry eyes I had one last glimpse of all the beauty around us, saw with a thrill the oak-canopied lane in which my very first basement flat nestled, and absorbed one last time the placid, fertile rural scenes. Then our descent into Adelaide began. I saw the warm welcoming motel where Carol and I had each started our quest for love. Now we were in the bustling city streets. In the back of the open truck you had to adapt to being ogled like hogs off to the abattoir. I didn't blame the people, it's a normal human reaction, but a few waves and a smile would have been appreciated.

By the time I hit the wharf most of the battalion were on board, except for a few with wives or lovers still hanging off them. Lucky bastards! I got straight on board with no waiting.

Who's Carol? That made you blush. Caught you out, didn't I. I'm taking you off to a war, and you're wondering about a name. I wish I could answer your question. But this is what I know about her that you should know.

It was at a nightclub in Adelaide, one of the new ones for the young. Live band, warehouse interior, mysterious scaffolds

and corridors leading to cavernous rooms with coupling shapes, the red flare of a joint. Robbie and Dennis were prowling among the crowd for women. I wanted a drink. Robbie had said it was licensed, but it wasn't. I stood looking at the band. It wasn't bad, but most of the dancers were having problems. Red light, blue light reflected off the tinfoil-draped walls. A tall black-haired beauty stepped into my field of vision.
'Hello. You've been drinking.'
'Yes, up until I got here.'
'Any left?'
'No. And Robbie said it was licensed.'
'I had friends like that. Here are yours now. They look like they want you to go.'
'Lunchtime next Thursday, the Botanic. Know it?'
She did.

Carol was taller than me in knee-length boots. Her legs were her best feature once you tore your gaze away from her face. I made next Thursday noon with fifteen minutes to spare, grey slanting rain driving me on. But she's not turning up, I thought. I knew the publican, Bill; he's dead now, I'd guess. Bill was then sixty-odd, bald, stooped and gangly. Played 'The Unicorn' unashamedly on the jukebox at night when he was pissed. Used to prance around the lounge like a big fairy—dancing, he called it. He claimed there was a message in the song. A crazy bastard, but I was glad to see him this day.

'You look like you need a beer, Barrie. She's in there.' Across grey-maroon Axminster, through heavy leadglass doors, and she *was* there, where Bill had placed her. I was out of my depth—she must have been blind when she'd approached me. Carol sat by the fire at a table set for two, dressed in an olive tweed suit and flat-heeled leather shoes, as only a grown woman can make alluring. Grey light highlighted her fine, even features, and the fire glowed in her auburn hair and hazel eyes. 'Another one of those and you choose the wine, Bill,' I said.

I sat down. 'I'm in the army, 19, you know the rest.'
'I'm 26, a model until three years ago, mannequin. Catwalk mostly, some photographic. I work for a law firm now, more stable.'

I drank her in; couldn't believe I might attract a woman like Carol. Lunch went unnoticed. She described past affairs with older men. I bragged. Then we were tumbling into the back seat of a cab, Bill shielding us against gusting rain with his umbrella. We held each other close until the cab dropped us for a moment into reality. Past prying motel staff hovering in Reception, then triumphantly back into our own secret time.

The MPs—the military police—prised the last of the women clear and we shoved off. On the HMAS *Sydney*. Not a bad sort of a boat if you're an off-duty officer. Officers had a beautiful messroom just below the flight deck at the stern. Huge windows right across, their own balcony to view where they'd just been. Fucking typical. Must have been a pig to handle! The accommodation for the rest of us wasn't much, though I wasn't too badly off. Intelligence Section, which is a designation not a compliment, were at least up on deck. For peasants that was well placed. We had air, we had our own outdoor railed section, we had views. We had our upstairs neighbour's arse pointed at us as we slept, but there was about a foot of freeboard and a thickness of canvas hammock between your nose and a nasty surprise from the tenant above.

I'm not complaining but the other poor bastards should have been suing. For most of them, the accommodation meant being down in the bowels of the ship or sleeping on the steel flight-lifts lowered into the holds. Flight-lifts were probably the worst because they were used during the day for PT and weapon handling, that sort of frolic. Not only did you have to pack your gear up each morning but you were a known face, and known faces get most of the shit jobs. We worked our passage, doing crappy cleaning jobs and training. No one with bastardry on their mind had enough intelligence to find our little hideaway—that's why we were called Intelligence Section, I suppose.

The cooks were at their spiteful best throughout the trip. They all liked to think they were comedians. Served pork chops the first night. They assumed that it made soldiers crook, but it was the best meal we had all trip. Just a pity they hadn't kept the pig alive to eat the rest of the slop they served up.

Our messroom was right in the guts of the ship. Ventilation and insulation had obviously been rubbed off at the drawing-board stage when this tub was slapped together. You could smell every dish cooked for the last month as you sweated, rolled and tried to eat a meal no better than the last thirty. We had to be there perhaps twenty minutes a day, if you were fit enough and hungry enough, and then only in three short bursts. The cooking staff were there a lot longer and it showed in the end product. They generally tend to be cranky bastards and not good at personal public relations, but they have my respect, if not my affection. Beer was rationed to one large can a night and there were few fights over the spares. We were staying alert.

A friendly sailor offered a few of us a look at the engine rooms. I had to see that. It had been my Dad's lot in the Second World War, only he was mainly on submarines. Here it was a strange environment: huge engines and massive spinning shafts and counterweights, gauges, conduits, all colour coded. Dim puddles of light, a constant throb, oil smells and silent, attentive watchers in overalls. Better than being a cook but not my scene. The *Sydney* was an aircraft carrier from which they'd removed the planes, and they were probably wearing out its last refit using it as a troop carrier. It may have boasted a meritorious past for all I know but it didn't reveal it in comfort.

The trip offered a few views for those who had access to them and the time and inclination to see them. Crossing the Bight there were views of moody skies, a dark blue sea and one night a well-lit cargo ship passing close by. Then a view of Fremantle harbour, where we docked briefly. Those with relatives there could get off for a last farewell. A number of wives and lovers had flown in from all over the country just for that.

My Mum, Dad and elder sister Lyn, with her two daughters, one barely toddling, were there. And David my young brother, then aged four and a great surprise to all except Mum, the cunning bitch. They'd all come down to see me off. The press published a photo of us, Mum, Lyn and me. It came out well, a bit contrived, the usual public interest slant. If I ever had a best it was captured in that photo. I've lost it somewhere along the way, and the cutting. There was only the dock to roam, no kiosk or anything open, which had Mum browned off—she needed tea like I need a smoke. It was a welcome interlude but no great wrench when we steamed off again.

We lumbered up the west coast, a few dolphins said hello now and again, then the call went out: 'Last chance to glimpse Australia'. I didn't figure on it being my last, but I went to have a look anyway. I was on the port side, and followed my mob through the shortcut—which was all steel ladders, bulkheads, dead ends and no-go areas—so by the time we surfaced back where we started from we were probably passing Timor! Missed the glimpse at any rate. Saw Krakatoa real close; half the mountain missing on our side, very eerie to see. It was big, but the devastation which it once caused I couldn't imagine coming from this little islet. Don't fuck with nature, it's bigger than it looks.

The *Sydney* passed through the Doldrums. We entered the area from an emerald sea under a brilliant blue sky. The Doldrums was a golden, glowing wonderland enticing you to step off the boat and walk away into it. As we travelled through the stillness it changed: the sky dimmed to copper, the sea paled to a milky beige. At dusk flying-fish broke the surface in flocks of thousands and flew, silver wings driving them on endless mirrored flight a metre above the flat, still sea.

We moved through a fleet of junks gliding between shimmering flights of fish. Large, hand-hewn, wood-planked craft straight out of the seventeenth century. Dun-coloured sails fanned out by bamboo battens waiting in hope of a breeze, kerosene lanterns glowing softly over castle sterns and up above on the rigging. Dark figures manning long heavy wooden tillers, burbling motors inching them away from our course. Night fell and the lights from the lanterns slowly winked from view.

Carol and I spent several frenetic nights together, crammed into my heavy program of exercises and duties. Whenever I could get away Carol found the time, somehow. Passion carried the days. Then Robbie and Dennis invited us to a group picnic. Anne and Andrea came, their teenaged girlfriends. Carol sat on my lap in the car, excited about the day ahead. Now and again she burst into song, operatic airs. I'd not heard that from her before. She was not well received, and by day's end my thoughts on Carol were exactly as my friends intended. I last saw Carol through the rear window of the car, waving me goodbye.

The love of my life? No. The end of the story is this: there was no end. I didn't see it through, didn't get beyond the passion, the ego, the pride. Didn't learn all that I could have from simply being with her. But I learnt all I needed about outsider interference in my life. Since then every fuckup in my life's been of my own making.

Our RAN escort now arrived—a destroyer, a supply ship, and a frigate, I was told. We refuelled at sea. Some thought that interesting. The sailors rigged a bosun's chair between the *Sydney* and one of the escorts and swung a few people back and forth, but no one looked like falling off except Tizzy, momentarily. And I wasn't likely to get a go, so who cares. Most days the rifle companies just blew shit out of large, weighted weather balloons bobbing in our wake. It was comforting to know they were honing already excellent skills. My little band were supposedly there for our ability to observe and interpret, not our ability to kill, so we didn't get a look in. Suited me. There was also piped music on board. I don't know what source it came from—bland unmemorable crud for the most part except for one song, a minor classic from the *Sergeant Pepper*'s album, transformed by Joe Cocker. Still kicks me in the guts whenever I hear it.

Vung Tau dead ahead! A wide blue sunlit bay, skirted by a ribbon of silver sandy beach with a dark unnatural patch notched into its centre. I'd climbed on to the flight deck to watch the port emerge. It was a scrap heap. Native junks similar to those I'd seen earlier were bullying aside small open-decked fishing boats of similar age, even a few ancient wicker coracles. That was lovely to see. The water tobacco-brown and glinting, the air full of strange smells and the raucous voices of the native crews as they recognised or bollocked one another. But the main harbour was a real shock. None of the sleek fighting vessels I'd expected, just a clutch of narrow-gutted old US destroyers, real ugly bastards, chained together. The rest was a very dreary scene. Every type of work vessel—dredgers, sweepers, cablelayers, coastal supply ships—all naked guts, rust and neglect, like a million tonnes of floating scrap-processing depots.

We came in close enough to see the crews. Hard to tell if they were US Navy or pressganged merchant crews. They were all guts, crazy, shifty eyes, funny haircuts, three-day growths and filthy clothing. For the snappy dressers, greasy singlets were all the go that day. Every breed and crossbreed in the world, it seemed. They were probably fine sailors but I can only judge by what I saw.

Bert gave me a yell to say an enterprising RP had stumbled on to our hideout and we were being organised for landing, so that was it, I'd seen enough anyway. The RP, Hipslops, was there sorting us out. He's worth a comment. Mid-thirties, tubby, stocky, medium height, greying curly hair, flushed saggy hound-dog face. Didn't look tough but he'd been in the job for years, so he must have been able to handle mugs. One good copper. The only RP I ever had time for. Never tried to be your friend, just friendly. Looked after us all.

RPs? Regimental Policemen. Soldiers recruited from within an army unit to deal with day-to-day misdemeanours and run the unit lockup for short-term minor offenders. Different to MPs, but normally out of the same stable—Coward out of Cunning.

We disembarked in landing barges, just like D-Day. Great views—grey steel deck underfoot, high grey steel walls, high grey steel drawbridge for'ard. Crane your neck to snapping point and you could see the landing barge crowd controller up on the bridge with the skipper. Lucky bastard. We could look up at the sky, but brilliant blue is just blue after a while and the sun's glare made me sneeze. A dull thump and a scrape, engines throttled back from reverse roar to idle. We're there. Get the fucking ramp down! Let's have a look!

Expecting something else? What we see is a shale and stone beach like much of England's coast, only sunny. Treacherous underfoot weighed down as we are—have to keep our eyes directly in front. Only when solid sand is under us can we look up and see Vietnam for what it is. Vung Tau is like a huge open warehouse. We're awaited on the red gravel road by identical trucks and personnel to those who started us off on our journey. We clamber on and start to weave our way through countless rows of tarpaulined, crated and containered equipment blanketed with red dust.

Nothing's moving that I can see—a trio of our Service Corps standing round an empty truck having a fag, shirtless, wearing berets. Not everyone changes for war.

Security is provided more by just being there than by real fortifications. A high, open-strand barbed wire perimeter fence, a high tower or two with an armed MP in it. As though mere occupation is enough, like a low-security prison. We pass through the gates of the docks finally, watched by two or three MPs, and into the city proper. At this point I notice the city's surrounding low green mountains, the communications networks threaded through them. International communications for Australia and the US.

Crowds fill the streets and alleys, servicemen in work greens or fawn dress uniform. The locals are in either military dress, Western-style but locally tailored cheap synthetics, or traditional clothes. The latter are mostly women. Conical straw hats here and there. Working men, porters and labourers are everywhere, dressed in ragged shorts and singlets. Traffic is busy but not lethal, people still walk in reasonable safety. Here and there police control the flow. They are armed, white-shirted, in smart military garb. Knee-length riding boots, khaki jodhpurs and Sam Browne belts, sparkling black, peaked hats. Arrogant and belligerent to my eyes. They are called White Mice. Why, I don't know, it doesn't describe their attitude. Near their stations stand sandbagged guard posts. Within them wait the relieving shift.

The city centre's streets are paved, mainly bitumised, and lit with electric street-lighting. Neon signs hang over the more prosperous and aggressive business houses. The suburbs generally have no lighting. As we reach the suburbs it is not as crowded as the milling throng of the centre, nor as cosmopolitan, military. It's essentially local people. Here our truck virtually fills the rutted dirt road. Trees line some of these streets but form a canopy over them, giving the air a diffused green-gold glow. Shafts of sparkling dust-filled light strike the chrome of the little motorbikes the street boys or cowboys mainly ride, or glance off the tin shacks crowded together in the poorest areas. From these streets narrow chalk-white dusty lanes branch off. Down these, single dwellings made of concrete blocks with iron roofs jam together—most in the process of collapsing in on each other.

Apart from motorbikes, transport seems to be mainly large scooters adapted to three wheels, with canopied seats fitted at the rear. On the flat they could carry incredible loads if the passengers stayed amenable. Lambro's, we call them. Ramshackle buses in some areas. Pushbikes too. People on foot; most locals seem to use that mode. Heavy-haulage trucks bear names like Alaskan Freight Co. on their sides and tailgates, or are military, wearing big white stars on the cab doors. Handcarts or scooterised deathtraps with trays behind serve the locals' haulage needs.

There are shops here, general stores selling food or household goods, hand tools, pots and pans; one or two basic cafes. Intersections often have service stations on one corner. Ramshackle affairs, one tall skinny hand-cranked pump with the glass measure tank on top. A few one-litre wine or soda bottles filled with red petrol and stoppered with rag are stacked on a trestle, ready for the bikes and carts which have small capacities. Handy if anyone you hate goes by.

We stop at an intersection for traffic, and a group of young children, mainly boys aged from seven to perhaps twelve, wave and call. Grinning like kids hiding a trick. We've been waved to a fair bit this far, in response to our communicators on the truck.

'Hey, look at that beauty! Hey! Sweetheart! What's yer name?'

'Got a sister?'

'Shit, look at all the gold in that old geezer's mouth. How're ya feelin' Granddad? Remember me? I'm your favourite nephew.'

From the front row of the group of kids a little boy of about eight gave us the 'V' sign as his older friends had taught him to do. A big fat RP on our truck heaved himself up off his arse and hurled a green apple at the boy's head. It atomised on impact, tracing a silver aura about his small cheeky face. It struck so fast and hard it didn't stagger the child. He looked wide-eyed at us, stunned, frozen. Some of the soldiers on the truck thought it humorous, but not many. As the truck ground off again, I saw the boy begin to cry quietly. Not as a child would but as a person who had encountered a great shock in life. Or perhaps it is my own emotions I am describing; it is now many years past.

As we clear the city's outskirts and head north, a different country emerges. The first part of the journey we travel through wetlands, large expanses of delta tributaries. The road is a continuous stretch of causeways and embankments, roughly paved and capable of carrying two lanes of traffic at a pinch.

One or two lengthy steel and concrete bridges sit over larger tributaries. The banks of the waterways are charcoal-coloured mud with here and there a copse of mangrove. Water swirls past the grey spikes of dead copses. Unnavigable or not, the fishermen are out in little clinker-built punts, fishing with small weighted cast nets. Some boats are motorised, most are rowed from the stern by the tiller oar, or they're poled. The fishermen don't fish close to the road. I found out later that soldiers going back to the Dat from a binge sometimes skipped a few rounds about them for a laugh.

As the wetlands recede we enter the ricefields for the first time. Harvest appears nearly completed. Golden stubble greying in the small paddies forms an unbroken carpet stretching beyond the horizon. Deeply rutted ox cart roads crisscross the fields. Gravity and manpower flood them, I know, but there is little activity today.

We pass through three small villages which straddle the road, their approaches signalled by copses of tall slender palm trees. Here the villages seem shanty towns. Tin shacks mixed with more authentic native structures—thatch-roofed, woven fibre-walled houses with glassless windows, wooden doors. Long-fronded palm trees provide shade. Kids are everywhere, old people squatting in huddles smoking, chewing betel nut and spitting. Women carrying baskets of shopping or washing, young men idling in the shadier spots, not as many of them. The odd pig, a buffalo sticking its snout through a wicker enclosure, ducks in thousands wherever water lies. A couple of shabby general stores cum fast food and beer cafes, a government building in more than one of the villages, small two-roomed buildings of rendered brick and tile. Lounging in the shade an armed ARVN sentry or two in tightly-tailored green uniforms, scarlet neckerchiefs, bright shoulder badges. I'd better tell you what ARVN stands for. Army of the Republic of Vietnam. More accurately, South Vietnamese government soldiers—the Republic didn't recognise the government of North Vietnam.

Parked nearby on the dusty street there's a drab green jeep with a mounted 30 cal. machine gun and a radio whip aerial. A coffin shop, displaying its glossy red and black wares, silver glints.

Almost at Nui Dat. Time to reflect on what we've seen.

To me, it falls roughly into line with the odd glimpse I'd seen on TV at home. The small pictures from the screen can be superimposed over the reality, much like ten or twelve pieces of a jigsaw laid over the complete 500-piece master. It takes time to complete a jigsaw, there are no shortcuts, mysteries unfold piece by piece. Be patient and you may see it all.

High wire fence coming up, several armed figures in jungle green uniforms. Diggers? Yep! Guarding barbed wire gates. Pull up. 'Make safe weapons!' Magazine off, cock, lock, check chamber, it's empty, release cocking handle, squeeze trigger to uncock, push extracted round back in mag, mag back on, safety on. Safe. That's weapon condition at the Dat.

No real warning that you're approaching Nui Dat. All of a sudden you're there. Nui Dat is our Task Force Headquarters, our field operations centre, from which all our active ground operations are launched. I'm sure you've heard of it, perhaps seen photos of it. At ground level it's almost invisible. Trees, bit of barbed wire—is that a tent among those rubber trees? Is that a shed through there? Nui Dat has been constructed to repel ground attack because our enemy are ground troops. It is superb. Nui Dat is huge—take a vehicle if you want to see the lot, but to really see it you still have to walk miles, poke around beyond where the roads stop. From the air you see the long red scar of the airstrip. It will take small-winged aircraft that the day-trippers from Saigon use: our military, political, intelligence and specialist support people. Choppers of course. And Caribous, which are big twin-engined people and equipment movers, capacity around thirty armed soldiers. They're fun, climb almost vertically, land like a kite, steep and quick. Aircraft seldom stay at the Dat overnight, though, they're susceptible to mortar attack by the VC, the Viet Cong—they're the revolutionary army of South Vietnam; communist, and our official enemy. Attacks aren't common, but our RAAF take few chances. A small, dusty, steel and fibro air terminal squats beside the airstrip. Elsewhere a small control tower, with a limp windsock coated in powdery red dust (to tell if it is wet or dry perhaps?). It isn't often windy here.

The roads pass the entrances to various unit base areas. Small signs occasionally give traffic warnings, others proclaim the unit's identity. Through the rubber trees a glimpse of khaki four-man tents covered in red dust, surrounded by a thick wall of sandbags to chest height. Some duckboarding for the rain, a shed here, a store building there. A few Diggers walking around shirtless, floppy giggle hat, rifle at the trail. That's the Dat. Attack this place at night or day, you're really in the shit. Who's who? Where are the targets that count? They're all here: artillery, armour, engineers, infantry (three battalions of those), medics, cooks, transport, stores, Task Force command—but where? Have to beat the lot of us to find out. Hang on! No you won't! Look, up on the hill, there's a Jolly Roger flying. Guess who! SAS. Well, that's alright then. They'll cope, you can be sure.

The truck pulls up. We're at BHQ, Battalion Headquarters. Let's get the gear off, find a tent, and crash. What's that smell? At Vung Tau it is exhaust fumes and adrenalin. In the villages it is warm hay, buffalo shit, spices, washing, warm damp earth. And babble. Here it is musty, slightly sweet-smelling, rotting canvas. And silence.

It is 20 November 1968, a hot sunny Wednesday. We are here for a year with Nine Battalion, an Australian infantry unit. Our mission: to seek out and destroy the enemy. Tough fucking luck! Tomorrow we get down to business.

CHAPTER 2

THE BUSINESS IS WARFARE. Warfare, or war if you prefer, is a fundamental component of what we term humanity or the human condition. At its best, and there is a best, war manifests itself in deliberate open debate, concluding in an enlightened, effective policy which we all abide by. You can call this process by another name. Democracy. It is a system of government that has never been properly tested. At its worst, and there is always a worst side, war manifests itself in the form of simple butchery. Know the true meaning of the term? You have put the muzzle of your weapon to a person's head and squeezed the trigger. You watch the brain tissue, bone fragments, fluid and blood spurt out and drop onto the soil at your feet. The body falls onto this mess, jerking and kicking until life is extinguished. And *you* don't know who you have killed, or why. Step back from the mist of blood still floating in the sunlight around you. Step way back. You fire a cannon from miles away, same thing; press a button, give an order over the phone from another country, go about your business without a care while your countrymen engage in war, same thing. But the further back you stand the less likely you are to accept how evil your own actions are. That's why every bastard's an expert on war. I've stood mesmerised while shopkeepers, academics, politicians, advertising people, media people explain to me why Vietnam was not 'won'.

But on 21 November 1968 I held no particular opinion, I was just taking it moment by moment.

My tent seems OK and there are no sandbags around it, so we must be way in from the outer perimeter. I'm in Intelligence Section as an interpreter and for whatever else I can do. The intelligence officer is a bit of a fruitcake but interesting to watch, no harm there. The troops are a real mixed bag and humorous bastards, if you enjoy the company of neurotics. The CO—the commanding officer—doesn't figure. He beats a path from his office to the mess, down to see the brigadier; his offsiders hang around the phone. The regimental sergeant major is an admin type, looks like he finally got dragged overseas again and is too old to want any more trouble. The RPs are the odious presence, they infest this place.

I'm taking a break from the arduous journey, working up to getting my bearings. Ducked the first night patrol, all the curious and the slow got sprung for that. Graham went, must have been caught asleep in his bed. Came back the next morning saying they'd had a contact, the ambush got sprung. A knowing grin spread all over his face. I wore the lying bastard down with Bert's help. Someone had got jumpy at being outside the wire late at night and had fired off a burst in panic. An RP had had an AD. Big charge over here, an AD. It showed you were a fuckhead. I'll explain later. I knew it was an RP. If it had been a Digger those arseholes would have charged him, no risk. Anyway, things are looking good. Boozer must open soon. I can handle this place.

But I was already being prised out of my safe little nest and only I didn't know it.

Back to the first line of philosophy. The business *is* war, but I'm not going to get away with an easy ride, I'm going down to the simple butchery end—the fucking *front*. I didn't know the field interpreter posted to my old company was going to dive under his bed and piss all over the floorboards as soon as he put his bag down. He cried, he babbled, said he was definitely too ill to stay. Had the strength of a python to resist when people tried getting him out from under the bed. He didn't want to look around, he already knew he didn't like this place. I believe the boys had to carry him to the homeward-bound plane. Cunning bastard: 48 hours all up and he's off, with the medal Canberra is so fond of in his grasp. And fluent in Russian too. I'd better shut up, he's probably a bureau chief for ASIS now.

That little comedy, on its own, might not have affected me. But a second intrepid field interpreter affected more than a few of us. This man, and I use the term reservedly, ran around at night naked—apelike tattooed body, apelike possibly tattooed slug dangling. Trying to suck soldiers' cocks. Had a mouth like a bear trap. Leapt out of bushes and trees, no fucking around, no pretence of persuasion. Shit, he was an ugly bastard, a Polish neanderthal. He also got a medal I suppose, and a flight home. He had to *walk* to the plane—he couldn't very well claim he was too weak to stand.

I'd better explain about medals. We got two over here. One from our own government, a big silver gong with two-tone blue, yellow and red striped ribbon. You qualified after staying 24 hours in Vietnam. Fly over, book into your hotel, see the sights, attend a meeting, hit the piss, fuck a whore and fly out next day, picking up your gong. Many officers on noncombatant missions were flown over from Canberra on one pretext or another to dress up their left breast a bit. It's been seen as a typical act of administrative peacocks preening their appearance. This view is wrong. It was an arrogant act which devalued a symbol of sacrifice for your country. The other medal was an imitation gold star with an enamel depiction of Vietnam on it, and a green and white striped ribbon. The Republic gave you that after six months' service 'in country'. Six months was a full tour for US troops. You got these medals whether you sat in an office in Saigon or scouted for an infantry platoon. There was no distinction, not in medal terms anyway. Many office workers who have them imply there was no other distinction either. They're not all lying—most of them wouldn't have a clue what war was. Many differing stories lie behind ordinary service medals. Some of them you will see along the way.

That's the quitters and shitters, so far. Let's go and meet some of the real people.

I am trying to recall the details. Two rifle companies had required replacement interpreters. Bert was posted to one of them but Graham was just here for a look around. His term was up soon, and he only knew about ten words of Vietnamese anyway. So I got the second company. God knows why, there were other options. Anyway, I was off. Never got to find the boozer. Without Bert and Graham, it wasn't going to be much fun at BHQ. And I could give the RPs the flick—they never went where I was going—and I knew the company, my old one. Or thought I did. There were only about thirty troops in the company when I left it to attend the Vietnamese course at language school. In my absence the ranks had been swelled by 13-week recruits who had done Corps training (infantry training, in other words) during the battalion exercises prior to shipping here. This mob I had to see, which was a good attitude to have given that I had no choice anyway.

I turned up at the company's lines on the perimeter wire next day feeling a bit gloomy. Didn't know a soul. All had changed. OC was the same but he was a bit out of my social range. 'Duntroon' was very much about, full of bounce. Staff I vaguely remembered, ugly old bastard, and Tizzy was still 2IC. The company clerk was still the same fat lazy bastard. Hello . . . new CSM. Big, mean-looking prick. Better play it cool with that one. I fucked up right from the start, though—I breathed.

Who are these people? They're the company power base. I'll introduce you. OC. Stands for 'officer commanding', in this case commanding officer of the company. Rank, major. Average height, arse always stuck out because he stooped, small blue eyes, crinkly grey-brown hair, buck-teeth with glints of gold in them. Carried his Armalite rifle absently, as though he was about to put it down. Looked about 60 for most of the tour but was about 36. Family man. Knock-kneed. It took Pete, the medic, ages to pick up on that. OC had a resonant baritone voice which he kept quiet. When he spoke to you he looked straight at you. Once in the field someone commented on the book I was reading—'Any good roots in it?' OC noticed the cover and discussed it briefly, mentioned others of similar standard and went on with his job. I judged him a cultured man, donnish even, but it usually only showed in his good manners to everyone. On the rare occasions he barked we did what he said, the same as we always did. His role? Leadership of the company—and judged by its conduct.

Regrettably, OC was also, weight-for-age, one of the fittest and most resilient soldiers in the Corps of Infantry. Consequently you needn't ask who came first to mind when a rifle company task requiring intensive scrub-bashing presented itself.

Then there was Duntroon, whom I've named after the prestigious academy that spawned him. OC on the other hand was a Portsea man, a perfectly sound school to have attended, but not if you planned to be a toffee-nosed prick, which Duntroon was. Duntroon bounced around quivering in anticipation of higher command. At this time he was a platoon commander. Most of the Diggers didn't let him worry them. It was just the way he'd been brought up. He was slightly taller than me but about the same weight. When I'd started with the company at the beginning of the year it was he and I who usually paired off for man-on-man exercises. He was no quitter. He looked like a hanging judge would as a young man. But more personable. Blond hair, college cut, high brow, long sharp hooter, striking blue eyes, pink complexion. Reminded me of a pixie. He struck me over time to be a young man whose breeding carried him through to where braver men mightn't venture. This was his one major flaw—the desire for recognition. It affected his decisions too much, and very often his attitude when reporting events. Ended up 2IC of the company.

Tizzy was the current second in command of the company. He was ex-British army, commissioned at Mons I believe. He was a captain, probably had been for years; he still wore the larger British pips on his shoulders. He may have been here on trial. About the same age as OC—looked like a Gurkha: short, squat, dark—and had a high-pitched British accent. He was widely acclaimed as an administration wizard, God alone knows why. We also had the laziest clerk in the Empire and the company records were a disgrace if my experiences were anything to go by. But Tizzy was a genuinely kind and caring man, who actually was a soldier, not an administrator. He was also a dickhead—he believed all soldiers were human beings.

His job is worth examining. He was responsible for base defence in the company's absence and support of the company in the field—including ammo, food and water, equipment, reinforcements, mail, what have you. He had a skeleton staff, a staff sergeant and a sergeant cook to assist. He got a gallop out in the field from time to time, not for long, just to keep him in touch. And if the OC was unfit or called away then it was down to him.

Next his offsider, Staff. A staff sergeant. Staff Daily. '*Fuck off!*' daily also comes to mind. He controlled the Q Store among other duties, perhaps food requisitioning and, I suspect, the beer supply. I doubt he'd trust that to others. He looked like a redfaced walrus. Might have been from all the piss he drank, but I doubt it. About five foot ten, a once massive physique now starting to dry out, knotted-cord veins propping up sagging wrinkled skin. Couple of tattoos, now just black-blue blotches. Grey walrus moustache and weary blue eyes above a great, puffy, wattled hooter. All his own teeth, well ground down. Must have knocked 60 over two years back. I heard he'd dropped from regimental sergeant major to make one more trip with his boys. I saw him once in dress uniform and his ribbons stunned me. Second World War, Korea, Malaya and Borneo. Was that a Military Medal? At least one MiD. Two and a half rows of ribbons. There was no boat he'd not been on. Hoary old bastard? Perhaps.

He took over control of our Q Store, which in material terms looked after all but food and ammunition. A bit of a comedown for him, a shopkeeper's role—but it didn't end there, not for Staff. He inherited his two store workers from the outgoing battalion because they hadn't served out their term of National Service. Queer as arseholes. How they ever got past induction had us all guessing. Zig and Zag. It was Staff's problem, he'd handle it. He did. He did nothing, told them to carry on, gave us the snake eyes if we looked like laughing in his store, which invariably meant 'NO!' to any requisition for two days. They sorted out their own problem. Zig re-enlisted because his time was up and Zag had four months to do and couldn't bear the thought of being parted. Then Zag threw a mental over a letter from home. Pete pissed him off for psychiatric evaluation rather than slap him, and the shrink said 'Son, you can go home'. That left Zig with his heroic gesture shoved up his arse and one hell of a lot of time to do, very much alone. He threatened to kill himself with a kitchen mop and Pete used the same approach with the same result.

Staff was now ready to run his Q Store, using Diggers in need of a break and a little peace of mind. Not many got a go, but someone's got to carry the gun. We missed Zig and Zag for a while—sort of homely having your own soapy unfold in your midst.

Later, when we were based for a while at another large military base, I bought a pair of baby ducklings to soften the atmosphere, but soon afterwards we returned to the Dat and other obligations took me away. I lumbered Staff with them. Who else would you trust? He was very gratified, not that he showed it, of course. They grew quickly and came to love him, enough to wander into his store and shit on the floorboards before nestling into the bundles of new socks. Zig and Zag he called them. They did well for a while but died bloodily one night on the grass between the boozer and the Q Store. Staff accused ferrets as being the murderers. Obviously it was the doing of some wild creature. I know it wasn't Staff. The look of regret I sensed was not one of guilt.

In the early days we had what we called Paludrine parades to ensure we took two different sized pills, Paludrine and Dapsone, each morning to combat malaria, and now and again we had skin inspections. The group I was with inspected each other, if we remembered—usually a verbal check. If your toes or your arse are burning, you're going to bitch, aren't you? One platoon commander paraded his men outside the Q Store in boots and towels, told them to drop the lot, then began to walk down each rank inspecting his naked troops. Staff was leaning against his verandah post, gazing into thin air. There was bugger all for him to do, he couldn't get many stores. No one would give him any. He focused in on the parade and after a moment or two joined it, trailing behind the lieutenant, looking vacuously over the troops. Suddenly he halted, squinted at our token well-slung warrior, marched inside the store, re-emerged with an issue boot, flung it at Horse in the front rank and said, 'Catch, son, you've been under-issued'. That was the last of those parades, and it illustrates how a true soldier thinks.

Staff only spent a week or so operationally out in the field with us, replacing CSM while he went on R&R. But he came out every time he could sneak on to the resupply chopper bringing in our food, ammo and mail, and new clothing if he had it. He'd have a look round, get the feel for what was needed so he could bring it out next time. Once we were out in open country, little shade, withering heat, no water to be found and none in our canteens. Resupply was denied. We were on the trail of a big, organised body of enemy pushing towards Saigon. Because of the open terrain we were expected to make rapid progress. We'd done that for days, and as we entered a scrubby, thinly treed area, Pritch, one of the gunners, a fucking huge bastard, suddenly chucked his gun into the scrub, pack and webbing after it, and charged into the treeline like a maniac. It took four of his section to ground him and they had a hell of a time keeping him down. From my position I could see bodies bucking and straining in the dust. Pete went straight over and helped sit on him to check him out. Pritch was bright pink, puffed up, dry skinned and demented. Others around me weren't looking too good.

Pete headed straight toward OC, looking hard, but he was already on the radio, trying again to explain our needs. We hid under what shade we could find, waiting for his next order. Within an hour a little two-man Bell chopper, all plastic bubble and skeletal frame, landed in the clearing beside us. Our battalion commander's popped in for one of his rare visits? Not this time. Out of it stumbled Staff, documents for OC in his teeth, company mail jammed under one sweaty armpit, two jerrycans of water clutched in each hand and one clamped between the cheeks of his arse. He and OC had outflanked the bastards back at base. Diggers took Staff's load and he went right through the company directing supply to the neediest, remembered it was rightly CSM's job halfway through and included him. Gave him the mail to hand out before the mob turned nasty. Pritch came good within an hour or so and we were able to go on. That was Staff. I knew him only slightly but I will never forget his actions—or his ugly mug.

Company sergeant major. Or CSM. This position is responsible for discipline within the ranks, some administration at the base, charges for misconduct, seemingly anything that involves work or grief for the common Digger. In the field much the same, with the added duties of controlling resupply, extraction of wounded and dead, and defence of Company Headquarters. Support Section came under CSM's control. His job was to die defending the OC. Some CSMs were utter cunts, but often that type never experienced war, too rat-cunning. Many were pricks. It's the sort of job that can make you go that way. Our CSM seemed to be a prick. Certainly when he and I mixed, we didn't. We were never destined to get on, I suspect because we shared some common values but were different physically, in age, personality and of course responsibilities.

He was a tall man, over six feet, big muscular bastard like a rugby front row. Just past 30 I'd say. Looked like a Yank—wore US-issue jungle greens and boots, crewcut hair. Square face, pug nose, strong jaw, hint of an overbite, pronounced when angry. Voice like a concrete mixer full of gravel and broken bricks but not loud, usually just above a whisper. He was truly gifted at knowing when people were thinking 'Fuck the book', and usually struck early, before it came down to a charge. He got on with those in his sphere of influence, from the OC down to his Support Section commander. Me, I was the pest, the fucking kid. In fairness, he usually warned me. Once he tried to charge me for falling asleep on radio picquet in the field. I didn't, I was daydreaming with five minutes to go by the watch we were using—but it turned out to be wrong. Mine was the shift that had to wake CHQ at 6 am. The first I knew, he'd kicked my boot as I lay (we all did) listening to the static and odd call signs coming faintly from the handpiece. 'Sleeping on picquet! You're on a charge!' Straight to OC, just climbing out of the bag and wondering what day it was. I heard OC say, 'Better give him the benefit of the doubt'. It made me feel good. CSM caught me back in camp once, snoring my head off about 10 am in the Nugget. That cost me a half day helping to lay a concrete path between the general office block and the company office.

I was by then a corporal and shouldn't have been involved. CSM reminded me that if I'd been acting like a corporal I *wouldn't* have been involved. Fair enough. Shit, he moved quietly when he was on the hunt! He could have caught me asleep on radio watch back at base more than once. Dave relieved me one night, woke me and said he'd had a gutful of my snoring, it kept him awake. He'd stayed longer at the boozer than I, staggered down the steps of the command bunker and slept, or tried to, on the ledge above the communication equipment I was supposed to be controlling. Never asleep in the field, though—exhausted or not we've all got to live.

Once, out in the field, we were waiting for orders to attack an enemy position and CSM stalked in among us, quietly warning us to be prepared to fix bayonets. No bastard laughed, so I told him that if that order came through my contract was torn up. The boys thought I was being funny and that made me laugh too. He looked at me drily and moved on without a word. The order was never issued. He had a very subtle sense of humour at the oddest of moments.

To me, one characteristic above all stood out about CSM. He was not a natural killer. He would kill on need, but not by choice. Once we were in a spontaneous ambush position, heard movement and dropped to the ground. Several enemy flickered audibly by, metres in front of us, screened from view by vegetation. I pointed and whispered, 'They're right here!'. He told me to 'Shut the fuck up and watch our rear!', as I should have been doing. A Support Section rifleman three up the line from us dropped one of the group; the rest got away. I know CSM chose not to fire. If the enemy had been aware of our position and attacked he would have fired. He was a complex man.

Let's have a quick look at the furniture shall we?

Mine is a very good tent. It is one of three, innermost from the perimeter wire, surrounded by banana trees and closest to the main internal road which goes past our company area. Dave had already considered the possibilities, but I hadn't met him yet. These three tents are separated from the rest of the company by a small service road which terminates at a topless, circular corrugated-iron incinerator about waist high and five metres across. You could burn a truck in it. My tent has a close view of it. Tracer and flares used to whine and erupt prettily out of it occasionally in the early days, courtesy of some twisted Diggers who were here before us. Banjo went to throw an old packing case in it one day and a flare ignited in his face. He didn't see the humour in it, and Banjo saw humour in almost any human endeavour. The rest of the company are tented close to the perimeter wire, under huge shady rubber trees, which is an added comfort, but there is no substitute for seclusion.

The company medic, the stretcher bearer, and the blowfly (company sanitary worker) live in the first of these three tents. It fronts onto the service road and within pissing distance of OC's tent, located just across the road from them. A minor zoning setback, to state the painfully obvious. Beside the medic's tent a narrow track branches off, leading up to the other two tents, one behind the other, well out of harm's way. Mine is the first of these.

All the tents are much the same. Inside the tents are floorboards elevated on spent howitzer shells, a naked electric light bulb, a couple of power points with twelve bakelite double adaptors piggybacked into them, metal cots canopied with green mozzie nets, sea chests shoved underneath. Also one or two grey metal lockers used as wardrobes or backdrops for *Playboy* centrefolds, and an improvised table of some description. Outside the tents there's a rickety packing-case washstand, a zinc tub for washing and shaving, with green plastic jerrycans for water stowed underneath.

These last two tents house Support Section, whose function is to defend CHQ in the field, control the company's arsenal, and help run night watch on CHQ's radio in the field, and down in the command bunker when back at base.

What's CHQ? Company Headquarters. OC, CSM, radio operator, interpreters (that's me and a Vietnamese national), medic and stretcher bearer. A sapper or two depending on how many bunker systems we expect to encounter. An artillery forward observer group which is usually two Diggers, an officer and a radio for calling in artillery support. Often a mortar forward observer, usually a sergeant. Plus Support Section and the OC's batman. Around twenty men all up.

Well, that's me settled. The mess is down the service road on the right, with the boozer, not yet open, just beyond it at the end of the road and Q Store to its left. Then an arc of platoons, tented and sandbagged, running around the wire back in my direction. On the opposite side of the service road from the mess there's a wooden, tin-roofed admin building with offices for OC and CSM and a recreation room with darts, pingpong and pool tables. The equipment's clapped out, but who wants to be playing outside the CSM's door? Those looking for work, that's who. Beyond that, linked by a concrete path I helped build, is the company Admin office, half building, half tent. That's where they make up the pay and fuck up the paperwork, if they can be bothered. Plenty of toilet blocks and shower blocks for everyone. It's enough. We'll have a better look around after the first real Op.

Griffo, Support Section Commander, put me in his tent, introduced me to Young Mick and shot off somewhere for the afternoon. Griffo impressed me as a pro, a bit officious but then he'd been in the service a while—had to wait for his hooks. My bed area didn't smell of a madman's urine, and no one's gear had encroached on my space so it appeared Griffo ran things pretty tight. Young Mick was a Nasho, good type, a bit quiet, seemed younger than me but was in fact several years older. He was a country boy from Victoria, had been in a government job since school, railways or some such, clerical. Tallish, lean, powerful limbs, crewcut, popeyed. Had a voice impediment that gave an elongated looping note to the middle of a word sometimes, but it wasn't a problem. He said bugger all usually. Good company if you liked to do all the talking. He'd already made close friends with platoonies and only shared our tent because that's where he was put. I unpacked, kept an eye out for any rank with a work detail on his mind, and read a book.

Next morning, after stand-to, Griffo and I were boiling up coffee in the dirt outside the tent, when a raucous voice cut through the air like a house brick. 'I luv's ya, fair dinkum, dinky di I do'—then some maniac tapdancing on a wooden pallet.

'What the fuck's that?'

'Ah, that's Dave back from Vungers. He came over with the advance party. Sent here and there for a few weeks to get him out the way.' (Vungers was Vung Tau, to us a place to get crazy drunk and also laid.)

'Why?'

'Came over as Duntroon's batman but it didn't work out. Got asked to clean the tent, clean the kit, that sort of shit, so Dave told him to take a course in self-reliance.'

'That's what a batman does.'

'Not Dave—but he likes to fly, and the advance party flies over.'

'Got it.' I peered around the fly of our tent and there outside the end tent was the craziest bastard I've ever had the privilege to call my friend. A Queenslander, of course. Tall, rangy, coordinated in a wild sort of way, with slightly protruding eyes. Dribbling toothpaste foam from a wide leer under a big busted hooter. He lifted his metal cup to his mouth, gargled like a drain, sprayed foamy water like a hydrant, then asked: 'Who the fuck are you?'

'Barrie Crowley.'

'And who *are* you?'

'Oh . . . yeah, the new interpreter.'

'Hope you're better company than the last cunt.'

He strode over, shook hands, bludged a share of our coffee and joined Griffo and me for a debrief.

'What did you find out?'

'I can get piss delivered out the back once a week. No limit, ice daily, but we might have to collect it ourselves now and again. I've got us a jeep, can we get fuel?'

'Nah.'

'OK, I'll swap it for fridges. Want one here?'

'Nah, better not . . . but the boozer could do with a big one.'

'OK. The Yanks go crazy for captured weapons, everyone wants to go home a hero. Good deals going if you know how and who. Spread the word.'

'What about Vungers?'

'All VC or crims. Couple of good knocking shops. The spirits are paint thinners, so stick to beer.'

Over time I found out that he'd grown up in country Queensland—Roma, St George, and places I'd never heard of. His Dad was a rural agent, wheeler-dealer type; it certainly showed in Dave. He'd worked as a youth in the justice system, administration of various sorts, mainly face-to-face stuff, Aboriginal welfare and the like. He was rooting his arse off in New Zealand (if he wasn't on the piss or gambling) when his ballot came up. I don't know if his *number* came up or not, but as he wasn't at home to register at the correct time he was in anyway. He told me once the best job he'd had in New Zealand was in a big commercial poultry concern, shovelling chicken shit down a chute in the floor. The second best job was holding the bag at the bottom of the chute to catch the shit. Got so much a bag. Did well.

'Why'd you quit?' I asked. 'Ran out of shit,' he said. Fair enough. Anyway, like most of his category, he came home when he was good and ready, turned up at the recruiting office and said, 'Here I am, you've got two years, make the best of it. I'm gunna.'

Dave collared me and we had a busy day ahead. Being Dave's friend was a lot of fun but he was an unpredictable bastard. I determined to be so close to Dave that what hurt me hurt him. I felt he needed someone to be responsible for and I liked his style. He was about 23 and married.

That day Young Mick, someone else and I spent scrounging polystyrene packaging to line metal sea trunks for beer chillers, finding wood for a card table and humping cartons of beer and blocks of ice through the banana trees. Dave directed, helped lift things, shifted his stuff, his cards, and his crown and anchor game into our tent, and the Golden Nugget was born. It had a beer garden behind under the trees, for nice weather or when big crowds turned up. The Nugget ran for seven or eight months until OC decided he'd put up with enough aggravation from us every night. He was a pretty tolerant man. The Nugget went the way of all over-indulgence, but the friendships stayed firm.

Next morning I met Pete, the medic. Six foot, solid, black hair, cheeky pugnacious face, level blue eyes under fine black brows which sometimes gave him a sinister look. He had a hint of Pommy accent, pushy sense of humour, often sardonic.

'Who's he?' He pointed bluntly at me while addressing Dave.

'New interpreter.'

'Don't give me any grief like the last weak cunt or . . .'

'Yeah, clamp it, we've covered that, Pete.'

'What's your name?'

'His name's Barrie, now what the fuck are you after?'

'Can't remember now. Every bastard's getting roped into work parties. Fuckin' CSM's on the loose again. I'm off, hang out at BHQ for a while. Give Chuck Baby the shits for a change (this was our battalion doctor, of sorts). Got any piss?'

'Got any money?'

'See ya tonight.' Pete merged into the bananas and was gone.

I hadn't said a word. But I knew who my next friend was to be.

Pete came from Elizabeth in South Australia, but that was about all I ever knew about his background. It was then a Pommy town, so he probably copped a fair amount of the same shit I'd encountered. Had a girlfriend, showed me the photo one time, didn't look much. It wasn't the looks, it was the mentality. Surly, bored, uncaring, to me not Pete's type, but he cared for her so I said something acceptable. Pete was the enigma in the group. He disclosed very little in conversation. He was talkative, but not a yarner or a bullshitter, he was an action man. Couldn't give a fuck about social position or formal authority, if you're a cunt you're a cunt and he made sure you knew it right off. He didn't discriminate when his help was needed, but everyone knew exactly where they stood with him because he issued constant reminders. A Reg of about 20, and the bravest man I've ever met.

The next few days were spent getting to know Support Section—not that I ever knew them well, their members came and went. I was fitted into the CP (command post) night radio watch roster and CSM began to recognise me enough to give me the odd job, nothing too odious. Beer at night was no problem. Dave ran things well, but I was still a bit lost. At last the boozer opened, limit of two cans a night supposedly, but it meant seeing the company in a social setting finally. I was relieved to see among the crowd of faces some I knew. Lenny was there, plus Banjo, Big Mick, Jock, Dusty, some others. Then I met Pigpen, Tank, Peaches, Woofer, and started to feel at home. Just as well: next evening we had our first official action.

We were to march as a battalion to a village, Anh something or other, and throw a cordon round it. It would then be searched for VC by a selected party. We trucked it to the outer perimeter of the Dat, then started to march off as dark descended. Why they bothered with the trucks is beyond me, as it took about two kilometres off a journey that seemed about twenty. We marched through the night in single file and reached our destination after midnight. Our company cordoned off an area of paddy fields, dry stubble at this time, spreading in an arc to a bridge over a stream. I drew the bridge watch with Pete, Dave and another. We were to guard it until morning, then check IDs and so on when the villagers were free to travel.

All that was a bit later and I needed a rest. Fifty per cent watch was ordered. Most laid out a groundsheet to lie on, with one member of each pair resting while the other stood-to (lying in a firing position, of course). I flopped back against the earth bund of the bridge. Forty-five degrees was enough, I didn't take my pack off. I chose the off-duty 50 per cent, ready or not. My pack kept my shoulders raised and my lolling head just touched the embankment, my eyes gazing at the stars. I felt a soft slapping at the back of my bare neck.

'Shit, what's that? Felt like a snake.'

'Probably a bit of stubble, Barrie,' Pete suggested.

I was now standing. Stubble, my arse! Then, from the paddy fields: 'Stop fidgeting!'

'I'm not.'

'Keep your fucking hands to yourself then!'

'What are you on about?'

'Shit, it's a snake.'

'Ooh, you've got one too?' This from Big Mick.

'Watch it, Tommy, I scared mine your way.'

'Keep the noise down, you cunts! Fuck, what was *that*?'

The field seethed with snakes. After ten minutes of butt stroking and stomping, things settled down, but many of the company didn't—they stayed on their feet. I certainly did.

There was a bang in the night. One of the villagers had stupidly tried to sprint through the cordon. Ran too predictably. Then nothing until dawn came. The villagers trundled by in their ox carts, some travelled in carts drawn by tiny little ponies, or shanked it with tools over their shoulder. We stopped many at random, checked their papers, for what I hadn't been briefed. None were endorsed 'I am VC, shoot me!'.

We dropped bits of biscuit over the bridge to the swarms of ducks swimming by underneath, then got trucked back. This load of bullshit was dignified by Task Force Headquarters as an Operation. Even had a name: King Hit One! War is hell.

Over the next few days we did some company exercises in areas outside the Dat, to limber up, find our place, get the feel of things. No trouble about, no mines or booby traps, none that we struck anyway. The only danger came from water buffaloes. They truly hated our smell. I didn't like it much either, but these unpredictable bastards took it to heart. On one of these trials we were walking through open farmland and one took a dislike to a gun group commander. Three tonnes of buffalo went for him. He sidestepped and the buffalo wheeled for another charge. He smacked it over the snout with his hat but that didn't bother it. It charged again and he sidestepped it again. The buffalo careered, straight on into a burst from Woofer's gun, dropping virtually headless to the ground.

'Listen!' Woofer addressed the company. 'These fucking things are deadly. Don't fuck around with them!'

Woofer, who by trade was a scout, not a gunner, had been in country some months already. We took his warning at face value. He didn't deal in bullshit. Crazy maybe, but no bullshit.

In fact, Woofer was an exceptional individual, and not at all easy to know. Stood about five foot nine, wrestler's frame, receding blond hair, strong, sensual, questioning face. His eyes were a piercing light blue, emitting searing grassroots intelligence. There was a tension, a physical, cynical aura about him. This man could give you the heebie jeebies. He came to us as a scout with a couple of personal kills listed to him already. He had been a psychiatric nurse, heavy cases, prior to his call-up, and I suspect he had been fast-tracked into Vietnam via the Reo—reinforcement—route. Some of these Reo's had only had a couple of months' Corps training before being flung into action. Woofer had already been in twelve months, a volunteer Nasho, but had spent much of that time cooling his heels in depots rather than receiving intensive training. We got Woofer from a battalion that had completed their tour. They'd passed him on because he had eight or nine months to go of his twelve. The name Woofer came from his habit of alerting unsuspecting enemy to their plight by calling 'woof woof' before shooting them. A curious trait, until you know that Woofer feared only one thing. Shooting the wrong man. He was an incredible forward scout. He used no second scout, whose job it is to relieve the forward scout when tired. Woofer teamed with his gunner, and did all the searching unsupported.

The forward scout is the bloodhound of the pack. He is the trailblazer who leads his unit to the enemy. He must be able to spot microscopic signs of human existence as he searches. A bent twig, a scuff mark on a track, a piece of paper among the dead leaves are signs that must be seen. Wilting vegetation, woodchips on the ground, a stump smeared with mud usually mean an enemy bunker system nearby. Scrub that imperceptibly thins at a certain point could very well be an enemy fire lane. Booby traps, land mines and concealed ambushes must be detected, or you bear the brunt of the consequences. Sometimes the scout uses secateurs to home in silently on enemy in thick country. There is no more mind-snapping job on earth that I am aware of.

I know of no other man who served in Vietnam as a forward scout unrelieved for more than fifteen consecutive months. When we rested, relatively speaking, at the Horseshoe fortress for a month, he detached himself to a special tracker group based at a village called Dat Do, not far from us—hardly a holiday. That kept him more than sharp until we all returned to Ops.

I'm off on people again now. Why? We're at the boozer. It is a very basic structure, timber-framed, clapboard and particle board, stud walls largely unlined internally. Bare concrete floor about twenty-five metres by ten overall. It is painted inside with dark green and bulldozer yellow gloss paint—whatever was available. Outside the door stands a wooden rack to leave our weapons against. This and the mess are the only places we park them; elsewhere they are always at hand. Through the door the servery is at the far end. It has a lockable metal shutter which hinges down at closing time—always a sad sight. Entry to the beer supply is through a stout, padlocked back door. Counter about three metres long, no bar stools but you can only prop the bar up on the rare slack night unless you want to fight off a brutally thirsty queue. The base boys, Q Store workers and clerks, man the bar, stock the two fridges and the ice chest. The bar divider is dressed up with captured weapons (AK47s, a few RPG rockets), Charlie Brown characters, some beer ads and a legitimate pub sign bearing the warning that drinking is forbidden to those under 21—then the legal drinking age in some States back home.

We don't observe that law.

Around the walls are long wooden trestle tables with unpainted bench seating. Above our heads billows a white parachute to break the monotony of the unlined roof. On the right wall, as you face the bar, is a door leading to a fenced outdoor area where we've held one or two barbecues. The boozer has been decorated over time by various predecessors. Our main enhancement is improved refrigeration; only the structure is provided by army funds. The boozer sells Australian canned beer, soft drinks, chips, peanuts, cigarettes, tobacco, razor blades and cans of sardines. Doesn't sound like much, I know, but it's surprising how common people can, just by their presence, transform it into something special. By being themselves, funnily enough. A place where mysteries unfold at ten cents a can. That's the boozer.

The sergeants and officers have a mess cum boozer behind our mess, well away from us. It's a big green canvas tent on a concrete pad. I rubbernecked in there one day. They had fold-up chairs and deal tables, a fridge or two. Depressing place. They are allowed to drink spirits, anything they think they can handle. We are allowed two cans of beer a day. I don't recall OC ever enforcing it.

Right. Got your bearings? Now . . . a few more people.

First, Big Mick. Six foot three or four, huge feet; his boots were custom made, there's not much call for that size. He was proud of that and also of his head, for obscure reasons known only to himself. Wore a bowler hat at all times except when deemed polite to remove it. He lost it in a contact and it was promptly replaced by the makers in London, accompanied by official approval from Task Force Command for him to wear it. In between the hat and the huge splayed feet was a big diamond head, tanned and freckled. A cavernous mouth, tombstone teeth, eagle beak of a hooter. Intelligent squinty eyes made pin-sized by a bizarre set of bifocals, granite jaw. Crinkly, cropped black hair. This bloke was a doer who could think. Big sloping shoulders, runner's legs, and arms and fists you'd want on your side.

I was walking to the mess one breakfast call and spotted a new face. Likely customer, six-footer, solid, and a cheeky Irish mug. Name of Patterson, from Perth he told me. Came in the previous afternoon as a Reo. He'd had a few beers at the boozer—I'd seen him there. I asked how he'd got on.

'Fine. Met some of the blokes, had a few, went for a leak, found a hole in the ground. Chose that, going well, then this Pommy bastard comes up and asks me what I'm doing.

'"Having a piss, dickhead, fuck off!"

'"That's a weapon pit. Our men have to stand in that."

'"Well pity them then", I manage to get out. Fucking crrunnch. I wake up in the middle of the night down the hole.'

'That'd be . . .'

'My section commander. Believe me, I fucking know.'

Patto went on to become a good gunner. I asked Mick about him. 'Oh, he'll do OK.' That'll do me, I thought.

Big Mick was the warrior. Reciter of epic poems, liver of an epic life. When needed, Mick's section was always ready to go. The other sections were ready also, but were sometimes hampered by Big Mick trampling them underfoot in his haste to get a look. I suspect he used myopia as an excuse for convenient lapses into clumsiness. Soldiering was Mick's life. He had a curious and very alarming talent: he could transform into a twerp. He'd developed the art in the British army as a light heavyweight boxer. Used to enter the ring in an old plaid dressing gown, hunched over as if his head was too heavy for his spine. Glasses on, of course, a pathetic little wire-framed pair he'd had made specially. Universal joint over the bridge so the lenses swivelled when he twirled them. A timid wave and a friendly vacuous grin at his opponent completed the effect. Few opponents, caught up in the swirl and roar of excitement, expectation and fear, remembered his incredible record, despite their coaches' warnings. Even those few who saw through him seldom went well. Mick knew all the skills. Even use of voice—high-pitched and giddy for socialising or for goading cunts, deep and penetrating for serious work.

He'd been a sergeant or higher in the British army, in REME, a corps of specialist mechanics, auto electricians and so on. He'd been discharged for decking an officer, I was told, which was probably true and was supported by his account to me of military prison. 'First day, you're in your cage looking through the bars and your meal arrives. It isn't bad food as such, just poor presentation. They hand you the bowl and it's got a fried egg on the top, but it's cold and crispy. The rice pudding beneath it is warm, but dark purple. The bacon beneath that has rind on and missed being cooked. Beneath that I don't fucking know. You don't eat it. Third day, you see a first dayer, watch his reaction and say, "Oooohh, don't you want yours then? I'll 'ave it."'

Mick arrived in country a lance corporal, whose job it was to control the machine gunner and his number two, or assistant. Seems a bit bureaucratic, but good gunners tend to be fiery bastards who treat attacks on their section as a horrendous personal affront, which is right. A good gunner well controlled is a gift from heaven when your world erupts in strange colours. Mick was rapidly promoted to section commander in the field.

Lenny was an Aboriginal, a three-year Reg. Curious thing that—I never met an Aboriginal of call-up age who was a Nasho, always a Reg. I'm not for one moment calling them stupid, I suspect they were preyed upon by the slimy bastards in recruitment, who must have been paid a bounty on each head: they were keen as shit to get long-term signings. Lenny was a forward scout, in fact I'd trained as Lenny's number two, or relief scout, before being sent off to language school. We had five Aboriginals in the company, several of whom 'passed for white' as it was termed then. They didn't readily acknowledge their Aboriginality, some even denied it. Lenny wasn't one of them. Lenny was a true blacktracker.

Just recalling Lenny throws me off on a tangent. It didn't seem particularly interesting at the time just how many Aboriginals there were in the army, or in the Infantry, to be precise. They didn't seem too thick on the ground in the safer, better paid Corps, but they were common in the Infantry—I'd estimate roughly three times their quota based on percentage of population. When I consider that they were mostly volunteers, I start to think there's a mystery there. Were they more patriotic than us? Naturally braver, more adventurous perhaps, or maybe just more cleverly manipulated by government departments? Don't expect an answer from me on that issue, not here and now anyway, but it's an interesting subject nonetheless, and not widely known.

Back to individuals.

Jock was a section commander. In large-scale setpiece battles like Waterloo or Tobruk, this position is pretty low stuff—count my troops, yep, all nine here; follow me, I'm following the platoon commander's order. In jungle warfare, and urban guerilla actions like those in Belfast or Beirut, it is the essential pivot of command. Everything that a higher commander orders should be and usually is based on the appreciation of the situation as his section commanders see it, because he usually can't see it for himself. He is too far back. In the jungle too far back can be three metres. A section commander is as good as his bond with his men. While Big Mick was the archetypal warrior-leader, Jock wasn't. He was, surprisingly, Scottish—no Glaswegian thug, more gentle brogue Edinburgh, grammar school type. He'd been in the Black Watch in Scotland which, if you are ignorant, was a very respected and much feared Scots infantry regiment. I'd known Jock since day one at recruit training. He was one of that experienced core of troopers who helped kids like me along the way when things got difficult. Not the technical or academic things so much as how to meet standards of dress, drill, cleaning, discipline—all the little taboos that an Einstein would fuck up on without help.

Jock was about 30. Medium height, medium build, grey blue eyes, mousy hair, freckled fair complexion, the tattoo on one forearm a bit out of character. Might have got on the piss in a strange port. His most outstanding physical feature was the lack of one. He was promoted to corporal within a year of enlistment, did his job over here without fuss or criticism from his men or his superiors. He would sometimes approach you and quietly discuss a problem which interested him—and draw you in, get you involved. After he walked off, the penny would drop. He'd been talking about a fault he'd found with your behaviour, and you'd provided your own solution. Like Big Mick, though, his wasn't really a warrior's background. He'd been a piper with the Watch, and a very bad one he admitted. Always got hidden in the middle ranks with a silent pipe. But pipers doubled as stretcher bearers in battle, a risky position. A position all future leaders should have some time in, to get a fairer perspective.

Well, the boozer's on last call, let's meet Pigpen and Tank, both Nashos. They usually went together as a team. Both Queenslanders, both played rugby, the brutal version, leagueandunion. Tank was just that. Six foot two or three, his massive frame made him look shorter till you stood right under him. He could run, jump, intimidate, wrestle, brawl, drink and root. As Dave once said, 'He excels at anything a big man can do'. He was Dave's mate. Tank and I didn't always get on too well. He once said to me, well, bellowed, 'I wish to Christ you were bigger, Crowley, I'd smash ya fucking head in', which indicated he had a sense of proportion as well as perspective. He wasn't much of a talker but he was good to have in a crowd, and not just because he almost made a crowd if there were just the two of you. He used to be a school teacher. At this time number two gunner I think, but he became gun group commander once the bullets started thinning our numbers. How they never hit him is still a great mystery to me—he was the biggest target we had.

Pigpen was a different type but in the same mould. About my height but powerfully built. Tradesman, boilermaker or fitter probably, had a grip like a bench vice. He was a forward scout. He beat Tank to gun group command, then became section commander about mid-tour. Real pocket warrior. Hard, a word I use reservedly, doesn't begin to describe Pigpen. Head like a melon, crewcut sandy hair, flawless white teeth, blue shrewd eyes. Until I met him he was called Tommy. The first time I saw him he was leading Tank up the path to the Nugget to say hello to Dave, and with every step he became noticeably dirtier. By the time he reached me he was a dust-covered shitheap and he'd only walked sixty metres. I named him Pigpen after the character in the Peanuts comic strip and it stuck. It had to, he was the real thing. His hygiene was as good as anyone's, it was just that he was a magnet for dirt and dust. Out in the field he was invisible. The times he appeared before me out in the scrub and startled shit out of me I'd rather forget.

He and Tank were great examples of mates in the army sense. Rough and ready maniacs who looked out for each other. Pigpen described to me an incident with Tank on a night ambush during training at home.

'We've been bashing fucking scrub all day, had ten minutes to eat dinner while you pricks've been lazing around all afternoon. We stomp off through the slop, reach the site, which is a track that looks like a buffalo wallow. It's pissing down, cold, no groundsheets (too noisy), fucking mozzies up your nose, in your ears. We're fucked. We're lying in ambush position, full alert, eyes out on stalks, no hope of any rest tomorrow. It's

3 am, still pissing rain and the big fella starts giggling. "What the fuck's up with you?" Titter, titter.
"What's the joke?"
"I've got a fat."
'I tell ya, Crowls, I nearly shot the big cunt!'
Now, you don't get mates like that in civvy street, do you? And that's where the confusion lies. Mates in civvy street do deals. What *we* mean by the term is friends, which is a very different thing. I thought a hell of a lot of Pigpen. There was a lot to him, mostly randy bull terrier.

OK, that's the last can, the lights are going out. Let's move on. We'll meet some more people along the way, and get to know some of them intimately. Life is experiences and people, separated by the impositions of wankers. Speaking of which . . .

Pete and I had to get up at sparrow-fart to conduct a 'papers check' on the peasants trundling by on the road the other side of the Dat. Had to walk there, of course, that's how I know the truck trip on King Hit One saved us two kilometres. And out further, to the road. Base sent Lenny with us to provide the muscle, along with a couple of others to shake down the 'enemy'. The entire local population were our enemies after we'd created a massive traffic jam and the oxen started getting cranky. Pete got out in the middle of the road like a typical fuckhead. Armalite cradled under one arm, fag hanging out the mouth, other arm creating a barrier wherever it pointed. Asked long questions consisting of three words. One French, the other two indescribable. Checked papers if the locals had any, kicked wheels, ignored answers, had a great time. Pete loved playing the arsehole. It gave him poise. Never thought to ask me to interpret. Lenny stayed near his shoulder in case people got too shitty. The others watched on silently, enjoying the performance. I took the photos.

We gave it away after a couple of hours. It was a long walk back and getting hot. A nice stand of timber outside the perimeter. The soil was red clay like our north, and the ants! Red, black, brown, up to two centimetres long. The brown ones had the biggest heads. They ran in channels, by colour, great big channels a centimetre deep and up to a metre wide. They'd obviously been at it a long while. I wonder if it all meant something ecologically? We were to encounter these little bastards time beyond count during the tour. Chompers we called them. They would tramp straight under your groundsheet at night in an unbroken stream and support your body on their backs until they finally passed through. Not as vindictive as our own breeds of ants, though.

I have pretty well described Nui Dat to you—for the most part invisible, some superstructure. It's important to note that it was Australian, run by Australians, for Australians. We ran it ourselves totally. The only Vietnamese on base were the National interpreters and perhaps a few spooks, but to my knowledge they came on base the day of an operation and went home at its conclusion. Visits to base otherwise were reasonably well screened. Laundry went out to Baria, a large nearby town; we drove it there and picked it up. The land formed part of the extensive Courtney Rubber estates, a French concern which no doubt valued our company in lieu of rent, and anyway we chopped down very few trees. It was the only base in South Vietnam like it.

When I started to travel around, the local military installations astounded me. They all looked positively feudal. Little forts like Roman outposts, only made of revetted corrugated iron, soil filled. Lean-tos tacked on the back for the garrison's families, pigs and of course ducks. Banners waving in the breeze, brilliantly coloured. Sandbags around machine guns, if they were lucky enough to have them. Ten-man affairs, roughly speaking, usually without radio contact. Not much hope and no support. That was in the country areas. The big regional bases were often joint ARVN and US affairs. Corrugated iron gave way to razor wire and concrete, gates and MPs prominent in white painted helmets. Not a blade of grass or a tree anywhere, masses of banners and bunting, even along the wire, like a presidential convention. The Yanks knew a bit about bunting, rest assured.

Now let me describe a base of similar size to Nui Dat to which an RAAF mate of mine was sent, to work there for a few months. It was a US airforce base that the Aussies took part in in a small way. Tony was sent there to help build our own bit of infrastructure. Fortunately he was a big fit bastard. The RAAF gave him a one-metre concrete mixer, a few shovels, some bags of cement, a superior officer, a crew of various skills, and orders to build a secure bunkered facility for a Canberra bomber squadron. The US flew mainly Phantoms and other fast fighter bombers from there. Tony was an ordinary airman in rank but he had a brain and a mouth and he enlisted the material support of the Yanks. He found out that their medical crew desperately needed a mobile operating theatre for the wounded US troops who poured in from the field. He got them one from our own sources without much difficulty. After that the Aussies got virtually anything they required in the way of transport, building stores, and equipment—from the Yanks. Think about that one for a moment!

The installation was inland from Phan Rang, about 240 kilometres north of Vung Tau. The site was overlooked by mountains and the VC they harboured. It was on a plain in the nearest country to desert that Vietnam has to offer. This was OK because a perennial river flowed from the mountains through the base, giving a reliable water supply. The land was 'owned' by the local warlord who doubled as the official ARVN chief of staff for the region. He charged rent, of course, for the land the base stood on, and for the use of the river. He also ran the camp concessions. There were three to four thousand men on the base, almost all US troops. They had to have laundry done, had to have food cooked, rooms cleaned, hair cut. The ARVN chief of staff provided the support services for a fee. He provided the 'Strip', which was along the lines of a knocking shop, bar, haircut & suck fuck $5, opium den, drugs arcade, and the nightclub. The latter a combination of them all. All of which he staffed for a big rake-off, off the top. The Yanks built the structures. Their troops provided all the protection for the base and environs. Korean soldiers manned the perimeter, living in pits dotted along the wire, because the US airforce personnel were ill-trained for the purpose.

Tony was a tradesman, a specialist, and a better trained ground soldier than the designated base defenders. The base, because of its ground space requirements, had a very long perimeter. It wasn't manned as we would have done it. They had fencing, concertina wire, mines, and gun positions where they could; but they relied mainly on a huge mobile arc-light installation that they could run up on the highest feature on the base. This could illuminate the perimeter at any point and was turned on through the night to search particular sectors at random. Tony planned and supervised its construction, and copped an MiD in recognition of his efforts. If any trouble was seen, armed jeeps would race to the scene to sort it out. If it was big, they could get a jet fighter up.

When the VC dammed and poisoned the river, and the camp was totally waterless, it was US troops who straightened out the problem. Airborne Cavalry were used for that. They were no bullshit fighting soldiers, no elite tags. Black, white, brindle, if you could fight they'd take you in. It took seven days to sort that problem out, a couple of days fighting, the rest clearing the poisons from the river. Couldn't use the ARVN, could you? Might jeopardise the warlord's, sorry, the ARVN commander's, sensitive agreement with the VC.

Phan Rang town was off limits to base personnel during the week, except for official business. At the weekend US troops manned gun towers along the beach and in the town, so their troops could play in more varied surroundings. Here the VC had a big hand in running the vice, but the rake-off rule still applied. Phan Rang was a fairly typical base for Vietnam at that time, overflowing with silly kids and masters of the art there to suck them dry at every turn.

Starting to get an idea of the politics at play here? Good.

Tomorrow we go into the field for our maiden Operation. It will be fun. It's called King Hit Two, very appropriate as you will see. Where are we going? Out! What do you mean, you want to know more? Who the fuck do you think you are? OK, sorry, I'm forgetting you haven't experienced this before. Anyway, you're travelling with a private, and a supernumerary at that. Let's ask an expert.

'Dave! . . . Hey, Dave! Where are we going?'

'Barrie, you are the One!'

'There's Griffo . . . Griffo! Where're we going?'

'Out!'

Just for you then. 'Hey, CSM! Where are we going?'

'On that fucking truck there! Get on!'

Get the message? That's how we travel. Not paid to think. That we do on our own time, if we get any. Want exact locations, numbers? Read a book by someone who saw the reports . . . and miss the point. Get on the truck.

Chapter 3

How do you like the truck? Yeah, jars your arse a bit, gets pretty dusty when we get up speed. The first truck in the column misses that, but I'd far rather cop dust than a landmine blowing my arse off. Do you really think I'd leave you like that, about to risk your life, not even knowing where you were going? Fucking oath I would, just like I was.

I have a map here from a book, a military one, so it's a bullshit view from carefully selected archives. I only have visions of where I've been, not the detailed eagle's eyrie view that a good map should provide. We operate in Phuoc Tuy province. It is a beautiful place. Its western edge is barely fifty kilometres from Saigon. Not that you'd know it—we're out in the sticks, no Western comforts out here. In shape it is a rough oblong with a large scallop cut from the top left corner. Nui Dat is pretty much smack in the centre of the province. It is, I am led to believe, about 60 km by 60 km in area. Seems much bigger, but that's probably because we often cross the border into other provinces without knowing it—at my level at any rate. Phuoc Tuy boasts all that Vietnam has to offer: jungle, rainforest, forested plains, grasslands, ricefields, rubber plantations, waterways, beaches, villages, forts and shit heaps. If we are in the green, the jungle, we're near to or over the border of Phuoc Tuy, probably in a mountain range. If we're in forest, we're probably in the foothills near the border. If we're in grasslands, we're in the interior of the province; if we're in the ricefields, we're among the people. If we're in a village we're surrounded; if we're in a city, fucking duck! The gang's all here.

Now, let's see. Yes . . . King Hit Two. Memorable little sortie, met the third of my mates, Peaches, there. Not sure when we went, but it kept us out all December until the 24th, I remember that. An Operation usually means thirty days out, fourteen days in. You lose a few of those fourteen days on pissant TAOR patrols. You're sometimes called back into the field in a pinch—someone caught the tiger's tail and can't handle it alone. Get pissed, lose your money, lie about your sex life, write to one if you have any, listen to music, clean your kit. Then out for thirty more. Ours started out that way, then management got excited over recognition, at our expense. Oh yeah, TAOR means Tactical Area of Responsibility. Short overnight patrols. More about that later.

Nineteen sixty-eight had been a good year for the combined VC and NVA (North Vietnamese Army). They had regrouped and rallied in '67 and in early '68 hit hard, hit every bastard. For the Vietnamese people, Tet meant a new year. The crop was in, a new start to a new year. It was celebrated by their revolutionary armies conducting massive armed aggression in the months of January and February, the dry season. In 1968 many US and joint US and ARVN strongholds were all but overrun by superbly organised attacks. Losses on both sides were huge, more so VC and NVA than the allies, by the time the assaults eventually petered out. It wasn't that the US troops were asleep, they just hadn't considered properly the feeling against them. It was a very close call for the US and the Republic, and after weathering the brunt of the attack they got out on the ground and took their revenge. And they decided to stay there.

Hearts and Minds, one of the programs was called, one of the greatest abuses of the English language ever perpetrated. It worked this way. Fly over some Nogs and drop some pamphlets about love and peace, fly back later and napalm the cunts. Schizophrenic behaviour; hard to defend allies like that, but we tried.

So here we are, our first real venture into the unknown. Tet of '69 about to get under way, what do we take? We need food, clothes, water, bedding, shelter. Tobacco? A book, matches, cards, writing material, a camera of course, spare socks, torch, watch, spare boots, hat, sunscreen, bug repellent, mozzie net, toothbrush and paste, razor, soap, pillow, deodorant, camp stool, collapsible canvas bath, TV . . . Hang on, we've got to carry this shit on our backs! Let's get organised. This is what we *must* take. Weapon, ammunition preloaded in magazines—no time to fuck around—claymore mine. Second weapon, an M79 grenade or M72 rocket launcher; add spare link ammo for the guns, marker panels for chopper landings, smoke grenades for same, fragmentation grenades, spare battery for the radio if you are unlucky. A radio if you are unluckier, one per platoon, one at CHQ plus the artillery forward observer who usually comes along. About 12–15 kilos there, plus a battery the mass of a house brick. The gunner and his number two in each section have to be fit. The gunner hefts the machine gun, the number two the spare barrel and parts plus his own rifle and ammo, and between them a lot of link. It doesn't pay to be among the strongest in the infantry. I have seen coils of concertina wire added to these beasts of burden while patrolling. Have I forgotten anything? Doesn't matter, we get resupplied every three days without fail.

Include in the must-takes your razor. Don't laugh, failing to shave daily is a chargeable offence. Charges cost you time and money. The solution's easy, you get organised. One takes cards, another a pocket radio; over time you cull out the bullshit. You take what you need and one thing you want, which you share. You have a weatherproof groundsheet roughly two metres by one and a half which makes a tent if you clip it to your mate's. If you're alone you wrap up in it but condensation's a bastard. You get a silk sleeping envelope with a nice chocolate-brown woolly liner which clips into it. Chuck the liner unless you're good at rubic cubes. Also, it's a nightmare to keep clean and tangles you up when you need to move fucking quick. Your rifle sights snag on the wool. Better a bit cold than stone dead. Sleep with your weapon, it's possible to develop a healthy impersonal relationship. Slip out on silk. Six to eight one-litre plastic water bottles will fit on your webbing harness and pack if you get obstinate. The weight makes your legs buckle a bit but don't be fooled by assurances, you will need them. Metal cups fit snugly on the base so take three of those; that's your cup, your oven and your basin. Don't mix them up! Ever been crook in the tropics? Take a machete if you have to, definitely your entrenching tool. And a field dressing or two, to plug up your mate's wounds. Tape them to your rifle butt.

Now, food. Two types, Australian one-day ration packs or US three-day ration packs. Usually we get a blend of both. The Aussie pack is about the size of a phone book. Three of them will fill much of your carrying space so get ready to cull. Each contains an 8 oz can of corned beef, vienna sausages in brine (squeakers, that's the sound they make when you eat them). Luncheon meat, tick, or if you're arsy, Irish stew. There's a 4 oz can of baked beans, omelette, one or two other choices, but you'll get omelette most times. Most of it still lurks beneath the earth, uneaten, the cans pierced with a bayonet to hasten death. We live in hope. There is a biscuit, a sweet petrified block of sandsoap some Diggers boiled into porridge, but for me that was for the ducks—what the fuck do they know? A packet of wholemeal crackers, a tiny can of soft Kraft cheese, a can of butter, and a 'condiment pack' with sugar, tea, coffee, sweetened condensed milk, pepper and salt and, very occasionally, a pack of curry powder. A pressed-tin can opener which can double as a spoon. Shiny toilet paper, waterproof matches. A rubber band. A small block of dry sweetened crystallised putty labelled chocolate. A sachet of instant rice—fucking bullshit!

The US rations come in three-day packs, each meal in a box within a box about the shape of a carton of beer cans but larger. The cans are larger than the Aussie rations and contain things like beans and meatballs, spaghetti and ground beef, sliced 'ham' in a semen-like substance, compressed white matter that passes for turkey. Cans of fruit: pears, apricots, fruit salad and apple sauce. These are good. The beans and spaghetti have sump oil in them. The meat is not animal. You get cake in a can too. Pound cake, which is a yellow sponge, the sort they make cheap foam mattresses out of, or a dry thing marked pecan cake. Canned cracker biscuits with a flat can of jam or burnt-orange cheesespread put in with them. The condiment pack is cute—a sealed brown metal-foil waterproof pouch containing chewing gum, instant coffee, tea, milk, toilet paper, four cigarettes, salt, pepper, instant drinking chocolate. A book of waterproof matches, a can opener with a short handle designed to give grief.

A plastic spoon. Everything in the pack tastes like chewing gum. The matches don't light. The peppermint on the toilet paper burns your arse. They're all OK until the novelty wears off.

Between the two ration packs you can select a diet if you're hungry and only eat in order to shit. But I take packets of instant noodles and some chilli when I can, to liven up the menu. So do others. Well, that's about it—you're lumbered with 45 kilos or so, unless you're in a platoon section where the weapon and ammo rating is higher.

You patrol like that, and if the shit hits the fan you'll fight and crawl and duck and run with it until you can safely drop some. What's the best position for your pack? High, low, in the middle, all are good—your back is going to get fucked regardless. Say goodbye to pain-free living. Don't whinge! No one'll listen. Just like me, you did it to yourself.

We clamber on to open trucks on the company service road and grind off, heading for the main gate. Dave, Pete and me as a group. The trucks could have bench seating in two rows down the middle of the tray facing out, but it's a hassle for the drivers. They have to rerig everything for the next load which may be general cargo, so they can't be fucked, it's all the same to them. We go out facing inwards: twist your back or ignore the enemy. We halt outside the gate to cock our weapons, put one up the spout, nice and ready. Dave sits next to me, Pete directly opposite us. We all cock, *zzzzitt clack*; Pete cocks, *zzzzitt clack crackcrackcrack!!* Prick nearly takes the top of my head off.

'Fuck, not again!' Pete cries. In fairness to him, he sounds genuinely concerned.

Fucking again! We've only been in country a dog's watch! Dave and I sit on the same side as Pete after that. The trucks move off. Pete now has another AD—that's an accidental discharge—to face, if he gets back.

The company is dropped off along a road and we head into the scrub, reaching our area of search around noon. The ground is reasonably level but heavily treed and visibility is poor through the shrubs and high grass. CHQ harbours under a thick copse of trees and the platoons head off to search their grids. For most of us in CHQ it's a matter of doing your turn on gun or other sentry duty around the perimeter, having a quiet rest, not moving around too much. The day is overcast and makes the small grassy clearing in front of me appear bleak. OC can be heard regularly on the radio to the platoons, tracking their progress, calling changes, plotting moves, a low burble in the background. All pretty tranquil. A blast of machine gun fire rents the air from the thick scrub, perhaps three hundred metres to my front. CHQ switches right on. OC's voice is our only source of information but it hasn't changed, a bit more protracted and questioning perhaps. No more shooting occurs. Shortly, CSM comes over to where I am with Pete, Griffo and some of Support Section. He advises us to be prepared for two platoons heading back through our part of the perimeter, bearing wounded.

Within minutes we spot the lead scout appear through the scrub across the clearing as he signals friendlies down his own line, then the first platoon silently moving towards us. We can see they are badly shaken. After the first section come the two litters. Two bearers to each. They come in through our position and Pete starts his examination of them as he meets them and begins walking alongside. The third man is dead, Peaches carrying the body covered in a sleeping silk. They were our own. The rest of the platoon passes, then the other platoon, in utter silence. All look the same, deathly pallid, filmed in sweat. Horrified.

We've fucked up!

No one knows all that happened. No one could be blamed; everyone could be blamed. Two platoons had converged in the thickly forested scrub when they should have been well apart. A radio message misinterpreted, a platoon commander changing course and not explaining clearly. A lead scout misunderstanding his section commander's bearing, wrong bearing issued, who knows? Who cares? Woofer missed the initial sighting, it came from toward the rear of his section.

Two gunners had opened up. One was Peaches. He was called Mick then, a magnificent gunner. Had to be, he was Woofer's gunner cum second scout. The soldier killed was Peaches' gun group commander, shot in the head in the act of rising to signal a friendly contact. Caught in the crossfire. One person thinks he knows who killed him—Peaches thinks *he* did.

I phoned him the other day, spoke to him for the first time in twenty-five years.

'Hello? . . . Barrie! I still have that ring you gave me.'
'I've got no memory of it, Peaches. I don't remember. What ring?'
'You know, the silver one with the blue stone.'
'Nuh, why the fuck did I give you that?'
'Dunno, fuck knows. Lost it a few times. Still got it though . . . Remember that clash? Ron . . . you know. Still don't know. Two guns opened up. Saw his signal as he was hit.'
'Who was the quicker gunner, Peaches?'
'Pritch or me? . . . Christ, how would I know? Ron was shot in the back and side of the head.' He talked in this vein for a while and it took me right back to the day. Peaches' voice sounded 22 still.
'How have you fared, Peaches? Fat and bald yet?'
'Bit of a gut, got a beard now. Don't drive, drink a bit so it's safer not to, you know. Must catch up, can't talk about this to people. A couple of blokes at work, otherwise they don't understand . . . the young ones, weak as piss. Don't want to know.'

I hadn't talked about it on the day it happened or during the tour. Being new I had no idea what the company's response would be. Didn't know who was involved, how those involved or connected through bonds of friendship would react. My only response was to listen without comment or undue interest if it was discussed in my hearing, which mercifully was a rare event.

Can you fly? Let's see what you can perceive through the dense canopy of time and disinterest. Look! You're stalking up a track and word reaches you that there's enemy stalking you. Woofer, Peaches, Ron and the rest of the section tear back down the track, hit the deck and splatter everything that sounds or looks like aggression. Not a hard decision, shit's pouring in at them by the truckload, murderously low. Woofer's behind a tree getting ready to hurl grenades. He seldom does that, he's used to controlling the situation. Lenny's yelling his guts out to stop and within five seconds it does. Peaches looks round for the living and sees his number two with a big chunk of red meat pulsing on his lower back. He instinctively touches it to find the source of the wound and it twangs away from his fingers and snaps back into a buttock again, bleeding but recognisable.

It belongs to Smithy. He's lost a chunk of his big toe as well but can't see what the fuss is about.

I missed the fallout that followed the incident. As in any organisation, people need to fix blame on someone, it takes the questioning light off them. Peaches and Woofer weren't officially questioned. Woofer probably would have shot them. Fuck knows what Peaches would have done. Pritch came over and Peaches and he had a bit of a cry together in the dusk. Lenny was the scout of the other section involved. He'd been scouting all day and had just called his second in to relieve him when the guns opened up. He was quick to realise what was happening, and as the first shots whipped past simply went to ground, calling out the warning. Lenny also harbours a nagging doubt about his own actions that day. Maybe he should have interpreted the situation just that bit sooner? One more second was all they had needed— one miserable second. When the inevitable grillings started Lenny corrected a statement someone was making and got a rifle muzzle held at his head by his own sergeant. Infantrymen never do that. Not to any one. Not when they're rational. The CO flew out in his little personal chopper to settle things down. Lenny, several of his section, the sergeant and the platoon commander met discreetly with the CO to sort things out. At this meeting Lenny had to disprove the assertion that *he* had held his weapon at his sergeant's head. I wouldn't be an Aboriginal in this army for anything! Lenny was as well liked as anyone in the company, but there was a basic difference. We all had a few people who didn't like us, but when you were black, dislike became hatred in some people's minds.

Nothing came of the CO's chat, of course. It would have taken leadership, a flickering spark of intelligence and an understanding of people to kick that sergeant's arse on to the scrap heap where it belonged. So Lenny soldiered on with enemy to the front and an enemy behind him throughout the rest of his tour. The company quickly set the entire mess aside for what it was and went on with their job. Even Young Mick, who had been very close to the dead man. He was found crying alone in the long grass, and Peaches joined him. Dave and Griffo were concerned Young Mick would lose heart and get careless, but he contained it very well, somehow. He wasn't a problem.

Several days later I'm out with Duntroon's platoon for a day of patrolling in the same general area. There are a fair few established tracks about the place and someone thought an interpreter would be handy in case we get some prisoners. Duntroon tells me to stick by him and off we go. Bé (pronounced Bay), our Vietnamese national interpreter, is with me. We strike a track and follow it. The scrub is too thick so we walk along the track. We move fast and cover more ground than I've been taught is safe by our instructors back in Australia, but you get used to that. Our main packs are back at base with CHQ so we aren't too loaded down. As we head up a slight rise into an open green forest glade, firing breaks out at the front of the column a hundred metres from us.

Word gets back by hand signals to Duntroon, squatting just in front of me, that the lead scout has sighted four VC and shot one dead. The other three are retreating to our right, downhill and into thick growth along a creekline. Firing is coming from both sides. Duntroon orders an immediate sweep to the right by the two rear sections, while the contact section tries to slow the enemy down with heavy fire. We're off like rockets, threshing through the scrub in a straight ordered line thirty seconds or so after the first shot was fired. Well, ordered except for me. Later, we regroup back on the track. Duntroon is crouching over the dead VC and rummaging through his backpack, with Bé looking on. 'Where the hell have you been, Crowley? Oh, never mind . . . stick with me in future.' He's sifting through handwritten documents taken from the dead man's pack. He focuses on one page and gets all excited about a phrase in it. Asks Bé, 'Does this say . . .?', and he names a village in the area which is suspect. 'It does, doesn't it?' Bé nods noncommittally. Always tell the punter what he wants to hear. So Duntroon is on the radio to OC with a major breakthrough. I collar my little interpreter mate, drag him right over the body of the young enemy soldier and pass him various documents.

'Interpret this!'
A quick scan. 'Letter to girlfriend.'
'This?'
'Poem.'
'Read..it..to..me!'
'Very complicated . . . OK . . . about trees, bird . . . sun.'

He's giving me a literal translation. He is right, it's poetry. This prick couldn't make this up in his dreams.

'Is this usual?'

'All time.'

'Ever any orders, that sort of thing?'

'No . . . like you, orders spoken.'

And that is how it was. Reports of valuable military documents being found on common foot soldiers in Vietnam were bullshit!

I tested Bé several times. My way, with no hint of what I expected. I checked with another of the battalion national interpreters who I liked and trusted and got the same answer. I don't deny that some information was enlightening and useful. Intelligence can come from unconscious slips and day-to-day trivia, but anyone who claims that regular and reliable military intelligence could be gained from body searches is hiding the truth. Most of the VC carried a lot of paper on them, pretty literate sensitive people for ignorant peasants, I found. I guess it's not important—we were there to kill the bastards anyway. I just hate charades, dressing up a kill as a legitimate intelligence exercise. Did we need that assurance? Surely, if your orders are to kill, that's it. Only liars justify. Switch on, we're being lied to already.

A few days later the company is travelling through tall dense grassland, quite near farmland, I suspect. The track we're on bears cart tracks. We're strung out in single file at ten-metre intervals. One minute flat out keeping up with the prick in front, next minute halted, watching your field of search, trying to rejig your pack so it doesn't cut chunks out of you. I'm in the middle of the column. Up front a few shots are fired; we go to ground, wait for orders. Nothing happens for a while, idle rumour-mongering breaks out, Pete gets into a few hands of cards with the sappers. Five Hundred's all the rage. Table talk fires up—slam no-ees, pair of tits, three scrags—all this means fuck-all to me. Cards are slapped down on Pete's sweaty pack. I get a call to go up front. 'Bring Bé!'

We go up the line four hundred metres or so, shrugging off curious looks. Reach the head of the column and there it is. Looks like a woman and a kid lying partly concealed in the long grass, dead. OC on the edge of the scene, half turned away like he wants to leave but can't. In the centre Duntroon, legs set apart, left arm cocked on his hip, Armalite in his right hand, pack off, in control. Nearby, three or four of our men standing guard around a squatting Vietnamese male, rifles pointed at his head. Hairtrigger tension. Sky grey and overcast. The man sits huddled in a foetal position, arms wrapped around his head and shoulders in a tight knot.

'We need to know if he's VC,' says Duntroon. I look again at the man. He's late twenties, dark trousers, light shirt, no weapon or webbing on show. Terror and loss howling, shrieking, from his blank black eyes; mouth locked shut and silent. He's cataleptic. Shut down. No one could interrogate a man in this state. I say, 'Too complex for me, best send him up the line'. I sense Bé beside me flex himself to move in and question the man. I block him with my elbow, then say quietly to him, 'We leave it at that'. He takes my warning, makes a show of trying to communicate, then backs me up. I grab Bé and head back down the line without asking, just in case someone has second thoughts and puts pressure on us to try again. I doubt that Bé would back me a second time.

OC was moving in as I left, and had the man sent up the line to BHQ for interrogation. Don't know how he was sent out. OC was not the man to misunderstand a person's mental state, but there were people present this day who wanted an answer on the spot. It was a problem dealing with a prisoner in the field. It tied the whole company up waiting for a chopper or an armoured personnel carrier to take them away. Original objectives then had to be rushed, which multiplied the risks to ourselves, as the objectives weren't reduced or cancelled. The vast majority of villagers were VC philosophically, if not actively. I later found out what fate awaited our captives.

It was our policy to treat prisoners fairly, but I guess we were pissing into the wind. It doesn't surprise me that a few were simply blown away by Australians, out of expediency. One of our own, a Nasho, pulled that stunt on a prisoner later on, but he was armed and shooting at us when captured. I wasn't called upon to interrogate on that occasion. I believe it happened straight after capture, possibly before the platoon commander got to the scene. Prisoner started to chatter, bang! Brains in the air. Who knows why. One or two of that prisoner's unit had died in the contact a minute or so earlier. Is there a real distinction between combat and murder? Yes. I don't know how anyone could execute another person. Faced with that situation I looked at a distraught Nog with a dead family and thought, Life! It doesn't always happen.

Our first good ambush occurred soon after. One of our platoons was stretched out along a promising track. Sure enough, near dawn, along the track stalked ten or more Viet Cong. When their scout reached the end of the ambush the section commander pressed the claymore tit and everyone opened up, Peaches flaying the group from left to right. It was a doddle. At first light the boys crept out, euphoric over their first clean kill, debating ownership of the captured weapons. They riffled through the packs and then, in some cases, reflected on the dead. Woofer didn't join in. He drifted undetected into the dense growth on the far side of the track, looking for something else. A sharp *crack* brought everyone up short. Woofer had contacted the one survivor too wounded to flee but strong enough, and determined enough, to fight back. The scout had done his job. The lessons were mounting.

Time to lighten up. Let's have a look at some jungle, maybe have a ride in an APC. An armoured personnel carrier is a wonderful thing if you're infantry. I'm sure you've seen them in film footage in one version or another—riot control in South Africa, Belfast, Gaza Strip, they're usually there somewhere. We use the US version, shaped like a shoe box on tracks, a wedge-nosed front with the driver's helmeted head usually sticking out of his flush turret on one side of it. When the shit hits the fan he closes his turret lid and peers through a tiny, bulletproof glass brick, and relies on his commander's better judgement over the earphones. It's square at the back, all door, which lowers like a drawbridge superfast to let the troops out. You have to fly out at lightning speed; when the door is down is when the troops are most vulnerable. A little door is set into it for discreet exit one at a time, for a piss or whatever—not for battle, thank you. A small gun turret on top towards the front is fitted with a 50 cal. machine gun or twin 30 cal. ones. Little bulletproof glass bricks set around its base allow you to peer out when things get ridiculous and you have to dive inside. The commander, a corporal, sits there, usually on top of the turret calling the moves, having a fag, a look around. The third crew member mans the radio and supports the other two. Inside there is enough room to carry ten grunts, with all their kit and weapons, seated on padded benches running down both sides. There is no view from inside unless the crew open the top hatches above us. This allows you to stand and get a firing position over the sides.

The vehicles are very fast and nimble over most terrain, fairly well protected against small-arms fire, but rockets and decent sized landmines can cause havoc within. Suspension ain't the greatest but it beats the shit out of walking. The crews are Armoured Corps—tankies, we call them. They call us grunts. A lot's said about rivalry between us, about tankies being elite. It's bullshit. It used to be true when Armoured was cavalry: gentlemen rode horses, the peasants marched. But these guys are great. They're basically Diggers who have better beds, don't walk much and carry more stuff with them. At a pinch they could do what we do, and we could do their job. We'd be short a few drivers and knob twiddlers, they'd be short of a bit of wind and leg condition, that's all. They transport us from place to place, strengthen our defence when heavy attack is likely. I've never had the need, but if you're short of water or food, ammo, whatever, and they're not, it's yours.

Pete came over to me one day all excited. 'Look what Normie Rowe gave me.' It was a can of slimy compound ham, the same as we ate.

'You don't even like this shit,' I reminded him, before realising I was acting like a prick.

'Fuck! I didn't read the label.'

He was just excited that a big name singer had spent time with him. Pete was just 20. He threw the can into the scrub, as he normally did that particular product, and pretended he hadn't felt honoured.

Some of us remember Normie for being the driver who pulled Peaches and Woofer out of a real nasty little battle later on, but it could have been any of them, and over time it was. The crews were fucking good Diggers.

How do I open you up to your first view of the jungle? Most Diggers, if you ask their opinion of Vietnam in one word, will say 'green'. It isn't always. It is bombed to the shithouse in parts, defoliated or strip-cleared in others, mainly hues of grey, olive, straw, red, with glaring hazy white sand in the dry season. In the wet it's mostly green. But if they say 'green' straight off, they've been in the jungle. For lead scouts it's the twilight zone, for other ground troops it's just as risky, just not perceived the same. I see it as a wonderland. I spend one minute in four having a look. I'm still on duty, but appreciating what I see. I'm usually in the middle of the column as the company travel. The total concentration that scouts employ is also expected of me, but I can't help myself, I take a risk. I see trees with trunks two and three metres in diameter soaring skyward, silver-grey, white with red slashes, grey-black. Canopies of leafy boughs towering overhead, vivid green, tinged with gold in bright light, moving and whispering in the breeze. On dull days it's dark green and grey, yet still embracing. The soil can be red, dark brown or grey-black clay, sometimes grey sand. The vegetation below the canopy varies. Sometimes flatweeds, low grass and shrubs, always head-height leafy plants, new growth. On occasion, dense, head-high, thickly matted grass, dusty and airless in the dry. Constantly, bamboo copses ten metres high, dark jade green, so tightly packed they're almost impenetrable. That's just the stems—each of them 250 millimetres in diameter. Then there's the tendrils snaking outward thirty metres or more, long tough thorns every few centimetres. More formidable than razor wire, denser, not consistent. The tendrils spread in all directions, a grey-green cloud covering hectares without a break. Sometimes, especially down in the gullies, the creepers join all this. Add deadfall—fallen trees—and you encounter real jungle. Our older members who've experienced Borneo are quick to recognise it.

Most of the time when we refer to the jungle we're more accurately describing rainforest, which is both better and worse. It is not dank and impenetrable, it is a beautiful habitat, comfortable even in the heat if you don't have to work too hard. The downside is that many others feel as you do about it. The jungle is crisscrossed by numerous paths, with many caches of food, weapons and equipment, halfway houses, bunker systems, and troops moving along the paths. This is where the hitters meet. There's no chance of shooting the innocent party here unless it's your mate. This is where the VC choose to come to fight us—we are not here to hide—as many who don't care to see for themselves have claimed.

Get the picture? Going well. Just look at that stream. Pale green opaque water trailing laces of white foam, whispering by, the throbbing pulse of its passage drumming underfoot. Over a metre to the bottom, except at the shallow stony ford that Kelsie's squatting on. Filling our water bottles. No shirt, dogtags round his neck, prematurely balding blond head, big moustache, big grin, big muscular frame. Very placid, he's smiling at me, the photographer, and the silver-green shrubbery behind him frames the scene. Until the rest of Support Section suddenly loom into focus, armed and alert, kneeling, guarding him from the background. And you remember that you are at war. Then, through the foliage behind them, you see the wide freshly trampled track of our passing, and you realise we are travelling too fast to take proper care.

Things have been pretty rough one way or another, but our first visit to the jungle is without major incident. Several days of uphill and down, following tracks, wading rivers and streams; best just before night harbour for a good damp sleep. We work our way down to flatter country and the going gets easier. We pass through heavy forest, with relatively open grass below, using available tracks because the cover beside them is negligible anyway. I can see the others up ahead, regularly peering into the leafy canopy above, checking for snipers. I'm doing the same, as much to determine what is greener, the lush grasses or the leaves above, as looking for enemy presence.

From the leaves of the higher boughs appear the head and shoulders of a monkey, upside down, about the size of a big chimpanzee, all black with a big white V on his chest. He glares down on me as I pass under his perch, barks and snarls at me with big yellow teeth, shaking the branches. As I look, a large tribe of monkeys appears around him, then start to swing unhurriedly along our line of march. There are fifty or more, ranging from babies to old timers, a real big one leading the way and the first one I sighted bringing up the rear. They are getting out of our way but not hurrying, long black arms looping out to grasp the next vine or branch, kiddies being kept in line. They could bolt at right angles to our line and disappear in seconds—just doesn't suit them. Our whole column stops to watch them. The last in line, the big angry bugger, tears off a bunch of huge seed-pods and hurls them right at me, just missing. They land with a thud at my feet. We watch the group disappear before moving on again. I've always imagined that monkeys would flee screaming in panic at human approach, but this lot didn't give a fuck. We were just a nuisance to them, best avoided but not to be feared or respected. We'd be gone from here before they were.

As we search this area we have another contact, just before dusk. It is a spot-and-shoot job. I'm halfway down the column and haven't done more than go to ground before it finishes. One enemy shot dead and abandoned by his small, fleeing unit on the track where he fell. We harbour for the night in a nearby copse of bamboo just as darkness closes in. It's a maze—tangled bamboo tendrils forming a dense thorny roof above our heads, the trunks standing in huge tight columns, creating corridors and chambers. Only the quick and the off-duty among us have hot food and drink before night routine douses all light. Those who shot the man have to carry him along to bury him, an unwritten law in infantry. They've done all the work and are still doing it; no chance of a coffee at this rate. The grave they've hacked down through matted bamboo roots is too short for the man.

'Machete ought to do it. Stand back!'

The sound of bone being shattered by a heavy blade five metres from where I'm eating takes the glow off things. I understand their motive: expediency, not cruelty or perversion.

Pete takes an interest. He gets up and strides over to the group.

'Best dig the trench longer.' A bit of muttering.

'Dig the fucking trench longer, fuck ya!'

That does the trick. Pete comes back and we finish the meal and drink our coffee in peace. At this early stage the feeling among the men is that this war is as we have been taught. There are enemy, they fight, it is honorable to kill them. If you do you are recognised, you get the enemy's rifle to keep, as proof of your deed. Pete always insists that honour works both ways and demands it be observed. He isn't alone, but few enforce it without compromise as he does.

It's been a bastard of a start to the tour. Fuckups, tough terrain, tough attitudes emerging. But you can't just suspend your life, you have to get something from each day, a joke, a view, a shared thought. In the restrictive world of a rifle company in the field your partner, or hootchie mate, is the difference between living and barely enduring. You are allocated a partner, usually dictated by the organisation structure. In a platoon the gunner hootchies with his number two, scouts work together, riflemen go in twos. Common sense dictates this.

It has been a bastard of a start for me too, never mind the company, and the contacts I made with various blokes in the few days at the Dat are useless out here. Visibility at most times is thirty metres tops. No moving around at night. Outside of your own section you are lucky to even spot most other members of the company once a fortnight. People leave and return to the field and you wouldn't know about it. In the field it is, for long periods, a time of poor communication, and your partner is vital. CHQ has its own order of hootchieing. A hootchie is your groundsheet; two clipped together make a two-man tent. Two is the base defence unit. The OC hootchies with his batman (if they can tolerate one another), the CSM with the radio operator or whoever, Support Section among themselves, the medic with the stretcher bearer. And the two interpreters together.

That's my problem, I hootchie with Bé, my little Vietnamese mate. I detest the cunt. I didn't meet him during my fleeting stay at BHQ when the other three company interpreters sought us out to introduce themselves. Canh, Dahm and Ahn. They said their names, and shook hands with Bert, Graham and me as we told them ours. Then the tallest, Canh, I think, said, 'Or if you prefer, Ahn, a Dahm, Canh.' I was the last to get the joke—he seemed too clever to say it—but we were off to a good start. All three were taller than me; mahogany-skinned, lean, fit, amenable, self-aware, confident. Been in the game for years. Sported early Beatle-type haircuts and snappy uniforms. They apologised for Bé's absence, he was busy elsewhere that day. We had a few minutes to chat together and I had no doubt I could work in with these guys, improve my language skills. Their English was basic but effective. I met Bé the day before we trucked out on King Hit Two.

What a letdown! He is an ugly little cur: five foot two, snaggle-toothed, face looking like it's been bashed flat with a shovel. That doesn't worry me. A whiny voice, round brown 'whip me' eyes, shithouse English—and a crawler. He's as greasy and fawning a creature as God ever shovelled guts into. This I can take if cornered, but he has no soul. His country is at war and he has one aim. Survival, at the best price. Love of country, concern for his people, these are alien feelings to him. Head down, make a buck, stay out of the firing line. OK, he's out in the field with us and it's rough, dangerous, but he's been with ARVN units before and knows the difference. We are united. ARVN are not good. Also there's no opportunity for blackmarketing in ARVN—the officers control that.

We're heading toward clearer land to meet up with the tankies. New orders have come through. On the way, our search turns up a cache of food—rice and other supplies, buried in the forest. A track, some other signs, a little resupply depot for the VC. That's when I see the Buddha. It's in the centre of the search area. About a metre high, a bust of Buddha; on a slight lean in the soft red earth, made of pewter or similar lead-grey alloy. It is all a filigree of intricate pattern: leaf, vine, eyes and tapered helmet. Vietnamese stylised. A large piece has been blown from the right shoulder by shrapnel judging by the curled, jagged edges of the hole. To me it is fascinating. Why here, in the middle of a forest? No sign of old building foundations, probably miles from habitation. It has been placed here, or hidden here. It looks too valuable to throw away and, anyway, why hump it all this distance? I stand crouched over it for some moments trying to solve the mystery, until Griffo says time to move on. Few in the company have more than glanced at it. The emphasis is on finding hidden supplies. Perhaps it's considered likely to be booby-trapped, and not wise to mess with.

We move on a few hundred metres to where a small unoccupied bunker system and an open shade lean-to have been found. The bunkers are quite shallow, covered, but not of the heavy-duty type we were to encounter later. All this we demolish before moving on to our rendezvous with the APCs. But why is the Buddha there?

The APCs are waiting not far from the bunker system and we rumble off on a short ride, probably thirty minutes, dropping off on a bush road. After a short hike through tall trees and scrubland we reach the edge of a huge rubber plantation. We might be near the Dat, but it's just a guess. Under the canopy it is silent and shady. The trees are mature, around five metres to the first bough, thick trunks heavily scarfed diagonally around for tapping. They are planted in rows ten paces apart and the foliage above overlaps to form a solid canopy. Green ankle-high grass, damp brown clay.

It's like moving through a sound booth, muffled. I can see our column moving ahead of me, the lead section sweeping a hundred or so metres to my front. Now and again we stop so the scout can check a sign he's spotted. I fiddle with the little bowls hanging beneath the spouts driven into the trunks to tap the latex. Before, they've been full of rainwater with solidified latex floating in them, but here they are dripping milky white and filling steadily. Workers have drained these bowls and scraped new cuts this morning, but there is no sign of them now. We start moving again and I see the line of four armed black-clad figures crossing our path fifty metres in front of us. Lead section kneel and let them have it. The gunner, scouts and two others fire together. Three of the enemy jerk through the air, one bounces off a tree trunk like a rubber dummy. The fourth member, who was leading the squad, has been missed by the first blasts. There wasn't time among the section to nominate targets. That was all the luck this man needed. He's now just a black flicker between black tree trunks. No amount of fire can bring this boy down, he's virtually out of sight almost as you sighted him—pack, rifle, rubber sandals, arse on choke, not a backward glance. Fucking good luck to him—they passed in front of us like a chain of black ducks in a shooting gallery!

We close in to watch while the bodies are searched. I crane over a shoulder to see the documents. There's nothing different. I see the wristwatches of the dead disappear into pockets, spoils of war. I look at the bodies, young, skinny, once stupid. All dressed in black, about the only time I've seen such uniformity. They must have read our briefings on VC dress, a couple even wearing conical hats. True stereotypes. The black clothing partially conceals the horrendous wounds, gaping holes in the bodies showing dark red against tattered shirts, the blood a greasy black sheen, twigs and mud sticking to it. Their weapons don't look much—assorted small-bore hunting rifles, quite old, the wooden stocks scarred and battered from years of use. A handful of cartridges each. Small canvas or cloth shoulderpacks containing a bit of rice, a couple of cans of mackerel and oddments of clothing. I move away when the cameras start clicking.

From there we move beyond the rubber plantation and encounter a huge fire break bulldozed through the forest. We follow this for half an hour or so and come to a dirt road running across it. As we halt and our decision-makers dicker over which way to go next, we get a visitor. Up the rough track drives a canvas-canopied khaki Landrover with red and white emblems on the side, probably Red Cross markings. Its progress is agonising, erratic; it comes perilously close to toppling over more than once. It seems to take exactly the wrong approach to every obstacle in the track, and there are many. At one point I think it will become straddled over the large hump in the centre and finish with all wheels spinning in the air above the deep muddy ruts, but at the last minute it slides sideways with a creaking thump and then scuttles crablike toward us, the engine slogging its guts out in too high a gear for the revs it is given.

'Who the fuck's this stupid cunt?' says some genius in Support Section.

'Give it shit, dickhead!' one of our car lovers encourages.

The vehicle lurches in among us, stalls to a halt, and out of the cab steps a Salvation Army man.

'Thought you could all do with a hot drink.'

He appears not to hear the remarks of the realists among us. 'Rather have a hot fuck.'

'Hot drink be fucked, got any piss on yer?'

I am too dumbfounded to think of a remark. What is he doing out here? He's alone, unarmed, has the driving skills of my mother, and he's out in country proven to contain armed active enemy. The product of our little shooting gallery episode lies buried not four kilometres away. He's blissfully unmindful of the dangers he is exposing himself to, and for what? A fucking drink. No hope of a conversion here, no time for a little prayer meeting, anyway no one's in the mood.

He unlatches the tailgate of his Landrover and two square stainless steel army issue hot drink urns are behind it.

'Hot coffee or milo, take your choice.' He beams.

He looks a decent sort of bloke. Dressed in jungle greens with red Salvation Army tabs on his collar and epaulettes, floppy giggle hat, GP boots, all standard army kit. Looks anything but standard on him, almost as though he's dressed back to front, and all of it too new to inspire confidence. Average height, slim, gawky, mid-twenties, innocent smile. As we queue to pour a drink he stands nearby, saying little, not pushing any issue. OC moves over to him for a yap and wills Duntroon over to them to keep the conversation going. Which he does—Duntroon is a good professional mixer.

I pour a cup of milo because I'd got in the wrong queue and couldn't just reach over to the other tap and block both lines without the risk of a punch under the ear.

'Don't fret about it Barrie, the coffee's not much of a punt,' says Dave. But the cunning bastard won't swap.

Some of the blokes have a quick word with the Sally man to thank him for his trouble, which is about all there is time for before we move out again, leaving him farting around with the tailgate catches.

He was underway again before our last section left the spot, so we'd seen him safely on his way to literally God knows where. God seemed to be his only guide, that's for sure. I hope he got back OK, we never met him in the field again. It was a stupid, futile, unnecessary gesture on his part, but I still remember him with a mixture of fond regard and concern for his mental balance. I haven't converted to organised religion and doubt I ever will, so I hope his motive was just a desire to be involved, to share in our experiences, nothing more. He was the only ordained man of God I ever saw in the field, with or without an escort.

That's it for King Hit Two. There's much more to the job than what you've just seen, endless slogging, more killing, but you can see it elsewhere on the tour. This stuff goes round and round and gets us nowhere after a time. Had enough? I have. It's 24 December. Let's get on the truck and get back to the Dat. I can hear the first can fizzing, smell the malty, white-foamy head, hear the burbling voices of contented mates drinking. Warmth and invitation. That's for us! Let's kiss this shit goodbye for a few days.

Chapter 4

We reached the gates of the Dat late in the afternoon of Christmas Eve. It was warm and sunny. Pete got through making his weapon safe without mishap, thank God; the trucks headed in to our company lines. All the omens were good. Time to put the feet up, get pissed, unkink. We got off the trucks, assembled to be dismissed, grinning like maniacs—and then got the news. We're on 24-hour standby, effective from now. Fucking brilliant! This meant being packed and ready to hit the field again within fifteen minutes if ordered. No booze, no wandering off, no nothing. It was done for a good reason—units out in the field sometimes needed help in a real hurry, so you had to do it. But fuck it!!

Nothing we could do but put up with it. The Nugget's bar hadn't been stocked in Dave's absence and anyway, a beer can fizzing open, even under three compressed pillows, would incite a stampede of slathering Diggers. We cleaned our kit and weapons, had a shower, took a crap in a halfway civilised lavatory, ate a cooked meal at a trestle table under cover, and slept in a decent cot for the first time in weeks. If it wasn't for the prospect of being hurled out into the field again at any moment, we could have enjoyed these simple comforts for what they were. Pleasures.

Christmas Day was spent either on normal picquet duty or hanging around your tent where you could be grabbed without difficulty. Dave and Griffo were busy most of the day restocking the arsenal and issuing ammo to everyone who needed it. So that left Young Mick and me looking at one another across the table. Tick tock, tick tock. About eleven he suggested we go down to the butts and test-fire our weapons. That meant cleaning them again, another job, but I hadn't fired mine for months, having been at language school and then posted to BHQ. That was a different world entirely.

I decided I'd better find out if it still worked. The butts was just a shallow trench right at our outer perimeter wire, used only for test-firing weapons. You stood over it and fired off a few rounds, no target practice involved. I got to have a look at our outer defences, something I hadn't yet seen. We walked through the platoon lines, ducking socks, webbing and shameful underwear hanging from the guy ropes. Between the outer ring of tents and the perimeter wire there was about a fifty-metre strip of land which conjured up visions of the Somme if you were educated. The tall shady rubber trees continued right to the edge of the wire, giving the area a sombre, depressing feel. We could have been walking through our grandfathers' old trenches. The ground was bare—dark greasy clay. Everywhere you looked there were two-man weapon pits, roofed, damp and musty. We had one at the Nugget just like these, somewhere, just couldn't find it under the tangled ground cover. Access to the main gun bunkers was by waist-deep fire trenches floored with duckboards so they could, in theory, be walked through comfortably in the wet.

Strung along the sides there were communication wires for the bunker phones used to communicate between guns and with the command positions in the rear. Wooden planks from packing crates had been used to retain the soil in places, particularly in the gun bunkers. These were sandbagged at the sides and on the roofs. The firing apertures were just above ground level. Most of them had elevated positions beside or above them which the picquets used normally, because the view from them was greater. Each gun bunker had a rough wooden-slat control panel with claymore mine and flare trigger-sets. Crude handpainted coding indicated which trigger fired what. The mines and flares were concealed out in the maze of concertina and trip wire which covered about forty metres from our perimeter out to no-man's land at our front. The ever-present transistor radio earplug and the 'flick zzip clack' of a Zippo cigarette lighter seemed the only links with the modern day. We warned the nearest gun picquet that we were about to use the butts.

'Hang on, Mick, I'll ring around in a sec, get you cleared—just wait for this song to finish. How are ya Crowls? Happy back in the fold?'

'Wasn't quick enough. How about you?'

'Ah, one down, eleven to go. Just like you. The motivated cunts were quicker to figure the game out. Serves us right.'

This was Banjo. I'd known him since Corps training at Ingleburn, where we'd learnt basic infantry skills together. He was tall, about six foot, strong frame, but a bit lean from training and field work. Dark hair, blue-grey eyes, cheeky smile which charmed most people; a dark birthmark or maybe a flat mole, about the size of a small coin, offset a handsome face. I saw him fleetingly on King Hit Two when his section passed by me on their way to set up a night ambush. I was getting my bedding 'just right' for the night as they creaked past. Banjo was bringing up the rear; he shot me a cheeky grin, muttered a hello which meant 'lucky cunt' in a friendly way, and moved on. He'd been that way since I'd known him. At Corps training he was always last on parade, pulling on his trousers, hopping into line, the man next to him having to hold his rifle so he could tie his bootlace. Always last over the obstacle course too. Criticism bounced off him—scraping through was his benchmark. The instructors took it from *him*, but not from any other bastard. He played Slim Whitman relentlessly on his record player. Over here I saw him only occasionally in the field, just a glimpse, and each time his position changed. From tailend Charlie to first rifleman, then gun group commander, then section commander, all within a few months. But typically Banjo, doing just what was required, no more; people couldn't influence him. Another Queenslander. Volunteer Nasho turned Reg, I think.

Banjo gave us the thumbs up, bangety-bangety-bang, then back to the Nugget and bright sunshine. I never bitched much about doing radio watch down in the command post bunker after that. Shit, the perimeter was a gloomy depressing place. It must have had an effect on those who manned it.

Feel like a bit of diversion? Why not. Let's take a shit. The toilets here are those dark green corrugated metal sheds you see scattered around. No, not that one over the service road from the track to the Nugget. It looks the same but that's a shower block. See the water tower beside it, with a great big bucket on top of the ten-metre metal and wood tower? That's how you tell. No point looking in there—just four shower roses, each with a tap, a concrete floor, the drain hole down one end. No bench, soap-holder, basin, nothing. Mirror? What for? You're a number, get it? Use mine. 55485. Oh, I hope you're not shy, or shitting's going to be a lost pleasure. Here we go, this is our preferred crapper, next to Pete's tent on the way to the mess. Like the flywired unglazed window around the top half and the top part of the door? Good for ventilation—it's needed. Don't worry, no one peers in. See why? Come right in. See? No booths, no doors, no need to peek; just four dark green metal-lidded thunderboxes set into the concrete floor. Below us the shit of those who came before us, in a big hole. Take the thunderbox at the far end, but make sure there's a roll of toilet paper within reach on the floor beside you. Most of the blokes here are fucking comedians; they like to see you scrabbling about, crouched over like an ape, clutching your trousers round your thighs, begging for paper. No, don't sit next to that big ugly tattooed prick there. Kill the fucking spider on the box I recommended. The prick never has learnt to lower the lid gently. Slam! See what I mean? How do you like that jet of cloying putrid air blasting up the hole all over you? The lid works like a bellows if you drop it. Don't bitch, if you'd sat closer to him you'd really have been doused. You can smoke in here, but it's a bit risky when clowns like him are about—the methane count's pretty high.

He works in the Q Store. Looks like a real tough bastard, doesn't he? I won't introduce you, no point. He goes barking mad shortly, shoots up a few tents, points his rifle at a few Diggers, sees enemy all around him. Fucking lucky that Staff doesn't shoot him. Gets sent home in a straitjacket shortly. Pete keeps those, maybe in that little tent next to his own. Hope he's got a few more. This isn't the last loonie we'll have by any means, but the others I can sympathise with. It's what they see or have to do here that makes 'em crack up, they're not just shit-frightened for the safety of their own gutless hide like that cunt. Where's the risk in counting blankets, for God's sake? OK, he did a quick trip out in the scrub with us, but Makka held his hand all the way. Got a rifle muzzle pointed at his head for his trouble.

All finished? Let's get some air, for God's sake. Best time to hit the thunderbox is straight after stand-to in the morning. It's cooler then. Still reeks of shit but you sweat less; you're not so likely to slip through the hole and down into it. Scary thought. There's some real humorous bastards around at that time. You'll learn a lot about people's honest philosophy over a crap. Peaches is good value, likes a debate. There's usually an incredible sound session too. If you're into fart jokes this is the place, no need to imagine. If you're very lucky you might get a tipoff about a work party in time to bolt and avoid it, but don't count on it too often. What are you looking for now? No, no basins or soap here, sorry. We'll have to go back to the Nugget to wash our hands. Lunch is nearly ready. Can't miss that, nowhere else to eat, I've checked. Yes, early is best. You come out feeling like singing once you get your breath back, and the air is golden, the road is red, the grass is straw coloured and everything else is green, or blue.

Well, here's the mess, but what's in a name? The same basic construction and size as the boozer, in fact almost directly opposite it, separated only by the company entry road and a rudimentary commercial kitchen tacked on at the front. The other major difference is that at the boozer you enter through the front door and the bar is farthest from you, so you get to check out the crowd before you commit yourself. At the mess you come in at the side door, passing the aromatic wet-garbage bin stand and the dixie-bashing penalty zone on the way in. You won't have to do that chore, I'm exempt—two hooks gets you clear of that shit. Through the door the servery hits you immediately, from the left side like a true coward. The servery here is similar to the boozer's, only longer, and its whole surrounding wall partition is painted a gloomy dark brown, much like the cook's frame of mind. There is no steel dropdown locking grille—what possible use would it serve? No decorations of any sort, just trestles and tables, unadorned except for pepper, salt, sugar in wrapped cubes, a dreadful vinegary mongrel of a chilli sauce courtesy of Yank rations—same as the sweet, acidy bottled shit called catsup. Oh yes, and jars of dill pickles in salted battery acid. Those are given to us free too, by the Yanks.

Anyway, we're getting on to food and we're not ready for that yet, we've just come in the door. And there they fucking are, all four of the bastards, gloating over their steaming trays and cauldrons of spite. The youngest one, short, slim, dark-haired, nearest to us, is a Nasho. Comes from Perth; his Dad owns a pub. Fucking useless. Too immature, never worked a day in his life, doesn't plan to. He came down with some grotesque disease that made it preferable he didn't play with the bread knife, let alone cough over the oysters. Or at least that's what we've been told. He doesn't last long.

Next one along, Cave-in. Just look at the miserable prick. What a sight! Greased-down late '40s haircut, ears like buckled banana leaves, creased sunken face with a long, bent bulbous hooter. All subtly highlighted by skin blotched with several painfully inflamed hair follicles in an otherwise sallow complexion—unless he's been squeezing blackheads, then he pinks up a bit. Boils on the neck. The physique of a stick figure with a caved-in chest. His jungle greens look grey even when new. Medium height, about 25 and of course a Reg. Acid tongue when required.

'Course it's steak! Would I be serving up meat to a dumb cunt like you?'

You could conclude he is a handy lightweight, and he may well have been, he shows no fear of anyone. Cave-in is a trier, in his job and as a soldier. He doesn't go out on Ops with us, isn't allowed to, but I think he has been on almost all the TAOR patrols I've been on, and I've done a few. He is good; a capable weapons handler, knows his basic fieldcraft, never gets windy, never stands out or fucks around. Must be volunteering to go out as often as he does. He never learnt to wear his webbing on his hips, always chafing under the armpits, peering over the top of his ammo pouches like a shy vulture. Christ, he looks a bag of shit. He should have been in the infantry, but he was a fair cook. Some of the Diggers swear he excelled more in the upmarket end of cooking, banquets and such, but that's just kind-hearted bullshit. He's well respected but we don't make much of it here.

Standing next to him is the Lance Jack cook, second in command. Medium height, solid, black hair, round pugnacious face, pencil moustache, married, 28 or so and a Reg. A good humorist when in the mood but apt to have tense moments. You'll learn to pick 'em if you're smart. I saw him kneading a huge slab of bread dough in a zinc washtub one mid-morning. He was outdoors and it was hot and sunny, sweaty. I stopped for a quiet inspection, purely personal reasons. I watched him knead away for a while, rivulets of sweat pouring off him, then asked if it was as hard to do as it looked. He said: 'Nah, there's worse jobs. It's tedious and sweaty, but what I like about it is the way the dough sucks all the shit and crud out of your hands, even from the tiny crevices.' His candour could take the joy out of your day sometimes, but it was he who solved the egg crisis. Eggs were flown in from somewhere, gassed up with formaldehyde or something similar to preserve them. Tasted like horse liniment, fucking dreadful, inedible. Anyway, Lance Jack was away from the Dat on the piss one day, propping up the bar and talking to a Yank caterer. He mentioned how the Diggers were bitching about the eggs. The Yank told him: 'Take 'em from the cool room the night before, let the gas dissipate, they'll be fine.' They were. It was about three months into the tour when he discovered that. It typified communication here—fucking hopeless.

Next to him is Sergeant Dahlia, the head cook. Six-footer, lifesaver physique, blond curly hair, blue eyes, good looks. The type they still use in ads for dentists and lawyers, bland-wanker-type good looks. Soft voice, gentle speaker. Poofter? I think everyone in the company wonders about that, from a safe distance. He has a habit of putting his arm round your shoulder if you stand close in quiet conversation. Pete warned me quite early on, but I'd already worked it out from mildly embarrassing personal experience. I didn't need that shit. With my size, looks, age and sensibly cautious approach to heavy, sweaty, dirty jobs a few of the company suspected I might be a bit on the gay side as it was, without being seen cuddled in public by a big and older senior man.

Look at the food. We have to sometime. Boiled corned beef, casserole this, stew that, roast beef for ten. We're twenty-seventh in line, so forget *that*. Cauliflower au white stuff, grey canned beans, red canned carrots, baked or boiled canned potato, mashed instant potato. There's another variety, too—see that tray of stew with the coating of grey plastic disks? They're dehydrated potato, totally waterproof. Stay clear of them, they crack teeth and gash gums. Right beside us is the best one, that insipid red and white puddle. That's chopped up canned US frankfurters with canned tomatoes, boiled chopped onion, and cornflour to thicken it. Stick by me and you'll eat a lot of that. It's a great favorite of the dedicated drinkers, or the last fifteen or so in line, which amounts to the same thing. At breakfast you can get the frankfurters mixed with baked beans, which is marginally better, but the frankfurters supply is overwhelming, you can't beat them. After a while over here you'll understand how the poor Red Indians felt. Breakfast cereal, tolerable milk but skimmed, dessert if you like custard with everything. Even the brave call it yellow peril—don't know why, I never touch the shit. Tea and coffee in those big square steel urns. Which is which? Don't know. They taste different, but I don't know which is which. Well, what d'you feel like? I've got a can of sardines up at the Nugget if you want some . . .

Some months into the tour a Digger stomps up to the servery with his plate full of stew, plonks it on the servery, and lets the cooks know what's on his mind.

'When are we gunna get some *fucking steak*!!'

The cooks all turn to their leader for defence.

'We don't get steak,' replies Sergeant Dahlia, with all the petulance he dares.

'What do ya fucking get then?'

'Huge slabs of flesh.'

'Show me! I'm a fucking butcher by trade.'

He's a recent reinforcement to the company and proves the best acquisition we could ever get. Three cooks to cater for over a hundred troops, with pretty basic equipment, very little fresh produce and virtually no days off for a year can't work miracles. Even the breadmaking is done by them. But the support of a butcher, when he isn't out in the field as a rifleman, gives them half a chance to perform well, and they try fucking hard. They could handle the frankfurters better, though, that tomato dish is pure spite. I'll never forgive them for that. They have drains to put them down! And bins! I'd gladly dig a hole!

Food apart, there is a good side to the mess—the company. Don't let their looks fool you. There's Tank, that huge bastard halfway down the mess, looking murderous. Over there, Big Mick with another huge bastard, yapping with Lenny. They're real tough bastards, but there's comfort there. On the other side, Woofer and Peaches arguing the toss over some bullshit, Pigpen sticking his oar in. Up the front here, Yabby and Kelsie laughing their arses off over something Young Mick can't fathom.

Reminds you of a prison full of maniacs. Harsh. Sit anywhere you want. Go on, find a gap and sit down, you'll be OK. No one'll snub you. There are groups within the company—people tend to gravitate to types they like, it's only natural. But there's no clubs here, just the company. We've got the lot here, healers, teachers, leaders, bullshitters, wankers, dickheads, thinkers, dreamers and cunts. Bloody good crowd, no smarter than any other hundred dragged in at random, but better tested. The shit's been scraped off. As long as you try you're OK. You'll get a prod if you step too far into your own bad character, but this environment is as fair as it gets. Because everyone is important, everyone counts. Want to die alone?

OK, Christmas Day's been a total loss, but we've covered some ground—you've had a look round and met some more people.

Early on Boxing Day we came off ready alert. Dave hadn't wasted his time either. He'd managed to squeeze in a bit of work at the arsenal in between restocking the Nugget for the grand re-opening. We got started around 6.30 am, just after stand-to. Stand-to? Half an hour before first light till half an hour after, in your gun pit, rifle aimed at the perimeter, everyone on full alert. Same at dusk. Half-light is the likeliest time for enemy attack because everything looks strange in the half-light, disorientating. Our patrols go out through the perimeter wire and search no-man's land while this goes on. We in CHQ don't have to do these sweep patrols, the platoons do it. We in the Nugget don't stand in pits either—can't find ours. If it was a can of piss we'd find it soon enough, but we got away with it. We do the next best thing, lie in bed in a firing position. Tough life!

The first can popped at 6.30 am. At 6.31 we were on our second can and Woofer and Peaches came stride for stride up the path headed our way. Peaches stayed for a beer and I got to know him better. He was similar to Woofer physically, another sawn-off oak tree. Massive shoulders and chest, powerful arms, strong lifter's legs. Dark brown hair, looked Slavic—wide cheekbones, blue eyes, granite jaw. Olive complexion with a pink tinge. Mouth slightly sunken. Out in the field he was intense, brooding and formidable, always ready to unleash. Now I saw the other side to him. He was childlike. Drank a lot of piss, carried a knockout punch in each fist if you got nasty, but if you liked a beer and a peaceful yap Peaches was your man. His real name was Mick, but within days I'd named him Peaches, after Peaches Parkowitz, a well-known American woman tennis player. He liked the name, which was a relief to me, and so did the company it seemed. He was Peaches ever after.

He was from Horsham, a fertile agricultural region in central Victoria. His father owned a small earthmoving and roadpaving business. That explained things—Peaches didn't look like the pastoralists' sons I'd met from there, a pretty heavily indulged private school mob in the main. He'd left home young, ratbagged around a lot and finally beached up in Melbourne, not interested in Dad's business, more interested in having some fun. Rented a flat, threw a few parties, got evicted. Repeated the process a couple of times until he ran out of bond money and gullible landlords. Then he moved in with some mates, threw some more parties, got them evicted. He was called up as he sat on his suitcase on a Melbourne footpath wondering what the fuck came next. Peaches was of the same intake as Dave, Pigpen, Tank and close to half the company members. A vintage intake, as it turned out. Peaches' particular quality was that he thought so deeply he looked dumb.

We hit the mess for breakfast. The creatures of habit choked down a couple of gassed-up eggs. There was bacon and frankfurters and beans for us cowards. Then a company parade. Bit of bullshit from OC, CSM gave the times for lunch and the opening hours of the boozer and advised that morning religious services were an option. That got a few reactions, typically adverse. Peaches sang a touching verse and chorus of 'Jesus wants me for a sunbeam'. His version ended with 'And a fucking good sunbeam

I'll be'—which buggered up the mood he'd set so well but was given a good hand. Perhaps twenty of the Diggers attended the services. I didn't—I went straight back to the Nugget.

Lunch I don't remember. A vague recollection of the officers and senior NCOs serving lunch to us—a patronising tradition. A debate at our table with Pigpen making a point that required him to strangle my lunch for emphasis. I suppose it was turkey—didn't get much of it whatever it was. But it must have been a good day. I woke up next morning with a mouth like a greasetrap, guts full of acid, a thumping head. And I had plenty of mates. Kelsie told me while I was nursing a cup of coffee at breakfast that all West Australians were getting a food parcel, sent from a soldier support group some women had formed. Turned out my Mum was one of them. She was into the Country Women's Association and that sort of bullshit then. Not now, though, she's lost her social position. A rumour must have got round that the packages were full of naked *Playmates*, judging by the crowd that turned up at the Nugget waiting to pounce. Don't know who delivered mine—he was mugged at the tent entrance and got lost in the milling crowd.

The parcel was passed through to me and I was allowed to open it. A box the size of a beer carton. Inside, half a dozen cans of Swan Lager, a good beer then before all the new improved ingredients fucked it up, but not so good in the tropics for some reason. They went under the bed without a fight. A can of plum pudding. I think Pigpen opened that and cut it up, passed it around. I got a bit, wasn't bad. Some cans of fruit, a chocolate bar, melted, a red beer can opener with Swan Lager printed on it. Don't know who got them. Some other stuff, a pack of cards—Dave probably whipped them—and a canned chicken from Canada. Beautifully printed can, a full page of bullshit on the back, probably a list of its chemical additives; the sort of presentation you like to pore over for the sheer pleasure of anticipating the exotic contents. Not with this mob! Dave had the can opener in front of my face. Got the lid off, looked in. A nasty clash of heads, Dave wanted a look too. He pulled back to give me first go. My vision was still a bit blurred but I could make out a white shape in the amber jelly that filled the can. I looked about for a tray to pour it onto. Dave's holding his bayonet in front of my eyes. Fair enough, in with the bayonet, stab the white bit, out it comes, a clean white chicken skeleton, the size of a small pigeon. Everyone left then. Too small to share, let Barrie have it, we mustn't be greedy—all very noble sentiment. That left Dave, Griffo and me.

'Turn the fucking thing out into this,' Dave said, handing me his mess tin. I poured out the can and there at the bottom was the meat, pinky white flakes. Tasted like frog, or perhaps snake, pretty salty. There would have been enough to go round the whole mob. It wasn't the greatest but we finished it anyway, out of boredom. Peaches came over too late to get any, so he drank a couple of my cans of Swan just to be spiteful. That was about it for the Christmas season.

Didn't see much of Peaches for a day or two after that, nor Woofer for that matter. Seems they'd gone off for a day's leave in Vung Tau, a bit of drinking and rooting, a punch-up, a few rounds sent past the fishermen from the rear gun of the Landrover on the way down and back. The snag was the vehicle wasn't theirs, nor was the leave sanctioned. Pity Woofer fired a burst through the brothel ceiling. Peaches thought it sounded great and put a belt through the gun. Shore Patrol found that very interesting. Took their section commander too, ex-Corporal Bob —that is, ex-Corporal after the charges were laid and judgement passed. For Woofer and Peaches it meant twenty-eight days field punishment, same period loss of pay. For ex-Corporal Bob it meant he'd blown three, four or more years' advancement— right back to square one. Field punishment back at base was a prick; you got no spare time and did shit duties for your sins. Serving it out *in the field* was easy—how could they make it much harder than it was? They couldn't, simple as that. It was later found that there was a law against serving in the field without pay.

Consequently Woofer and Peaches had a wicked time on the piss down at Vungers without much penalty at all. Couple of days mess duty. Peaches persevered, though. He got the record for the most misconduct charges in the company. Not for any crime that affected us. He only punched idiots—just fucking the system was Peaches' private delight. He was caught for only a fraction of what he did, but he reckoned he was the only one to pay his passage there and back in fines.

Ex-Corporal Bob wore the lot. It surprised me he'd been in on it; out of character, I would have thought. He was a conscientious sort of soldier, a bit like Griffo, amenable but just that bit aloof, professional. Quite young. Anyway, he stuffed up in a mad moment and went back to arse-end Charlie.

He had another problem at about the same time. He had a brother serving in another regiment over here who got killed. Bob was flown home—his mother was naturally distraught, one son dead and another in the same war. I don't know how he sorted it out but he did. He was back in a matter of days, bringing up the rear, working his way back up the ranks. He had to do it hard. This was no slap on the wrist—give it all back to you next week deal. OC and CSM promoted quite a few Diggers before they looked at Bob again. Bob made Lance Jack after a few months, and finally got back to section commander late in the tour. This was at a time when promotion was quite rapid for the right type of soldier, and I don't think anyone doubted he was the right type. He could easily have sat it out at home, one death in a family is usually a valid way out. Some people are funny. Bob certainly was.

Normal duties began to crowd in again: TAORs, work parties, preparation for the next Op. Diggers started going down to the PX, as they called it. It's an American term for military shop, but I think it was run by ASCO, the Australian Services Canteen Organisation. The blokes started coming back with great radios, cameras, watches and hi-fi quality reel-to-reel tape recorders—stuff we only dreamed of owning back home. The prices were fantastic, affordable. But I never went down, I was hopeless then with that sort of thing. Kelsie did it all for me. He knew I liked good sound and picked out what I'd be happy with. Got me a big powerful transistor radio, tape deck, speakers, earphones, tapes, all the things I wanted that I would've been too ignorant to pick myself. When I think back now, he did a lot for me, and for the others. He was the guy in the stream filling water bottles—I'm sure you remember.

So, we had music. Mainly pirated. We had about fifty record albums floating around the company lines and two or three record decks. I had Sergio Mendes, Feliciano, Sgt Pepper, Sinatra, Ellington and Ray Charles to offer. People taped them, believe it or not. Kelsie organised our taping, it was too complex for most of us.

A lot of the blokes took to taping messages home rather than writing. I did that too. It never occurred to me that my parents would have to scour the neighbourhood for a machine to play it on. I sent them a small tape recorder later, then lost interest in the project. One of the Diggers in Support Section was newly married and really got hooked on the concept. Sat for hours pouring out every heartrending bullshit emotion he could dredge up onto tape for his bride's ears alone. He used to fall into embarrassed silence if any of us tramped in for a yack. I left him to it—didn't see the possibilities. Dave did! He and some other heartless prick, I bet it was Pigpen, tampered with a tape the Digger had ready to mail off. Jazzed it up. Nothing too harsh. A bit of lust and depravity, turgid wet pulsating flesh, throbbing donk, swallow and drool darling—that sort of tone. Now a mature more experienced woman probably would've got a laugh out of it, but this bride was a youngster, the golden glow of the big day still played giddily through her mind. On top of which she was half inclined to believe it *was* only her husband's voice on the tape, and was fearful he'd been turned into a deranged monster. The poor bastard took months to weave together the tattered threads of his once idyllic marriage. Of course Dave was very penitent and supportive. He still brays like a fucking donkey at the memory of that stunt. Reckons he taught the fawning dickhead to write.

As the company's interpreter, I was officially still with BHQ even though I was living and getting paid through the company. That was my hope at that time, at any rate. It put me in an uneasy position. Back at base I had no real function. I did radio picquet, everyone did that, or perimeter picquet. I got caught up in a few work parties, everyone did, unless they were cunning. But like Pete, the medic, I belonged to somebody else. At least Pete had company duties, listening to all the whingeing bullshitters on sick parade, sticking needles into us, puddling around with his drugs locker. My real duty was to spend time with Bé, improving my interpreting capabilities. I had a couple of problems with that, and nothing to do with me hating the little cunt. First off, he couldn't teach a bored dog to dig a hole. Secondly, he was seldom at the base. When he did show up other than to go out with us into the field, he was on the scrounge for goods to sell on the blackmarket.

One morning I get the idea I could make myself useful at BHQ, so I walk over with Pete to present myself. Pete is headed there on routine business at the medical centre. I find Intelligence Section's building and hang around at the counter for someone to turn up. One or two faces walk past, totally ignoring me. Fuck you then, I'll go over to the lines—have a yack with some of the boys. But there's no one about, unless you count an RP who stops long enough to ask what I'm up to. It doesn't take me long to figure out there's no place for me here anymore.

But while I'm here, let me tell you a bit about the battalion structure. I think you know already that there are four rifle companies. I'm with one of them. There's also Support Company and Admin Company. Admin Company contains all the clerks, the drivers, senior blowfly (the expert shit drainer cum drain unblocker), the stores people—that sort of role. The type who prop up the bar at the RSL and tell all the war stories, show all the photos. You've met them, surely—true war heroes. Medical Section are lumped in with Admin too, to give them a home. Similarly the catering mob, though neither are infantry. Also the armourer, who looks after weapon maintenance. Support Company are infantry in the real sense of the term. They form the permanent defence for BHQ out in the field, so that a rifle company isn't always tied up looking after it. They have a mortar platoon and also an assault pioneer platoon, who are infantry but trained to build defence structures and temporary bridges, to disarm mines—whatever is required of a practical nature in the field. A poor man's engineer group I suppose. There's also the battalion sigs, or radio operators. There's an anti-tank platoon who fire things that look like bazookas, and odds and sods like tracker-dog teams, special tracker teams and such. Field soldiers with specialised skills. That's enough to know in order to get by. For a rifle company the sigs are the most important; in my experience the rest are a good idea but mainly self-serving—we're usually too far away to call on their services. The sigs are vital because they can link us to air and artillery support if we're in the shit. They also convey the orders that *put* us in the shit, but that's not their fault. Oh yes, the RPs are attached to Support Company too—there goes an otherwise good neighbourhood.

I'm about to head back to my company lines when I see Canh walking towards me.

'How you go, Lé?' he calls. Lé is the name I was given at language school. Everyone got one. I believe Lé (pronounced Lay) means something virtuous or wise—just my luck—can't eat that shit.

'Not bad Canh, what're you doing?'

'Oh, hiding . . . work, things, you know.'

I mention the captive we sent for interrogation, and ask if he's heard anything about him.

'No, probably in Tiger Cages now.'

'What the fuck are they? I've heard of them.'

'They . . . er . . . interrogation place, question for VC, not good, very bad.'

'What do they look like?'

'Oh, how to . . . long trench, prisoner crouch, can't stand, barb wire, bar on top . . . very . . . crowded? . . . Guard beat and kill. Not so many come free . . . none maybe . . . I think.'

'Who runs it?'

'Oh, there are few, near Saigon. Government runs.'

'Our prisoners go there?'

'All go, I think, no place here.'

Did they show those camps on TV at home? Very interesting. I later saw photos of them in a book. They were real, don't worry about that. Canh knew what he was on about.

Next Op coming up, time to skip. The Nugget took on a business atmosphere at night. Dave got his crown and anchor game going at the boozer which gave him the cashflow to gamble. If you don't know the game it's played with dice and you bet on one of six squares—crown, anchor and the four playing card suits. The banker can't lose. Dave was the banker. I didn't gamble, so for me this meant less people to talk to at the boozer, and after that closed, a tent full of fucking idiots playing poker in the Nugget. Christ, gambling for money bores me shitless! I didn't kick up a fuss, I had nowhere else to go. I lay on my bunk reading, drank beer on the house for being good. When they played till three or so I got nice and shitfaced. There was no way you could sleep sober with all the bullshit punters drivelling on to bolster their egos, while they were being fleeced.

New Year's Eve came and mostly went while we packed our kit. Griffo, surfacing out of a daze, said: 'Dave, better pull Jock's strides back up. Find him a bed, eh.'

'Pity . . . fuckin' hilarious if you ever get to see it.'

Dave turned the light back on and put his torch away. Some time in the night Jock had blundered back to his own lines flinching and whimpering with a merciless hangover. He had a section relying on him out in the field in the morning. He'd saved the quart of malt whisky for months to celebrate Hogmanay, and true to his race he'd passed out over the sandbags, spewing and farting like a tuba, at three seconds to midnight—toasting out the old year with us. Dave had whipped his strides down, killed the light and trained the Big Jim torch beam on his arse, so we could see one pout sticking out like an elephant's trunk.

A very memorable New Year's eve—I stayed sober throughout. Just as well with Dave around. And we were heading out again in the morning.

At 7.30 the trucks were waiting. OC called quietly over to Duntroon so most of us could hear: 'He was VC.'

'Confirmed, is it?'

'The prisoner, yes, VC alright.'

Well, I'll be fucked. What is the point? Why do you have systems in place to dispense justice when no bastard in the system does the job? That little prick never had a hope. I don't know if he was VC or not. How could I? But the cunts he got sent to didn't either, and had no intention of finding out. He was a hick, a peasant, that was enough.

Let's get on the truck. We won't take many more prisoners—it just works out that way. Not that it matters, there's only one way out for them in this system.

CHAPTER 5

THE TRUCKS TOOK US TO A DESTINATION out on the flat where we were soon on choppers and well away. The Op was called Goodwood—either that or Federal. Doesn't matter anyway, one followed the other and we did them both, followed by several others. We didn't see the Dat for three months. I don't know what caused this—no reason was ever given for the length of stay in the field, but I can speculate. It isn't that hard to work out. Tet '69 was upon us and the Yanks weren't going to suffer a repeat of '68. This war was being beamed back to the United States for daytime TV. Many of the common people were starting to question the performance of the military, even the need to be in Vietnam at all. Tet was the time to show how a war is won, that's when this enemy traditionally showed itself. But the Viet Cong were a bit thin on the ground this year— weren't living up to the Pentagon's expectations. It was probably caused by them being bled white from their efforts of '68. It could also have been as a result of seemingly promising peace negotiations being conducted in Paris by all the warring factions. Not us of course, or the Kiwis. We were not at war, officially.

We weren't exposed to media coverage the way the Yank troops were. Too small a picture but we still had to play the game, get the numbers in. We got the numbers in towards the end of the stint, but a lot of hard slog went into it before we did.

I now hootchied with Pete. Out in the field, that is. Back at base Pete and Brian, the stretcher bearer, got on fine. They weren't close, didn't like each other for a start, but they respected each other and were known to sit around the table in their tent and talk for hours. Mainly shop. Out in the field, forget it. Couldn't see eye to eye on anything except their work. Have I described Brian yet? Don't think I have. Six foot, slim and sinewy, black hair, long face, prim mouth, black moustache failing to conceal it, wise blue sunken eyes, big hawkbeak hooter, bulldog jaw. Got himself in a deep pile of shit as we went along, but he was OK. He features quite a bit in my memories. Brian was a Sydneysider, a motor mechanic by trade. Used to race a red hot FJ Holden at Randwick raceway, when he could afford to rebuild the last buggered-up motor. At night, when he wasn't fixing knackered donks in his garage, he drummed for jazz bands. Any jazz band that would have him I suspect, but he'd been in some good company. Growing up in Sydney, in this environment, he appeared to me sophisticated, but it still didn't stop him landing in the shit. He was a Reg. Twenty-two or so, and married, which held the seeds of his problems.

Brian decided he and Bé would hootchie together and I would have to suffer Pete's obnoxious habits. Oh God! Shoot me now before it all changes back again! The relationship between Bé and me hadn't improved. I had gone from being Lé, to Barrie, to Crowley. At least he'd stopped fawning on my shoulder, but he'd taken to teary outbursts which I found equally tiresome. One day out and Pete and I were firm hootchie buddies—it worked. Pete was a bloke who did his job, wouldn't be fucked around, pulled his weight along the way and liked a laugh in good company. Bé got passed around without a taker after Brian got sick of the sight of the cunt and booted him out. Slept without a friend, slowly drifted out of sight. He was still with us at the moment though.

We're back in the jungle and we're following tracks. Hiding, as the journos like to describe it. They much prefer the approach of some US units, which allow them to drive to the village, snap snap, get back to the bar for the afternoon, their copy filed. Either they're not capable of knowing what they're seeing, or their editors have them by the nuts. Otherwise you wouldn't read all the bullshit that gets printed on this place.

We come to a creaking halt and, after an eternity of glaring into the foliage looking for would-be killers and reshuffling harness and pack off our raw patches, we are called forward. We enter a semi-clearing, one obviously thinned by men to make vision and movement easier, without being too obvious from the air. At its centre stands a house, a halfway house, used as a comfort stop by the small bands of VC troops on their way to a rallying point or returning from battle. Or just wondering what the fuck to do next. We were told about these buildings at Corps training, but they weren't described. This first one is very much a place of rest. A one-room construction about four metres by four, dressed forest timber poles for the supports, flush floorboards supported on log joists, intricately woven fibre walls and a thatched high-pitched roof. The door and the windows are apertures with flaps of matting which could be rolled up and tied. Not unlike our own tents at the Dat, only not defended by sandbags and much airier—more natural, golden, smelling of warm straw, rice and spices. Away from the house are a number of tiny, recently tended kitchen gardens, a few plants growing in each: herbs, chillies, leaf and root vegetables. Our search turns up buried rice—some of it local rice in any old packing; some of it bagged in plastic; the type readily available from any local store, instant processed US grain. Boiled for an hour it's rumoured to be tolerable. Times must be tough for Charlie if he has to eat that at a rest stop.

The gardens have to be trashed, the rice slashed and ruined. The house has to be torched. The platoonies have to do that job. We move out, having watched the house slide off its supports in a cloud of dense red sparks and smoke.

We march on and soon the country changes. We leave the forest and enter what was once forest. Bomb craters and limbless grey tree trunks, turned rust-coloured at the gaping rents on the trunks, stretch out before us to the limits of sight. Bomb craters ten metres in diameter, eight metres deep, almost overlapping. It is overcast and humid, migraine territory. We might be on the moon. There is no going around it, our compass bearing says straight ahead; so we cross this open grey field, unsuited to troops crossing it without detection. It's too vast to skirt anyway.

It leads into defoliated forest. The defoliants used are systemic, like cancer they go from the leaves right through the plant to the roots, which they kill. These places are petrified, no bark on the trees, no leaves, weathered grey splitting trunks, shrubs long gone, punk and decay underfoot, a few weeds struggling. We've never seen devastation like it. It dulls the senses. We march through this landscape, clambering over fallen trees, careering down craters when we tread too near the edge and it caves in, clawing our way back up again against a tide of collapsing powdery sand.

A lot of silly bastards who were there at the time reckon they got sick from patrolling through areas like these, or from being involved in the process of destroying areas like these. They've been known to die in order to prove it. I don't know—I'm still kicking, and most eminent people reckon they'd have died anyway, so who's to know?

Have I described the wildlife of the jungle? The pristine jungle, that is. The monkeys, yes. You were lucky to see that much, especially travelling in the middle of a column of ninety men. The scouts saw more. They had to, they had no choice. The fleeing arse of a small silver-grey deer, a bird perhaps, something small scuttling up a tree or bamboo stem. Otherwise you shot at it, unless you recognised the form. There were tigers in the jungle. We heard one on our first Op, just after dusk it started roaring its guts out. Kept it up half the fucking night. A Yank grunt got dragged out of his perimeter by a tiger and was eaten, around the time we arrived in country. I wouldn't have cared normally, but he was in our territory when it happened. Dave loved that sort of shit. 'Imagine one of them cunts dragging you off. Wouldn't ya shit, eh? Wouldn't ya!' Thankfully Bé bore the brunt of his humour.

We never saw one, though—a tiger. Which is probably why we old Diggers bullshit a lot about the insect population in Vietnam, didn't see much else. It's true, we had a lot here, leeches, ticks, spiders, ants. Mozzies? A lot, but no more than many parts of Australia. Flies? Nah, compared to home they barely existed. And we had scorpions, centipedes, and a few little nasty surprises that I never saw. Some of the Diggers talk of the RTA bug—one bite and you're Returned To Australia.

Never saw it; if I had I'd have wagged my bare arse within biting distance of it right away. The youngest member of our company got bitten on the knob by a tick or some other thing. Had a cock like a torpedo for a couple of weeks; left the field by chopper to get it treated. Otherwise, insects weren't usually a major problem, I've been in worse country back home.

There was a big strange Norwegian with us, a sapper, engineer. We usually took one, an NCO, plus his offsider, with us on every Op—to blow up bunker systems, burn huts, or disarm dangerous devices if we spotted them in time. The big Nord, Sven, that'll do him, was a good bushman. He used to pick grasses, leaves, berries and seeds to cook with at the end of the day. Can't say it smelt good—Dave never stole his food, there's a tip. But Sven looked fit on it. Tall, lean, muscular and tanned. Going thin on top, blond of course, big mangy ginger handlebar moustache, a face you usually see on totem poles.

We were sitting in a bamboo copse not far from the defoliated area, brewing coffee, a bit of a gathering. Sven, Pete, the Kiwi forward observation officer and me, waiting for the water to boil. We were still dwelling on what we'd just been travelling through for more than a day. I thought of something that cheered me up—decided to share it, like an idiot.

'No snakes here. I thought the place'd be crawling with 'em.'

Sven, sitting opposite me, reached over my head with his machete. *Tock!* In the bamboo tendrils just above my head. And a jade green snake a metre long dropped with a plop at my feet, right by the little tin stove we were boiling our water on. Stone dead. Otherwise I'd have been too far away to hear Sven say: 'Oh, always plenty snakes here, yoost haf to look.'

I didn't see another snake until I was waiting outside Task Force Headquarters, watching it crushed to death and thinking of how best to protect my arse over yet another big fuckup. But I now knew the bastards were here. That took the pleasant edge off sleeping on the ground for quite a while.

Sven had a way with technology. Dave and I were brewing coffee shortly afterwards. He'd dropped by between patrols. Sven came over.

'You using Hexamine!' he gasped, as though we were using DDT. 'Dat shit fooking useless, good for only ants in yoo pack!'

Hexamine was the solid fuel capsules we burned to heat our food. It resembled candle wax. We burned it in a little collapsible tin stove about the size of a thick sandwich.

'Here . . . use dis!' Dave took the dull green shrink-wrapped bar, measuring about thirty centimetres by five by three, from Sven's hand.

'PE?'

'Yes, PE. Is fookin' good.'

Dave knew what it was, so did I—plastic explosive.

'Yeah . . . fine, *you* boil the water. We'll wait behind that tree over there. Call us when it's ready.'

'Ah, bullshit, Barrie. It safe. Put a detonator to it, you got a bit of problem. Burn it, it fookin' magic.'

Dave was game, but I've told you he's crazy. He told me to stay right where I was. Sven knew what he was on about. I thought Sven was crazy too, but what the hell, I was getting curious. Dave broke off a two-centimetre piece—it looked and felt like white plastic cake icing—put it in the stove, put the metal cup of water on top and lit it. What a sight! Hexamine burnt like a candle, when you finally got the shit to light. This stuff burnt with a brilliant blue flame like an oxy welder. The water boiled in seconds. Had to be careful with heating canned food, though, unless you ate molten tar by choice. PE made a big difference to our lifestyle. We showed Pete, he told Brian, and within two minutes the whole company had stripped all the PE supplies that Sven, CSM, Griffo—anyone—had set aside for demolition work. CSM never ordered Hexamine again. He saw the benefits quicker than anyone did. Out in the field, this discovery meant the difference between having a hot brew and a meal and not having it, for most of the platoon Diggers. Those poor pricks often had just minutes to get a meal organised before last light, and Hexamine was too slow-burning.

While we're talking coffee, how did you like the water? It was chlorinated, stored in PVC jerrycans at the Dat—that's why it tasted like a swimming pool. Amoebic dysentery is common in the streams no matter how clean they look, we were told. We use water from the streams anyway, in the field—it was that or die from thirst. Usually we boiled it. And we were issued chlorine pills. Nobody thought of herbicide runoff—who knew of that sort of problem then? A lot of people, it seems—none that spoke of it then, though. Stick to the resupply water, much smarter. It's safe. Comes from base. Where's base? The Dat. Where does the Dat get it? Out of a river I suppose, I doubt it's flown in from the Snowy Mountains.

Questions of chemical contamination have been asked for years. Many eminent men say it's all bullshit—that it was harmless, never hurt anyone. In my experience most eminent men speak through their fat pay cheques, or their research grants, which amounts to the same thing—so set those weak bastards aside for what they are. Look at the figures. Vietnam Vets do have more health problems than their civilian counterparts. I don't think it is many times more, but significantly more. I don't query whether Agent Orange and all the other shit that was dropped all around us affected us, but what happens to populations outside a war zone? This one or any other. That's the real question. Of course the chemicals used in Vietnam were deadly. Check out the health of the population of South Vietnam. There's all the proof you need. But think about my question—that's the one that must be answered.

Dave hounded Bé relentlessly, kept stealing his meals. Bé brought rice, spices and herbs, and took food from the jungle to add zing to the ration packs. Smelt good. He showed me how to find young bamboo shoots at the base of a copse. They looked like a rhino's horn, about ten centimetres long was best, beyond that they got tough. Bit of stuffing around involved, with nothing but a blunt bayonet to cut with, after you found a flat rock. I showed Dave. He couldn't be bothered with cutting them either, not while Bé was around.

'Where my food go, Lé?' Bé asked me.

'Dunno.'

'This your cup, Bé?' Dave asked.

'Yes, where food? You eat it Fwenchy?' (This was how Bé pronounced Dave's name.)

'Ease up, what sort of a cunt d'you think I am. I found your cup, here take it!'

Bé went hungry.

'Hey, Bé, OC wants to see you right away.'

'Now? I eat now Fwenchy.'

'Now!'

'What did OC want Bé?'
'Nothing, not know what I talk about. Where Fwenchy?'
'Good question.'
Bé wouldn't fall for that stunt again. But Dave had options—limitless, credible options.

Dave was becoming a real irritant to me. He got fed and I got Bé crying and whining hour after hour. The little shit was starving to death. I intended to fix things—not for Bé's wellbeing—for my own peace of mind. But I didn't get the chance. Dave, the thieving bastard, got shot! I was sitting down sorting out what rations to keep from the latest resupply and Pigpen turns up behind a prodding finger.

'You tell that bludging, fucking mate of yours when ya see him I'm fucking sick of him!'
'Who?'
'Dave! He flew back to base in the resupply chopper just now, smug look on his face, the prick.' This was news to me, Dave leaving, and him being *my* mate—Pigpen and Dave were like brothers.
'What'd he fly out for?'
'Wounded, of course,' Pete chipped in.
'Wounded? Pete, you're fucking handy to have around.'
'What am I, the gossip column? Thought you were there when I packed him off. Must have been Brian. Fuck-all anyway—couple of pellets in the arse.' Pete turned back to reading my book.
'What happened?'
'Ah, fuckin' joke. Support Section came out with us last night to up numbers on the ambush.'
'I didn't know. Heard the shooting.'
'Yeah? Where do *you* live?' Pigpen squatted on his haunches. 'Anyway . . . Dave gets link spot next to Jock's section. We hear movement just before first light, spot a few. Jock presses the tit, every cunt opens up, then we do the search. Time to check our own position. "Anyone hurt?" "Yeah . . . ME! The fuckin' Scotch cunt shot me with his claymore" says Dave. He had too. Still hobblin' around, but Dave knew where he was going. Hospital bed in Vungers, already plottin' a way of getting stuck into the sluts. And here *we* are. That your coffee there?' He pointed.

Dave was gone for weeks. He missed the sight of our first big bunker system. We'd found a few bunkers up to now, either not in use at the moment or the occupants had run off when they heard us coming. Up to six or so well-dug bunkers to house enemy units about the size we could realistically handle without support. All our contacts up to now had been against small bodies of troops on the move—suited us. If we'd walked into this one when it was fully manned our company would now be just a name in a file in some dusty corner of the military archives, not for public view. It was huge.

We struck it in the late afternoon, after a day of stop, start, stop, fucking start; uphill all the way, through jungle. Our feet throbbed, our arses were chafed raw, and so were a lot of our tempers. At our last halt we were on a track that could have been cut by a bulldozer. I'd had enough! My pack and webbing were killing me. We could be on the Ho Chi Minh Trail—who gives a fuck! Give me a break! Imagine our scouts up the front, more loaded down, following bearings, searching everywhere, likely to be shot, responsible for the lives of ungrateful, uncaring cases like me. Finally we were called forward, guided along tested paths by members of the lead platoon, placed in harbour positions for the night. It was still two hours to dusk, and the care with which we were placed gave me all the orders I needed. That and what I saw on the way in. We were in a gigantic bunker system in which the Viet Cong, presently absent but due to return, might have left some nasty traps for us to find. I crashed on my pack on the ground, went dead for five minutes. Got up. Checked the ground for nasties, helped Pete finish stringing the hootchie up, fluffed up the farter, got coffee on. Plenty of time for two cups before dinner. Crept over to OC's radio operator and organised the ten till midnight radio watch. It wasn't my turn but it was the best shift to have and he believed my lies. Went back to the hootchie floating on air and got stuck into some dedicated spine-bashing.

Human nature is incredible to observe. Every bastard who wasn't on picquet was out scratching among the thinned undergrowth, finding and then peering down bunkers. Hundreds of bunkers. Sunk deep in the red clay, roofed with three layers of logs laminated and then covered with rammed earth. Built to withstand anything but blanket bombing. Fire pits connected many of them. No communications tackle—nothing other than earthworks was left behind. Saw it all on the way in.

Night routine took over. Yapped with Pete till ten, went on radio picquet. Listened to the transistor radio, heard Buck Owens and the Buckeroos sing 'Rocky Top Tennessee'—written by Dolly Parton, I think. It blew my brains out. The rest was shit, whining old cowboys sounding like old women, young women entreating you to tread on their head, steal the housekeeping, take the car and fuck the barmaid. This shift wasn't great for music unless you were patient. It just gave you five hours' straight sleep from midnight.

In the morning it started.

'Barrie, come and take a look at this!' Pete's calling.

'I'm busy.'

'Stop fucking around, just . . . get over here, fuck ya!'

I went, knowing what I was going to see. And there it was, about forty metres away from my tent through the scrub—the entrance to an underground bunker system. The entrance was cut out of the clay, a steep ramp fifty metres long, sloping down a fifteen-metre incline to an arch-shaped doorway high enough for a small man to walk through, straight into Hades. The sappers would go down it of course, but I knew it was going to involve me. It had a sign above the entrance: BARRIE CROWLEY WILL PASS THIS WAY.

'Just going over here for a look,' I said to Pete, and shot through. Fuck you lot! Found a quiet spot and looked for somewhere to hide.

Meanwhile OC's briefing the two Sappers on their mission. 'Thirty minutes you've got, then we come and get you.'

'Nah, we'll need forty.'

'OK, forty.'

Off they went, down the tunnel, with me peering at the scene from cover. The offsider I can't recall at all. The team leader was roughly my height, stocky, brown hair, round face. He was with us at the Hill, later on. What he said and did remain with me; the man himself I could now walk straight into and not recognise him. They were gone thirty-five minutes, I knew they would be. The company started looking for me. I knew that too, being officially the smallest in the company. There were several as small, or smaller, but they lied about their height and weight. Even Pete joined in the hunt, the heartless bastard. I was considering hiding under a pile of leaves when some prick grabbed me on the shoulder from behind and yelled out. I shrugged free and walked to the entrance as though I'd just caught on I was needed. Duntroon was organising the show at the top of the ramp.

'Hi Crowls, we'll need you to go down and check on the sappers,' he called cheerily, the cunt.

'Not forty minutes yet.'

'I know that—just be ready.'

Forty minutes came. I'd said nothing. Duntroon kept me in sight, but otherwise left me alone. Then the guillotine creaked.

'Crowls, better get going, they're overdue.' Operatic concern written all over him, but it suited the mob to agree. I would've too if I was six feet and hefty.

'Yeah, sure, who's coming?'

'Just one, you.'

I thrashed that one out for all it was worth. Duntroon himself was ideal—only slightly larger than me, an officer, proven sound in battle. But he didn't like holes in the ground any more than me, it seemed. That wasn't what he said. He was running the top end of the show, already had a role, meant to keep it. I appreciated his position. Fuck, did I appreciate it! Still, the debate bought time. It was now forty-six minutes. I grabbed my rifle, stepped on to the ramp, farted around for another three minutes, checking the magazine, gnawing at a hangnail, adjusting webbing, asking a couple of stupid questions. Trudged down the ramp. Stopped halfway.

'Anyone got a spare torch?'

Five were held out within easy reach. That buggered it. Inched my way to about three metres from the entrance—and out they popped.

'Ya should of fucking seen what we've just seen!' blared the senior sapper, eyes like saucers.

'I very nearly did,' I said.

'Shit, they weren't sending you after us? Fuck, don't ever do that. We said forty minutes, it took longer. We go down, we get back, we'd have fucking shot ya . . . Ya should have fucking seen . . .'

I tell you, communication was shocking over here. I didn't get to go down the tunnel. I was content with the sapper's description to me later, when I'd unkinked a bit.

'Ya should have seen it—went for miles, no gear in it, all stripped like up here, but you could make out what they had. There's a hospital, kitchen, huge fucking galleries for hundreds of troops, storerooms, offices, everything, a little city! Ducting . . . chimney system . . . fucking brilliant.'

'Any traps?'

'Nah, none we saw. I've seen most of 'em in other systems—not a system this big though.'

Some of the boys had a quick look around, just inside it, for the experience. It was a dark hole in the ground.

Satisfied? Go ask a Tunnel Rat if you're not, if you can find one that's recovered his sanity yet.

We had a number of contacts during the Op. One platoon or another ran into an enemy patrol from day to day—law of averages, they walked far enough to find trouble. If it was a straightforward contact it meant a bit of a brass-up, count and bury the enemy; people in my position didn't know much about it. Unless you were hanging around OC's radio when it happened and listened in. Usually it was close by and you heard the shooting. But there was no regular briefing on events. You caught up on the details later if anyone was talking about it, which was a rarity.

Two contacts I recall because they happened as we moved along in company formation and I got a chance to see the results. The first occurred when Lenny was leading the company through forest. The ground between the trees was screened by scrub and occasional bamboo clumps. The sky was dull and overcast. From up at the front we heard the *brraaaatt!* from an Armalite, Lenny's. A bit of return fire from a couple of AK47s cracked through the leaves above our heads in CHQ, about 150 metres back down the track, then what sounded like Lenny and his second scout firing more shots. All this took thirty seconds or so. Then nothing. A minute or so more and we were called up to form temporary company defence around the contact area.

I arrived on the scene just as the contact section were starting to mill around Dusty, Lenny's section commander, lying on the track. He lay partly under a low, wave-shaped sandy bank, half a metre high, right in the bend of the track his section were following when they met a band of VC coming the other way. Lenny had dropped the first one, hit the deck, passed back the signal to his section commander: enemy directly in front! Then he fired again, supported by his number two scout who'd come up beside his position.

By now orders are coming forward and the gun group have hit the deck, giving the enemy a shitload of grief, and the rifle section are sweeping through to join Lenny's line in support. The rest of the platoon are driving forward to kill. It's all bullshit because Dusty's hanging off the end of two bamboo spikes, or punji stakes—totally out of it. The whole system's jammed up because the section commander was smart—went for the best cover and the best view as soon as the first shot was fired. But some cunning little bastard had anticipated that—he'd set six two-metre-long bamboo staves into the side of the wave-shaped bank looking right up the track at the bend. The staves had been sharpened to barbs and were all but invisible. Dusty copped one deep in the thigh, another in the upper left arm, not as deeply.

As I approached, some of his section were just easing him off his perch. Dusty was in pain, having a nice old whinge. Partly because of the pain; but also he'd lost the picture, that's what was gnawing at him. Without him to set things in motion, Lenny and his mate were on their own until someone stepped out of line and took over. That takes time. Out here the lowest level of command is vital.

The enemy didn't exploit this break in communication by attacking. Instead, they chose to drag their fallen, shoulder them at the gallop, and get out. Lenny and some of his section sorted out what they could. Then the choppers came in. I thought it was a dustoff for Dusty. Pig's arse! We were needed elsewhere. Lenny carried him to the chopper; at the other end Lenny carried him off again. The choppers had more pressing tasks. Dusty would keep. They made an odd couple—one whimpering in pain, the other wondering if he was expected to continue to scout with Dusty draped over his shoulder. Dusty recuperated in country, returned to his section for a while and then went to AATTV as a sergeant. AATTV? Australian Army Training Team, Vietnam. They were hand-picked soldiers who went out in small teams training up Republican Vietnamese into units, then taking them out to fight. That might have been when Big Mick got his second hook.

The second contact was much bigger. Here we're in real headache country—high dense grass, three-metre-high scrub, closely packed forest. Following a track more like a narrow road, hilly, and you guessed it, humid; grey as granite overhead, with sporadic soft flickers of lightning. Then—*brraaaatttt!!* from an Armalite, the *back!back!back!* of an AK47, then the guns of both sides open up and their RPG rockets and our M72s start whizzing one way and crumping back the other. We're all on the deck. The rest of the contact platoon get up and reach a position where they can shoot at the enemy.

Then one of our reserve platoons roars through the area to the front at right angles to us, spread out in a straight line covering 200 metres or more, smashing through deadfall and heavy growth at a frightening rate, letting off a few shots at whoever they see that isn't us. One rifle is heard above it all. *Boom boom boom boom boom.* It's an SLR with a matchstick under the trigger mechanism; easy to do, turns it into a machine gun. But just try holding on to the cunt of a thing when you fire it! Wheels you around like a mad dog, so the fifth shot hits you in the arse.

Not this bloke, Boom Boom, a farm boy from Pingelly in my own adopted State. He holds it like I would a torch. Looks like Lee Marvin. Probably has the bullets notched too. Cut a groove in the point of a bullet and it opens up like a jagged dustbin lid on impact. Get hit with one of them, you really get hit. Good man to have on your side, Boom Boom. Good company too. I drank a fair bit of piss at the boozer with him—not much of a talker but funny when he did, and safe.

Time for a bit of weapons instruction. The SLR, self-loading rifle, was our standard issue weapon. It could drop a rhino without much trouble if you held it steady enough and remembered the safety catch. Not bad for maintenance, bit of a prick to cock—you had to reef the cocking handle back hard and fast with your left hand and let it snap back as you continued to reef. It was a knack, took practice. Don't do it right and the cartridge wouldn't chamber fully and it wouldn't fire, and that could be the end of you. Twenty-round magazine, so you did it every twenty shots, unless you chanced a thirty-round mag, but they could jam. Not a weapon for a mug.

Our scouts, section commander and gun group commander carried Armalites. Also called M16s. Revved up small-bore semi-automatic rifles you could set to single shot or fire in bursts. Usually twenty rounds to the mag, thirty if you wanted. They were very light, plasticky, had to be kept spotless or they jammed up. Some Diggers didn't trust them, not enough hitting power; tended to go through people without dropping them. When they came out the M16s were given lots of TV news coverage worldwide. This little marvel was supposed to have a tumble action to the bullet, or projectile, so it could rip a human body apart on impact. Bullshit. It couldn't, not possible. That lie was later revised to say the bullet travelled along bone when it hit, causing massive tissue damage. Bullshit. Any bullet can do that, but you can't influence it—it happens or it doesn't. The makers had even shonkied up demo footage and graphs, interviewed experts, the lot. US-made and US-marketed, of course. You can put any bullshit on TV, it seems, people soon forget. Woofer, Pigpen, blokes like them, thought the M16s were OK, learnt how to master them. Hit 'em with a good burst. Hit 'em again if need be. One positive: they were much lighter than the SLR and so was the ammo, but you needed to carry more of it.

The Viet Cong had AK47s. A Russian-designed weapon. Same bore as our SLR, same capability as the Armalite, automatic, a rough and ready weapon that was pretty reliable. Dust and crud didn't affect it too much. Not super-accurate, tended to scatter rounds a bit on auto but that could be a good thing when you were shooting at a moving target. I'd have chosen that weapon if I'd had a choice, ideal for the jungle.

Guns? We used the M60 US-issue machine gun. Same 7.62 mm Nato round as the SLR took, which was handy. Good gun. Bit tinny. They weren't rated for continuous firing because they overheated and had no cooling system, but I never heard a gunner complain about the M60. Don't know what the VC used. Any gun they could get, I suppose. Often their gunpower was superior. Rockets? They went *voooossshh . . . carrummppp*. Shrapnel, shock and searing flame everywhere. Ours were more portable, telescopic, US-issue. The RPG, which the VC used, was launched off a steel tube nearly two metres long, a prick of a thing to lug around. That'll do for now.

Back to the contact. The shooting and crumping have gone on for two minutes or so. CHQ move up behind the contact platoon as they make ground on the enemy. Now we're in a bombed-out section of the forest. The enemy have been swept off the track they were travelling along and into the scrub, then driven back the way they had come. I can see some of the contact platoon taking cover, using fallen tree trunks. This area is a mess. Bombed within the last month. Ground churned up, craters everywhere, the few trees still standing surviving on one or two shattered limbs; all the others upended and mangled, lying in heaps where they fell. I'm in a clear patch. I can see now it's Duntroon's platoon that made the contact. Duntroon's crouching with the contact scout, Pigpen, getting a briefing on what his scout saw. Next minute the two of them are off in the direction the enemy fled, following something, Pigpen leading. Pete disappears, looking for wounded. I slink over to Boom Boom, who's crouched behind a stump covering Pigpen's back.

'What're that pair up to?'

'Following a trail, might be a body out there.'

'I'm gunna take a look.'

'Don't go past that big line of deadfall. We hit a big group. They might turn up again.' There was thirty metres of open ground to the pile of shattered tree trunks he'd indicated.

'Start here, Bazz.' He's pointing at a blood trail almost beside him. I've been standing on it and haven't noticed. This one goes straight to the tangled line, an evenly spaced trail of big blood spots going right over the tree trunks and into the heavy going over the other side. Back I come and on to the next one. Find that easy enough. Chunks of guts and gouts of blood and tissue as if someone had poured it from a bucket as they went. That's the one Pigpen and Duntroon have followed. The third one is further on, one of the platoonies points the way for me. This trail is all blood, three centimetres wide, almost an unbroken line, easy to follow right up to the tangle.

The one with the guts in it was judged a certain trail, but the body wasn't found. The other two were judged blood trails. I doubt that any of these men survived. They weren't choppered out to well-equipped medical treatment stations within an hour or two as we usually were. The VC death toll was very high because of this. Our death toll was remarkably low compared to theirs, and also compared to past wars we've been in. Choppers, that's why. Check our casualty lists, you'll see what I mean; they were long enough.

Soon after, Pigpen and Duntroon return, and we get sorted out to move off. I move back to where CHQ are forming up, near the point where the contact started. Griffo, Brian, Young Mick and Pete are up the track a bit, looking at something. It's the body of the scout Pigpen dropped at the start of the contact. His pack and AK47 are already being taken away by some of the platoon to OC and Duntroon for examination. The body lies twisted on its back, with the legs splayed sideways. Dark blue shirt, black trousers, rubber tyre-tread sandals.

'Check this out Crowls,' Griffo murmurs as I draw up to them. The VC had been stitched right up the side from the ankle to the head, eight or nine wounds. And not a drop of blood. The two wounds on the left foot and lower calf are fully visible. The flesh around the bullet holes looks like pink boiled pork. The skin yellow-white, peeling away from the flesh, like a big blister or a scald after the skin has dried out.

'This guy must have been taking that Vitamin K or whatever they use to clot blood—slows down the bleeding,' Griffo says.

'Fuckin' powerful vitamin,' Pete adds.

'Slows 'em down though—their reflexes—they reckon. Certainly did to this poor cunt. Better get sorted out, we're off once he's buried.'

Shortly after this, Dave came back into the field. I was out at the LZ, landing zone, just having a nosey around. It was a natural clearing among the trees so no chopping had been required. Down came the chopper with Dave's leering mug stuck out of the hatch. As the supplies got dragged off I followed Griffo and his team, Dave in the middle of them, back to their position. Caught up with them just as Griffo said, 'What the fuck have you been up to?'

Dave looked like death warmed up. He'd lost at least fifteen kilos, pasty yellow colour, sunken face like an old man. 'Couple of pellets in the arse,' Pete had said.

'Glad you asked. I've been up to a lot. What about you lot?' We told Dave what we knew, plus a bit of what we suspected. Pete joined us and filled in some gaps.

'Wound OK now?'

'Wound? . . . Ah that. Down to Vungers, two days in bed, back to the Dat. Staff didn't know what the fuck to do with me. Looked at his list, and I'm off to Heavyweight. It's OK—take them out in the scrub for a couple of days, come back and fuck around the base. It's Tet, big celebration, the good tucker comes out, people dance, get pissed. Don't tell me you lot missed it?'

Heavyweight was a battalion-strength ARVN training camp right on the Dat's doorstep but outside our wire. Diggers like Dave were sent there to train them in fundamental infantry tactics.

'Nah . . . much the same out here. Does this story get any better?' prompted Griffo.

'The feast was dog—killed the Corgi, tasted alright, made a pig of meself. A bit off when they cooked it though, killed the dog a tad too early. I'm out in the field next day shitting nonstop, couldn't get me pants up. Got carried in, then down to Vungers again. They know about my problem, the ward's full of us. Real eye-opener. Sixteen beds, five crappers and a queue. Some of 'em just shit the bed, thank God, shortens the queue. There's a bloke in a bath of ice making the walls tremble, probably still there. I just get comfortable, whip an extra pillow from the bed next to me while he's having a shit. Doctor's visit—means you visit him. Nurse drags me out of bed, points the way. They're not much either, heads like a rat's arse in a thunderstorm. I go in. "Hi Doc!"

'"Don't you salute officers, soldier?"

'"Yeah, but not my fucking doctor. Which are you?" We wrestle over that one, then the usual checkup. Next thing three cunts come in the door and line the walls. Doc trundles out the Great Silver Stallion.

'"If you're planning to do with that what I think you think you are, you can stick it up your own arse."

'"It's got to be done, Private, that's why the assistants are here. I understand. Don't take it personally." He smiled, the cunt.

'"Nah, it's you who doesn't understand. I take this real fucking personal! Forget these cunts behind me, they don't exist to me. It's you, no other cunt, you! Touch that arse-crippler, I'll bite your fucking nose off and eat it."

'I was let out—thank you, back to bed. Thirty-six shits in a day I had to beat. Made twenty-eight two days straight. Thirty-six shits and you headed back to Australia for radium treatment or some other fucking nightmare. When I walk out there's three other new boys cowering in smocks in the passage. "How'd it go?" "Ah . . . piss easy." Fuck, I tell ya, I shit my bed hearing the shrieks coming outa that office. Anyway, here I am.'

Chapter 6

Let's talk about flyboys for a moment. Ground troop chopper support. We generally used our own RAAF for resupply. For troop movement in the field it could be them or Yank Air Cavalry, and for dustoffs—extraction of wounded—whoever we could get. Generally there wasn't a lot of difference between the two.

There's a dustoff I remember well. Three of our Diggers were wounded, one of them badly. Pete was fretting. We had to rush a few patrols around to find some fairly clear ground in the forest for an LZ, then a group cleared away what they could with machetes. Dustoff was called in.

Over comes an RAAF chopper, hovers above us, fucks off. 'Not enough clearance,' yells CSM, 'let's get into it!' Everyone with a machete hops in, Diggers pushing over the tall saplings in gangs. The call goes out again for dustoff. Back comes the chopper, fucks off again, not enough clearance. By now CSM's spraying ground-up chips of teeth over the area. 'Let's have another go!' he manages. OC signals him from the radio: hold on. Word comes through that a passing Yank has picked up our signal, wants to give it a go. Seconds later he's coming straight down through the canopy, leaves, twigs, bits of branch flying everywhere, and lands. The pilot sticks his head and shoulder out and gives the thumbs up. Pete, Brian and the crew carrying the litters race out, slide them on for the gun crew to grab, and up she goes showering shit and leaves and heads off toward the horizon.

Some time later, same scenario. The ground is the same. This time we get three little chainsaws winched down. Unfortunately we have no sappers with us. Dave knows how to work one, I used one five or six times as a kid, docking boughs off fallen trees, and someone else is game to try. I get mine stuck straight off in a dead trunk full of shrapnel, one other keeps stopping, Dave wields his like a maniac. The RAAF turns up, not enough clearance. Dave keeps going. RAAF turns up, not enough yet. Dave goes berserk. By the time the RAAF comes back he's cleared an Olympic stadium. Down comes the RAAF, Dave roaring in fury from the edge of his clearing: 'That big enough for ya? Ya weak cunts!' Pity they couldn't hear him above the clatter.

We had both types of air support. The RAAF were competent and safe air transport; looked after their machines properly. The Yanks didn't take account of their equipment, they concentrated solely on their job. That's the only difference. That and the fact they could outfly any airforce in the world.

After one of these dustoffs I was sitting with Pete and Brian waiting for the order to move out. We'd shipped out a Digger very hard hit. Pete had had the saline drip going—the man had lost a lot of blood, coming out of first shock and moaning involuntarily. Pete wore a couple of khaki-coloured plastic morphine ampoules tied to his dogtags at all times in the field. You just ripped the sheath off the pointed end and there was the needle attached to a squeeze bubble, like a small toothpaste tube.

'Why didn't you use the morphine, Pete? He was in real pain.'

'Can't, Bazz—he'll be on the operating table in an hour from now. Can't use conventional anaesthetic if a patient's full of morphine, it could kill him.'

'Why carry the shit then?'

'Would *you* like to die in agony, Barrie?'

I started to appreciate how complex Pete's job really was.

'Do you carry it, Brian?'

'Shit yeah.'

Fucking hell! Pete was a trained nurse. Brian had only had

a fraction of his formal training, which is why I suppose these two worked so closely when illness or worse struck. About this time they started to really have some work to do. We were two months or more into the Op and the company was starting to get clapped out. Clothing was falling to bits faster than Staff could find, borrow or steal and get it out to us. The ration packs weren't ideal for the heavy relentless slogging we were doing.

Hygiene in the field was a constant struggle—lack of water, lack of every bloody thing. There were the usual problems you'd expect: foot tinea, infected blisters, sprains, cuts, infected toenails, insect bites, fatigue, shock, depression, and twanging nerves. Pete and Brian did their best with their small hipbags of Bandaids, scalpels, antiseptic powder, codeine, mercurochrome, tinea ointments and whatever. It was a battle; their own equipment got pretty tacky before long. Then the worms started hitting the troops.

'Clean ya fucking act up!' Pete ordered, more to tell people to keep trying than out of any hope that it was really achievable.

Then the 'tinea' struck. Some of the poor bastards had this so-called tinea from navel to mid-thigh, as though they'd been scalded with a steam hose. The skin blotched a purple-pink-grey and erupted thicker than orange peel. The surface was cratered, weeping and raw. That had Pete worried. He sent a description back to base. Chuck Baby sent some little bottles of clear liquid, US-issue—had acid in the name, it's all I remember. 'This'll fix it', Chucky had said in the brief—'just tinea, tropical style'. The liquid burnt like acid, said some of the users, but made a change from the constant burning itch that went with this tinea. I wouldn't know, I didn't get it, but I'd say half the company were affected, from bad to appalling. I do know the treatment didn't work. Pete dropped it after a while unless a Digger wanted it. They stayed in the field regardless of the condition, learnt to walk with their legs and the cheeks of their arse apart for the month or so it took to go. Rest didn't speed the healing process, so they didn't usually get any.

Then some got monsoon blisters, or infected prickly heat—Chucky's term. Pete hadn't heard of that one either, not the version he was seeing. Blisters from the size of matchheads to the size of peas, some as big as coins, full of yellow pus. The treatment of those, Chucky directed, was to prick them with a needle and wipe with surgical spirit. If you had a spare hour of course. Not as many got those, perhaps 20 to 30 per cent, and for some they were not too bad. But most got them on their backs where the pack rode, and they were raw meat at the end of each day. Shirts stiff with dried pus and fluid from raw skin, as well as sweat and grime. One or two may have left the field for this condition, I'm not sure. Again the prescribed treatment was useless, and liable to cause other infection in these conditions. The blisters dried up after a month or so usually.

What sort of a dickhead am I! I'm running you through all this shit and you don't even know how we live day to day. I'll address that now—give you a short rundown.

At the end of a day's hunting, usually around last light, we harbour. The site chosen is invariably in the best cover available. We deploy in a cartwheel formation, all nine guns evenly spaced around the perimeter, CHQ nestled in the centre. Before we relax, security has to be attended to—undergrowth thinned at our front to allow enemy to be seen, comm's cords strung out, and tracks cut so that gun picquets can find the guns they have to man throughout the night. Shit pits, or latrines as some wankers call them, are dug outside the perimeter, for some inexplicable reason. Claymore mines are set out from every gun position. Then you get down to setting up house if you don't get first gun picquet or radio watch, or, worse, forward sentry duty. That only happens if we harbour early or stay in harbour position after first light. Forward sentry duty—how could I ever forget it! A hundred metres or more out from the perimeter, armed with your own weapon, a claymore mine in front to activate at need, and a length of nylon twine to tug to let the boys know back at the gun that you're coming back at the gallop. Two hours is your stint outside the perimeter, before blessed relief quietly pads up behind you.

That aside, harbouring is heaven. Clip up the hootchies, clear the ground you plan to sleep on, string and peg the tent, unpack and roll out the bedding while the brew's heating to the boil. Select the night's meal, have a fag while you quietly bitch the day into history and hope another mate you haven't sighted for a while comes past to say he remembers you. If he does your dinner's likely to get burnt, but who gives a fuck. Then it's stand-to while three-man clearing patrols sweep the ground outside the perimeter for enemy. After that, shutdown. Picquet duty, whispered conversation, sleep, that's it. Want a fag? Learn to stuff your head in your empty pack to light it, then suck hard through cupped hands—any light and you're on a charge. Nicotine soon tans the palms of your hands to saddle leather but if you want to smoke it can be done. Most Diggers do smoke while they're over here.

At first light, stand-to while the clearing patrols sweep again. Then, if you're not on picquet, you might get thirty minutes of normalcy. No need to dress, you sleep fully clothed. Put a brew on, then half-fill your bathing mug if you've got any water left. Brush your teeth, then shave, and if the remaining water's not too murky wash your face and hands. Then smear them with fresh camouflage, charcoal or dirt, whatever's to hand. We don't have camouflage creams issued to us, but the ground provides products just as effective. It's a pissoff—you never feel clean out here, but a European face glows like a lamp in the field, and that's the face most likely to get switched off. By now the brew's ready, so put a can of crud on to heat while you stow your gear in your pack, then clean your rifle. Don't do this together. One at a time please. You need to dismantle the bloody thing to clean it properly. Rust is a big problem out here, and it's nice to know someone on your side can fire at an attacker while you concentrate on fitting yours back together correctly.

Right, OC's on the blower, haul your pack on, grab your rifle, we're about to move out. We're going in the APCs and they've just pulled up.

The hatches are closed and we can't see, but we're travelling with a bit of a lean for a while, so we're back in the jungle. Hatch open, yep, it's the jungle. We stalk up the hill through the tangled undergrowth and bamboo, reach the top, have a bit of a blow, start down the other side. Griffo grins and says, 'Now *here's* fucking jungle.'

We descend into the gloom. What a nightmare to get through, even when you're thirtieth in line. And it goes up slippery clay hills and skidding down to the valley floors where the rivers and briars are. Five days of this and I'm stuffed, head hanging down near my nuts. We're crossing a huge fallen tree trunk over a stream concealed ten metres below in the tangle of vines and briars. Off I shoot. Straight out and straight down—through briars, vines, spiders and all. The stream bed is studded with rocky fangs. I land on my knees, in the only two patches of sand in sight, straddling a rock that would have done the knee in nicely. I claw my way back up the bank, wet as a shag, and no bastard waiting for me. By the time I surface I'm arse-end Charlie.

Dave was right—who would be crazy enough to seek us here? We did have a contact or two, though, nothing special. One I remember because I had to lie pressed against a wet, red clay bank for an hour or so. Rifle jammed in mud, ammo pouches caked in it. It took days to dry enough to be brushed off. The trees were absolutely magnificent. Grey-black trunks reaching twenty metres or more to the first bough, millions of them. My two hooks came through about then, not before time. That raised a few eyebrows. OC and CSM seemed genuinely surprised.

'You've been promoted to corporal, Crowls,' said OC, then he choked and became silent on the matter. CSM jerked his head to signal 'Fuck off', so I did. The rank came from passing an academic course, you see. Bringing skills to the workplace. In this workplace you learnt on the job, nothing else counted, and you progressed up the ladder on performance, nothing else. I'd gone up the easy way, and I knew it. Still, I hadn't sought out the job I had, it was offered out of the blue. The officers were commissioned on their performance at a training academy, not performance in the field, so OC had nothing to grumble about, but I felt for CSM.

Few Diggers over here were ambitious; if it happened you did the job. Some took great personal pride in their own advancement but I didn't know any of them—can't remember them now anyway, no reason to.

We leave the real jungle and only come into it briefly now and again going somewhere else. From here we are off in APCs into different country, quite flat, patches of tall grass dotted among a forest of saplings, the odd taller tree here and there. We travel through the grass patches as much as possible. Rotting deadfall lies everywhere between the saplings, calf-deep powdery punk, a legacy of defoliation years earlier. It makes for slow progress on foot and we have to cover a lot of ground fast all day. It is faster to eat the dust and heat of the grassfields. We go through a bomb-cratered open area and start into the tall treeline—and shit happens.

A couple of shots, a gun opens up, two guns, three guns, six guns; here come the rockets, the grenades. We've found a live bunker system. A big one. Everyone's pushing forward, fanning out, disappearing into the undergrowth. I'm still not in the shade, so we're obviously not going too well. An hour or so of this, seems like three minutes, and the platoonies are falling back around us in CHQ. One scoots back carrying his dead section commander over his shoulder, someone comes running back with the back of his shirt red with blood. Pete's coming through, tending someone worse hit who's been borne back on a litter. Brian's helping another group. Peaches bolts back, teamed with Zarbo, towards the tail end.

'Did ya see that back wound, eh? Pissin' blood and not a hole in the shirt that we could find. Fuckin' weird.' And they drop to their knees to fire a few defensive bursts. We're retreating back on to the plain.

It's dusk now and OC knows what we've got cornered, knows it's too big. We're down one and three wounded, and lucky that's all we're down. Our retreat stops 200 metres from the treeline in a belt of spindly scrub. The land between us and the bunkers has been blanket bombed some time back, shattered tree trunks and limbs lie in tangled heaps everywhere. This is great. It means the enemy guns have to clear those, so by the time the tracer passes us it's mostly head-height or ricocheting harmlessly metres above us. We harbour and the three guns closest to the bunkers keep the bastards cautious about coming after us while we cook dinner. Pete gets his cold—he's further back with Support Section, getting the wounded onto the chopper. OC's on the blower, setting up a movement for the battalion, standing up all the while, taking chances because he has to see what's happening. Our Kiwi FO's hard at it on his handpiece, calling in artillery, standing to see when needed. And I'm sitting down with a fag, watching the fireworks go back and forth. Gunships clatter overhead, their miniguns barking solid red streams of tracer metres wide; rockets flash yellow-white as they whizz from the pods mounted beneath the craft. Then sighter shots from artillery and the barrage begins to crump into the bunker system. The treeline becomes illuminated by the flash of homing shells, at first fitfully, then almost without flicker as the barrage intensifies. The gunships have moved on by now to the rear of the bunker system, flaying the forest, seeking to cut down fleeing enemy. From then on—our task accomplished for the time being—it's two hours sleep, two hours picquet, until morning.

I know it seems tame. Where's the heroics, the blood and guts, the dead bodies strewn in spastic poses as far as the eye can see? Ask any Vet about a bunker system. A platoon-size one with three guns can cut a company to pulp without serious loss if it's well entrenched and disciplined. These little bastards always are. A company-size bunker system with nine guns can hold off and even destroy a battalion, if it's pure infantry. Being in bunkers gives you enormous advantage over an onground attacker. This installation we ran across is company-plus. Pure numbers are against us.

Time to get back and call in the big boys. That's what OC did. And he booked tanks for the morning to help with the second assault. A number of our company commanders took the hero's approach to this task—pushed their troops through without support. It seldom achieved more than excessive casualties to their own troops, but many commanders were decorated for their valour. Getting wounded while in command always seemed to excite the brass; don't ask me why.

We were fortunate: our company commander knew his job and did it superbly. He was a phenomenon. The role of infantry in this war was very poorly understood. We were not here to roam the countryside in groups of eighty or ninety men shooting every armed VC soldier who crossed our path. Of course we did that, most times anyway, but the number of enemy we personally killed was of little tactical consequence. Our real task was to find the main bodies of enemy. If it was a small group we killed what we could and followed after the survivors—tried to locate their main unit. If we did find them we were invariably at a disadvantage. The main unit was usually larger than ourselves, and well entrenched. Our job was to engage them in battle, keep them occupied, until the support units arrived to pound the crap out of them—hopefully driving the survivors into an ambush set up by brother companies and tankies working from our radioed field reports. After the bombardment we searched through the system and reported the results. Sometimes the little bastards were still there. That's when our own bodybags really started filling up. Tanks were handy for this second pass at a bunker system.

They turned up around 7 am. Big Centurion tanks, three in all. Great for bunkers. They could trundle in first firing canisters—shotgun cartridges about 13 centimetres in diameter. They had a 50 cal. machine gun on top of the turret. Rockets couldn't get through the armour plate unless they were big ones, but they could throw a bit of heat around inside, give the crew nasty burns. The tanks weren't the fastest of creatures, never mind what the movies show.

We started our advance, some of us flanking the tanks, some behind. Our blokes stepped over the tree trunks, around the bomb craters, straight on again. Not the tanks. They'd crawl over a log, crash down a crater, reverse out, shunt, lumber on and go straight down another crater. It was painful to watch. What had started as a straight line advance soon became a halting, stuttering straggle. How the crews didn't smash their skulls against the tanks' armour plate amazes me. Tanks are cramped, tangled contraptions inside. Hellholes when the gun's firing. By the time they clawed their way into the treeline our enemy had fled. By the time I reached the treeline the tanks were shunting back towards me, they'd had enough. We turned back to the old harbour and dumped excess baggage. Then the company took the sappers back to blow the bunkers up. I got to mind the bags, as well as Pete, Brian, OC's batman and a gun group. CSM deployed us: gun group west of a bomb crater; Brian and the batman east, noses stuck into spindly scrub as dense as a canefield; Pete and I north in the trees, lying on the spot in the track where our Digger had fallen. CSM said, 'If there's anywhere to watch they'll come through that scrub.' I thought, 'Then what's the point of putting the gun way over there behind us?', but when you're a kid you think without speaking.

Twenty minutes later, crash crunch yabber yabber—a party of Viet Cong were passing across our front ten metres away.

Often they were noisy, but this lot were loud. Pete and I could see a flicker of legs through the screen, then nothing, so we doubled back behind and to the right of Brian. He signalled 'Four' and turned back. I called quietly, 'Shoot!', but Brian signalled something followed by 'Silence!'. The batman threw me a look saying, 'He's a corporal, he shoots first or I don't'. Pete was lying beside me having nothing to do with it except to stay on guard. Then the Viet Cong decided to take a break right in front of a very silent Brian. They had a bullshit session for a few minutes, a stomp around, then headed clear of us, chattering like monkeys. Fuck this, I thought, I'm calling everyone in. If you won't shoot I can't make you. Everyone into the crater. Let's redeploy. I was just opening my mouth to sort things out when CSM came down the track, leading the company in.

'Look what one grenade'll get ya' and he walks past smirking.

What a bunch of dildos we must have looked. All crowded together in a jumpy little knot, like a bunch of kids listening to a ghost story. I decided not to report the sighting.

When the company had done a search of the bunker system they'd found it far too extensive for our resources to blow. They'd checked it for enemy, dead or alive, for stores, blown them up, then left it to follow-up experts to sort out, which is why they returned early. We headed into the forest, looking to find where the garrison had headed. At a break along the way I asked Brian why he hadn't fired.

'They were stretcher bearers with wounded, Barrie. I signalled.'

'I don't know your signals, I'm infantry.'

'So am I, Barrie.'

I still don't know the rules we operated under to determine categories of enemy and how you dealt with each. We were told we operated under the Geneva Convention but no one spelled out what that meant to us, not in my hearing. I believe what Brian did was right, but I've no idea if what he did was policy. He wasn't alone in his actions, though; it was more common than you think.

Let's take a closer look at killing.

Some individuals' callous actions caused us some concern. We were in the business of killing and when opponents clashed in the field the rules didn't count, they were not a consideration. You didn't even think about it. The aftermath was another thing altogether. After a contact there were enemy bodies to be dealt with. Were they bodies or were the VC just lying still? Make no mistake, people can be very hard to kill. The smart move was to put a round through their head unless you were certain. One of our riflemen was having a quiet beer with me one day and blurted out what was troubling him. After an ambush he'd been watching a body for sign of life, so as to avoid firing needlessly, and his partner knelt down, grabbed the man by the hair and slit his throat with a hunting knife.

'Shit, I was in the same intake as him. We've been mates right through, I hootchie with him. Would you trust the cunt? He gives me the creeps sometimes.'

There weren't too many such incidents but a few go a long way in a small population.

I know what you're thinking. If they're alive they're prisoners. But it wasn't always so simple. These guys were prisoners if they surrendered. Very few did. They'd stay quiet, still as a corpse, and take you out with a grenade, a pistol, a knife, as you bent over them. These blokes were soldiers. We'd been taught to tie a toggle rope around an arm, get behind the nearest cover, then pull on the rope to turn the body over—just in case there was a grenade under the body with the pin pulled out. We streamlined a lot of our methods as the tour wore on, but time-consuming as it was we kept to that one. I'll leave you to work out why.

Then there was Makka's story. I didn't like him much at that time. He was way too fast for himself and always moving on before he fully understood his own experiences. He was speaking to Dave and Tank—I was there because I'd been holding the floor until Makka barged me aside in mid-sentence. He told of an ambush he'd been on recently.

'We'd sprung the ambush a bit after midnight. Three of them caught in it. One bastard's moaning, like a cow mooing, all fucking night. Just before dawn, fucking *crump!* The moaning stopped. First light, we do a search. The bloke who'd been doing the moaning was an old bastard, had his legs almost chopped off by the gun. He'd held a grenade primed all night and let it drop when he lost the strength to hold it any longer.

We searched his pack and it was full of citations and medals from fighting the Japs, the French, this fucking government and the Yanks.'

During our pursuit of the running enemy we were told to look for disturbed ground. Our other companies had engaged in several contacts with fairly large enemy groups on the move days earlier. Few bodies had been found at any of them; we'd found only five or six, hurriedly buried in temporary shallow graves, at our last bunker system. And only bodies counted—the more the better. Halfway up into the hills our scouts found a grave, hidden under leaves and deadfall. By the time I reached it the boys had cleared it. A reddish-coloured garden plot five metres by fifteen, rising into a clay bank. I looked on as the platoonies started to dig, watched over by CSM, Duntroon and me, among others. Soon the bodies began to appear, shattered bodies clothed in black and grey and blue, stacked in tiers. They had to be dragged out to be searched and counted accurately, our orders stated. Several days had passed since they'd died and they were putrefying. No hot showers and baths out here, so the Diggers used their toggle ropes to drag the bodies clear. I saw men stagger and fall on to the wet clay when the arm or leg they were hauling on tore off. I watched about eight dragged out, saw the tiers of bodies yet to come. Then, the easy part completed, the exhumation party started wading in among the dead, mauling them loose from the stack. The faces of the dead frozen in grins. Grimaces. Near-shut eyelids shooting glimpses of white staring eyes. Rubbery limbs shuddering to stillness as the body settled where it was dropped, as though still capable of movement, even after death. This affected me most. It was as if these people were imprisoned in torment. But they weren't, they were just dead. I took no part in all this. I quietly walked well away from the scene in case my help was needed. I know Lenny left the scene real quick to do a gun picquet, and I suspect he'd found them in the first place. Yet it was intelligence. Somehow the number of dead meant something to our government. What the still-living thought seemed of no consequence; don't be concerned with the living, don't measure their determination—count the dead. Keep counting till they're all gone if need be.

I could really get into this body-count shit, point the finger at the arseholes who feed off statistics like these . . . but, no! I refuse to get philosophical! Let's instead go back and pick over the charnel; I was there long enough to remember the detail. Let's look at the slime covering what's left of the skin. Brown-grey and pink. Except for the intact faces, which are just grey. The red-brown pulverised stumps, the purple rents in the flesh, the crumpled lifelessness. Colours and forms strike you obliquely through an emotional prism, so that you wonder if you are really seeing what you are seeing. If you can suppress your shock and see things dispassionately, you see what you'd expect to see when you're confronted with butchered bodies, covered with dirt and dug up three days later. I see my friends and my company wading through all this in a big pit, and I've never seen so many people with their senses locked up in chaotic disbelief and revulsion. These dead were probably the result of our own bombardment.

So few among us bear the full brunt of war. Politicians say: 'Get over there and win this war!' Then the bureaucrats take charge. It's just a policy to be followed: 'Count the dead!' So our dickheads in High Command pass it down to us. That's why schoolteachers and plumbers and bank johnnies and shop assistants and farmers are down a hole dragging their counterparts out of graves and wondering what maniac issued the order. And those above us apply the pressure and plan their parades.

Days later we came down out of the hills and met up with the tankies and their APCs again. We didn't travel far—they were there to support us, to stick with us for a while as much as transport us. We trundled through scrubby grasslands for a day, heads sticking out of the hatches having a look. The scenery wasn't much and it was overcast, a dull glare in the sky. Next day we went into the trees and CHQ harboured. The platoons fanned out, the APCs went for a bit of a mooch around. It had turned out sunny. In the afternoon our platoons started finding what we'd come for, something to shoot at. As enemy were discovered the other platoons would dart over to support the one in contact. CHQ followed up so that we didn't get too strung out. APCs whizzed this way and that, carrying troops, trying to get their guns going for us. Real 'prop, turn and chase' shit. The forest was dense but in patches, not big enough to melt away into, so the VC were continually running into one group or another of us. OC had his mind working flat out keeping the picture—he had to run the lot, us and the APCs.

Late in the afternoon the chase focused on a dense patch of jungle going uphill. The APCs couldn't go up; they stayed just inside the edge watching our platoons go. CHQ stayed with the tracks. A couple of sightings occurred quickly, and one section of about eight men were sent out to the right, over a dry creekbed to follow a hunch. Woofer led it with Peaches as his number two scout, carrying the gun. They hadn't gone far up a track when Woofer spotted a VC scout coming his way—took his chest out with a good blast. Then the whole front opened up on him: AK47s, RPG rockets, machine guns, the lot. Platoon-size unit. Woofer dived sideways behind a fallen tree trunk, Peaches threw himself beside him and set the gun up on top of it. Shit was flying so thick that the rest of the section were cut off from them further back. Cover back there was thin scrub and a bit of deadfall, so they were easily pinned down. It became the deadly duo's battle. The rest of the section fired at whatever they could see—when they could get their heads up. Peaches couldn't sight his gun, the tree trunk they were behind was being pulverised by gunfire. Woofer crabbed around on his back till his feet faced the onslaught, then raised and lowered his head so only his eyes and a bit of brow showed above the log. From the glimpses, he told Peaches where to fire, and helped couple the gun belts when he could. They were getting nowhere. The VC came closer by the second, using fire-and-movement—up for a split second, gain a few metres, then down and firing while others took a sprint. Peaches flayed the area in an attempt to cover a retreat for the others, but they were too well pinned down.

It all came to a head when one of the VC did what many of us had heard about but never seen. He ran straight at Peaches' gun, looming above the trunk as he closed in, so that Peaches could see him clearly. Peaches hit him with everything. He finally fell dead, half over Peaches, stifling the gun. Woofer accepted that it was 'get out or get overrun' time, and shook Peaches to say, 'We're fucking *off*'. No response. 'Fuck! Peaches! *Go* mate!' Grabbed Peaches, the gun and his Armalite and made to drag the lot back the way they'd come. Peaches snapped out of it as he was dragged upright. The rest of the section scattered when Woofer moved, heavy enemy fire forcing them apart into ones and twos. Peaches came good on the run and Woofer and he ducked and dived down the hill hoping for the best, with the pack howling after them. What probably saved them all was that the tankies below on the flat knew what real trouble sounded like and reckoned they could get more out of their machines than the maker intended. Decided to give it a go. Got to them, managed to drag them all on board one vehicle or another, then, gun turrets blazing up the hill, headed back down on to the flat and across the riverbed, where the ground suited them better. The trip back was perilous. Woofer and Peaches added their eyes to the commander's search of the ground, spotting an unexploded 500-pound bomb or two lying in the dead leaves and shrubbery. The VC were chased by the platoons, but they found an escape route and withdrew eventually.

Next morning, about eight, after some final patrols of the area, we moved out on foot. As I walked out of the harbour position I noticed Peaches sitting on the ground. He was dressed in decent clean greens which must have been newly issued, plus his boots. That was all. No webbing, no ammo belts, no hat, no pack, no gun. Four or five Diggers, loaded up and ready to go, stood around him as if guarding him. Peaches was staring at a patch of ground in the near distance, head averted from the line of men I was following. Total silence enveloped the scene. It was stark and threatening. I pulled out of line, stopped, and looked at Peaches, not game to address him, just willing him to look at me, to explain. After what seemed a minute or more his head swivelled round and he looked straight into my eyes, shrugged almost imperceptibly, and signalled with a look, 'No more, mate'. Then he turned away again and I had to move on.

Peaches was the only man in our company to lay down his weapon openly in the field. There were other ways of avoiding killing if you were cunning or had a choice—and good luck to all those who did, well done! As a field soldier your options usually were few: kill or get killed, go insane, or lay down your weapon. Another member of our company later took quite a strong stand, but Peaches said straight off, 'I've killed for the last time, I won't do it again!'. OC respected that, and so did we. I was told shortly afterwards by one of the guard that

Peaches had said, 'You can't kill them!' It was interpreted by some to mean that Peaches felt the VC were in some way superhuman and to be feared. But fear played no part in Peaches' decision, he didn't fear anything, except his own conscience. He'd figured it all out.

I think Peaches left the field that day; probably went with the APCs back to Battalion Headquarters located elsewhere in the field, and from there back to the Dat.

On we went, looking here, looking there, and then out of the blue we had a day by the river. We came across a wide, shallow, gently running river with a sandbar forming a beautiful golden island at its bend. The water clear as crystal in the shallows, turning gradually to translucent light green in the deeper pools. On the far side was a plain of long golden grass wavering in the light breeze. We stood on top of a small ridge skirting the near side, under the cover of trees not unlike river trees at home, small with dark leaves and papery, silver-grey bark. I stifled the urge to yell out, 'Hey, let's have a swim!'. Pete turned round and said 'We're gunna have a fuckin' swim!'. I didn't believe him of course, I was considered a pretty easy mark for a wind-up at that stage of the tour. Then Griffo came by and said we were setting up Support Section's gun where I was standing—the company was going for a swim.

The sheer bliss of kneeling naked in clean flowing water! Up to your neck on a sandy bottom, scrubbing yourself with clean sharp sand while you pestered Pete to pass the soap.

'Nah! Get fucked! Haven't done yet!'

OC was not intending to go in, or at least not as soon as he did. He was standing by the bank grinning at all the grudge-sorting and rough play, making sure the noise didn't get too out of hand, really enjoying himself. Next minute he was arse-up through the air and crashing into the water nostrils first. Duntroon had set that one up with a couple of the Diggers. Purely selfish reasons, of course; a subordinate commander couldn't enjoy a dip when the boss was still on duty, could he? Then Duntroon dived in fully dressed, not a bad entry under the circumstances, just as his own pack turned on him. It was good to see OC laugh when he finally surfaced. Tore off his greens and boots and did a few laps, a bit of a float, held Duntroon under till the bubbles rose, then stood at the water's edge for a moment, letting the water dry from his wiry, undernourished frame. That's when Pete noted he was slightly knock-kneed, and his imitation of him from then on was cruelly perfect. Bé paddled in his parachute bloomers at the water's edge, he didn't trust us. No reason to. That was far and away the best day in the field we ever had. For three or four hours we enjoyed a peaceful golden sunny day.

Now, I must warn you. We get stuck into a bit of knackers, cocks, tits (the bigger the better) and pussies on our next jaunt, so if you're squeamish about the baser side of this subject simply skip the next part. And get out of the company, too—if you've listened to me this far in comfort but find sex distasteful you're sick! Get your mind moving now—come with me or stay chaste.

Chapter 7

WE HIT THE DAT EARLY IN THE MORNING—a glorious day weatherwise but who'd notice? Get real! The choppers dropped us at the battalion football field, which some arselickers referred to as the Battalion Parade Ground, and we were off through the trees faster than a contact drill—we'd got a truck to catch. Into the Nugget, slung the shit under the floorboards, grabbed the civvies, wiped the rifle over once with Dave's towel, and off down the service road to wait for the truck. Dave was beside me and we picked up Pete and Brian as they jostled out of their tent. Dave turned his thoughts into words: 'Piss supply's a bit down on when we left. Better get stocks up when I get back, and get the cunt that's knockin' it off . . . need ice too, remind me.'

I hadn't had time to even check if my bed was still there. We'd had a parade, of course. OC gave us a bit of bullshit. Duntroon got the job of preaching abstinence or at least moderation in all things—delivered, I might add, with no hint of personal conviction. CSM jerked us around for a while. Then we were gone in a cloud of red dust, with our rifles, some ammo and a small bag with our civvies. On the truck we faced inwards as usual. Peaches was earbashing Ronnie in a one-sided debate on an obscure topic—democracy or some such bullshit. Ronnie wanted to talk about rooting and tits and wet pussies and coming like a wild fuckin' Indian, and Dave was briefing the rest of us on the delights of Vungers and convincing us he knew where the best harlots were. I recall catching a fleeting glimpse of the fishermen in their little boats, casting nets off in the distance, and very picturesque it must have been. Then the red throbbing haze descended again. Next thing I knew we were in Vung Tau; not the outskirts, the centre. The nob. What did I say! We turned off down a dusty, chalk-white, weed-bordered road with barbed wire strung out everywhere, and stopped at the Badcoe Club. An amenities centre for resting Diggers. Fucking gloom.

Let me tell you a bit about Ronnie. Built like Peaches; golden blond hair, darker brows, the features of a young Errol Flynn before the booze struck back, piercing blue eyes and a voice of similar shock value. It was almost a screech but I'll be kind and call it a high soprano. The combination made you laugh on sight. His type of looks was well sought after for singlet ads, toothpaste, anything healthy and wholesome. He was a scout until he joined Support Section late in the tour. Decked a couple of big mouths while we were over here, one of them a red-headed sergeant who wandered into the company after Dave and I returned from Phuoc Loi. Wish I'd seen that punch land.

So, we're at the Badcoe Club. It was OK. My old mate Tony helped build that too, so I have to say it was well built. It had a pool with a high tower and springboards, a boozer with an outside beer garden, chairs and trestles, and a few umbrellas and awnings. But it sold understrength Yank beer so that was the kiss of death right off. Ever tried getting pissed on Budweiser or Schlitz? Don't waste your time. Dedicated drinkers know these things. There were pale green dormitory-style huts in rows, shower buildings with hot water in the taps, and lights, wash-basins and mirrors. Grey gravel everywhere and MPs wherever you looked. It was rumoured to have a chapel and also a recreation hall with table tennis and writing desks, but I never met anyone who saw it. Didn't keep that sort of company. There was probably more to it than that, but that's all I saw.

Officers and senior NCOs stayed where they liked in town; they had no curfew.

Right, I'm on the grid at the gate and ready to go, money changed to the local piastra, name checked off, every arsehole saluted, everyone who shares my need is here at the grid and they're mates enough for me. The MP controlling the gate starts coming the cop act, looks at our front row, decides 'Fuck this!', and opens the gate. 'Remember . . . curfew 9 pm!'

We're off. The battered, sputtering little Lambro's reeling up the dusty track with enough of us on board to more than pay for any suspension damage—if the driver can shake us down for the fare. By the time we hit the Grand Hotel which is at the centre of the action, we're down to about twelve. The cheapminded bastards have jumped off at the next to last corner. (In my recollections I always thought this was the 'Grand Hotel' but it wasn't. Pete said it was. I'll continue to call it the Grand anyway, because there's no way I can find its true name now, I believe it's been demolished.) The Grand looks fabulous. French facade, eight stories high at a guess, large intricate Roman-style marble fountain with a moat dominating the circular gravel entry. Slender wrought-iron spiked fence keeping the masses from the low, unimaginative garden. Nope! Something a bit livelier please; haven't got that sort of time yet.

Top End Mick, who's come all the way from somewhere way out of Darwin to be Support Section's gunner, spots a horse. Runty little thing: black-brown, plaited mane and a jiggly headpiece with little bells strapped on its head; bells hanging off stalks on the horse collar too. Barely reaches my shoulder, buckled to the shafts of an open four-seater carriage with the coachman sitting on an outrigger seat at the back, holding a big whip on a long stick. The little pony has its ears laid back as though it suffers constant migraine from the jingle of bells. The coachman, dressed like a barber, thinks he has a customer, of course, and he has. But Top End Mick wants to ride the horse, not go for a ride in the carriage, and can't make this stupid nog understand. He asks me to translate his desire that the horse be uncoupled and handed over to him for a fee and a promise to return it. What am I? A fucking lawyer? We leave him to it. Young Mick stays to watch the outcome.

So now there are ten of us. Brian and some other sly bastard say they're going shopping and disappear down a side street. The arse will fall out of Brian's world after that little white lie. That leaves eight: Dave, Peaches, Pete, Pigpen, Ronnie, Fuzz, some fortunate bastard whose name I don't recall who can deny being any part of all this, and me. As we head straight into the deepest shit heap we can snuffle out, Top End Mick careers round the corner astride the tinkling little pony, spanking its arse to a gallop, while the carriage and its desperately clinging coachman, reeking abject terror, slews over on two wheels behind. Don't know what became of Young Mick, he wasn't on it. Not by this time, anyway.

Seen a sleazy strip before? We're standing in it. Tacky as shit. Some neon, luminous-looking poster paint signs, bars, massage parlours, steambaths, restaurants—? Crowds milling outside, harlots beckoning, the dull roar of humanity at play seeping out on to the pavement. I'll describe the rest tomorrow; we're out for a root. We have a funny way of getting one, but you should be used to us by now. Into a bar and guzzle three quick beers. Yank piss again! Better have a steambath, sweat the crud out. Next door: 'One steambath for us lot, thanks Mama San!' This title is a throwback to the Yank term for madam in Okinawa, but widely used over here.

We grope our way into a cramped and dark concrete enclosure reminiscent of a country football ground's shithouse, all crazed grey concrete and cold, mouldy puddles on the floor; threadbare towels around us for modesty and to hold the wallets. We sit along the narrow wooden-slat benches against the walls. A lone, thin, pallid Yank is sitting there too, in silence, trying to hide. But his luck has changed. He's now wedged between Pigpen and Peaches. For probably the first time in his life he's surrounded by physical risk. We sit there and wait for the steam to come on and, when it doesn't, Dave does the only logical thing—pisses on Pigpen's foot. Pigpen can't decide whether he likes it or not so, fair enough, he grabs another opinion by pissing on the Yank. The Yank doesn't appear to like it much and gets quite verbal. Several of the group judge his comments to be an unfair personal swipe at Pigpen, so they also stand up and piss on the Yank. He gets shitty, then suddenly gets scared and leaves quietly; so the rest of us piss on the floor in criticism of the surroundings and general service.

During the shower afterwards, The Plot unfolded. Dave would do the dance of the flaming arseholes in green thongs at a Yank bar of his choosing if someone would demo a suck fuck for the rest of the gang. Just consider that prospect for a moment!

I walked into a dim massage booth and lay on the high

narrow cot which was covered with a musty grey sheet. Opposite my head was a partition painted light green—in the odd patch where the fungus hadn't already won out. Above it appeared Dave's leering mug. In thumped the love interest. Must have gone a hundred kilos; stood five foot six. Christ, it was homely. I was looking at my first blind date again. Don't snigger! You'll give yourself away. She was wrapped in an arse-length light blue smock like a meat packer. We're talking thunder thighs, with angry red sweaty patches to prove it. I forget the face; I didn't look into the eye of this disaster. Then I heard the scuffling start up behind the partition. Somehow I did my job and she did hers.

I could see nothing exciting in the experience at the time. Nor did the others, as it turned out. They all got their heads over the partition, just having a look, and then Pigpen, of all people, lost his grip and crashed in a meaty smack on the floor. He tried leaping back up but Peaches elbow-gouged him, so Pigpen took a swing at Peaches and Fuzz grabbed Pigpen in a stranglehold as he leapt on him. Then Dave and Ronnie joined the scrum. The thin Yank chose that precise moment to come back looking for something or other, but left instantly without it. The big heifer shot through and Mama San started shouting the odds until Ronnie roughed her up for being a nagger. Mama San was small and aged about sixty, had black permed hair and a tough preserved face; wore a green silk top and a red skirt to match. She talked money and restraint in a high-pitched whine and didn't provide service. You've now met Mama San, so you've met all Mama Sans. Pigpen won King of the Mountain and we dressed and left.

We went into another bar. This one looked likely. There was a long flimsy plywood bar covered in dull green lino on the left as you entered. Above it was a decorative cane screen fixed to the ceiling, coming down to head-height. From that hung split-bamboo blinds for closing time, whenever that was. The back of the bar was mirrored and stocked with spirits. The bench below this had bowls of sliced lemons, olives, cracked ice; shakers and tongs on top. The room was narrow but backed deep into the gloom, with brown vinyl booths on either side packed with rowdy Yanks in various army uniforms, some having a grope at bargirls sitting and squealing happily enough on their laps. A couple of fair-looking bargirls were sitting on stools down the bar a bit—mini skirts and big tits, plenty of makeup.

We filed in and fronted the bar. 'Eight beers please!', to the nog behind the bar. Another Mama San was behind the bar too, having a peer, a vulture probing for signs of life in the carrion. So was every other bastard in the place. Dead silence. 'What the fuck are you lot looking at?'—Peaches attempted to lighten the mood but it didn't, so we flicked the lot, got into the beer. Dave said he'd forgotten his green rubber thongs, which buggered the dance of the flaming arseholes. We had another beer and the bartender was getting jittery. Mama San came over, all grinning and nodding and wringing hands.

'No trouble boys, just enjoy? . . . OK?'

'Fuck off, you old bag!' Pete suggested. I wish I'd thought of that.

Then Peaches said something to Ronnie which he thought was hilarious, until Peaches explained it was intended to be insulting. Ronnie hooked him on the jaw and Peaches cartwheeled over the bar, taking the ornate overhead cane fixture with him to the floor on the far side in a dusty, splintering, clattering pile. He was up on the bounce, draped in bamboo blinds, as the first of the top shelf bottles hit the floor. He leaned across the bar and inquired: 'Anything special for you gents while I'm over here?' Peaches could take a punch but not a hint. Mama San went loopy. Her wailing finally drove him back over our side—but not until he got a replacement for the beer he'd lost in midflight. Mama San had to settle right down and get him one, because the bartender had long since fled. He drank the can he'd lost while she tried desperately to remember where the beer was kept. After that we gave the place the arse. It looked dull without the cane divider, the Yanks had no sense of fun and all the girls had scattered anyway.

Time for lunch, it's past one o'clock. We walked across the square and along a row, looking for a good restaurant. The first few turned out to be just bars, but they weren't a total loss because we were thirsty. Then we were shown upstairs at one of them to a steakhouse which the barman said was very good. They all say that, don't they. Sydney all over again. But it wasn't bad. The upstairs room was a rickety structure, just clapboard and wooden stud frame nailed on top of the ground floor, but the dining area was screened off with ceiling-to-floor bamboo screens and the thin, creaking particle board floor was covered in seagrass matting. Barring a typhoon we were OK. No other customers. We sat at a rough wooden table for eight with red or white paper placemats and drank beer until the meal arrived. There wasn't much choice: 'Biff Stek' or go hungry. When it arrived it was a plate with what resembled a fillet of beef, sliced canned champignon mushrooms, pan juices all over and some panfried pieces of potato to one side. It was fair; the steak was too well done. As we ate we could see the staff through the bamboo screens. Five or six of them sitting around smoking and muttering among themselves, dressed in dark trousers and grimy singlets. Another one was washing a pile of plates in a tin basin on a small table. Couldn't see the kitchen. The food wasn't very hot; maybe they'd sent out for it.

Some Einstein among us had worked out that it wasn't worth paying the bill for the meal. I have an uncomfortable feeling it was me. At the signal we stampeded down the rickety staircase and fanned out at the main door. I was at the head of the column but got jockeyed into a straight line across the square; didn't have the strength to gouge a diagonal run through this class of field. Consequently I had the proprietor and two of his thugs hard on my arse and the crowd slowing me down a bit. I might have stood a chance even then—but I ran smack into a big MP—one of ours, worse luck—while I was taking a quick peek behind me. He held me by the shoulder with his paw until the hounds caught up. We had a squabble in Vietnamese while the MP stood there impassively. I offered to pay the bill, but when I checked I was short ten dollars worth of piastra. I offered the difference in MPC (I'll explain later) which suited the proprietor, but my MP mate reminded me I couldn't pass MPC to the locals. 'OK,' I said, 'I'll fight the prick for the bill.' The proprietor and his two friends shaped up, so that was off the list of options very smartly. 'How about you turn your back while I pay these cunts then?' I suggested to the MP. Nothing doing, the arsehole was just waiting for somebody to collar. Then I noticed Pete's big frame among the growing crowd around me—pissing himself laughing. He finally came over and weighed in with the rest of the bill.

'Just as well you've got a mate, soldier,' the MP said to me.
'I'm only doing it to shit you off, ya big prick!' Pete snarled back.

I returned the favour he'd done me and got Pete away before he could wind the MP right up and start a riot with me in the middle of it.

We caught up with Peaches and Fuzz, then Dave found us in a bar, and the group slowly disintegrated, pairing up with bargirls that Dave said were clean and fair. Dave, Pete and I lurched into another joint about eight o'clock. Dave pointed out two bargirls sitting at the deserted bar and said, 'Pick two out of that lot, they're good here,' and staggered off into the night. We'd given the spirits a fair test by now and Dave's vision was going, and it showed. They didn't look any better than all the others really, just tired. Both of them. Pete and I moved over and bought them a drink each. Saigon tea—coloured water. Bar whores the world over drink it in one form or another; it pays management for the rent of the stool. Fixed a price for the night—we planned on staying out—told Mama San to stick the round of tea she was carrying up her arse and dragged our girls round the corner to the Grand Hotel and booked in.

The hotel was a disappointment. From the outside it was imposing, old-world luxury. I can't remember the foyer now. You walked up a few stone steps to a pillared portico, through a big door, and that was about it. A couple of armchairs against a pale green wall, a potplant in a brass bucket, a wooden counter with wooden key-racks behind. An old black bakelite phone, a blotter, a register. A bored Vietnamese night porter leaning against the far side of the desk, picking his nose with the long nail of his little finger. He signed us in, gave us a key to a fourth floor room. We tried to fight off a porter wanting to carry the key. Walked up the stairs in the gloomy stairwell. The corridor to the room was vinyl tiles, dark green walls, lacquered dark doors with room numbers in oxidised chipped gold paint. Sombre lighting from a shaded bulb here and there. A bathroom on the landing but I didn't see inside it. Into the room, slamming the door shut on the porter's nose. Two beds, a bit bigger than singles, a cloth counterpane on each, dark beige with a white towel folded at the foot, green lino on the floor, old darkwood wardrobe against one wall, walls painted light drab green. A window looking out over the dark roofs of bars and knocking shops.

Let's take a closer look at the girls. Mine's about my height and slim, dressed in a gold, scaly miniskirt dress. Pete's is smaller with a red miniskirt dress which is probably what attracted him to her. It did me. They're pretty enough. Young, twenty or so, both have good hips and jutting breasts, golden skin, black hair of course, straight and shoulder length. Exotic oriental temptresses both. Bullshit! It's a myth. They're like any other whores anywhere in the world, tired beyond caring and too fucking idle to change. That's no guess on my part. As we begin undressing, the love banter starts: 'Me very tired. Bad heart, doctor say I very bad heart, not so much jig-a-jig. I very bad heart.' The jutting breasts thump on the floor with the bra and she flops on her back on the nearest bed, turns her head to face the wall, spreads her legs slightly and stops moaning. I take this as a signal and clamber on. As a fuck it rates better than being cornered by an investment counsellor—at least she says nothing. Pete's girl is much livelier, he's pinched the skin of her shoulder with his elbow getting on, and she shrieks and bucks trying to get free for a second or so. Also causes a bit of motion while she looks to see if it will bruise. In case you're curious, Pete is bigger but I have the staying power over him. Pete sticks his head out the door and roars the porter back, ordering beers: 'Lots of beers, Aussie if you've got it!' The porter comes back with Budweiser and screws us for a double tip for being cheap bastards about the key. We drink a few of these while the girls whinge and whine about their weak hearts and how we are 'So big—not good for us to jig-a-jig so much'. As if we care. But the 'big' bit is nice to hear.

A quick belch, another root; back to the beer. About eleven we run out of beer so Pete says he's off for a shower and then to bed. 'See if you can fuck this pair off, Bazz.' Off he goes, wrapped in the towel he's ripped off his girl and I notice that her tits must be on the floor too—she isn't wearing them. She starts picking at her toes, which churns my guts at the best of times, so I have a look at mine. She's leaning on her right elbow having a scratch at her armpit, yabbering to her mate in between attempts at a hacking cough I haven't noticed before. Neither of the girls now possesses that essential feminine mystique; in fact, mine is starting to appear disturbingly masculine to me. Time to shut off.

Next thing, Pete was back in the room.

'That was quick,' I said.

'Bazz—just see what *I* dragged back.'

'What are you on about?'

'Fucking Shore Patrol, all over the place—big cunts.'

'What the fuck do you want me to do about it?' Can't I ever keep my mouth shut?

'You're small, this is a runt's job. Open the door.'

Pete had the wind up alright, so I thought I'd better take a look. Opened the door. Fuck!! This gigantic bastard in greens, a blue armband with SP in white, a 45 Colt automatic in holster and a blue enamelled steel helmet with SP on it was just about to knock my teeth in. Not intentionally, he'd been about to knock on the door but I'd beaten him to it. From where I stood I could have bitten him on the nuts just by leaning forward slightly. He stood back and I saw the really big bloke just behind him. Black, about six foot eight and 180 kilos. The one in front was white and personable, in a professional way. The 'Hi, I'm smiling and talking quiet and I'll stay that way while you do exactly as I say' type of professional.

'G'day, what do you want?'

'What are you guys doing here? This floor is secured.'

'Having a fuck, and the desk Johnny gave us the key. We're staying the night.'

'There's been a mixup here. I'm sorry, we got the Chief staying on this floor, you'll have to go.'

'It's too late.'

'Oh, we'll organise a lift for you. Better get dressed now.'

We had to go—this pair could have carried Pete and me around in their pockets. I said, 'Hold on a minute,' and went back into the room. My new buddy pushed the door ajar to see that we weren't getting cunning. Pete and the girls were already dressed, so by the time I found my stuff the girls were gone when I joined Pete in the hall.

'Come on down and we'll get you a lift back,' said the black mountain. He could talk. We kept up the chat going down the stairs but he wouldn't say who the Chief was. As we hit the lobby we said, 'Thanks for the offer but we can get back just fine on our own'. They didn't push the issue, so all we had to do was get past the Shore Patrol jeep parked at the entrance, but that proved OK because the driver was helping the girls into the back. No rest for the wicked—I bet the girls didn't whinge to *that* lot all night. It was only when we'd made it down the now quiet street that we considered how to get back to base without getting sprung coming in—or rolled by the local thugs on the way there. A Lambro came by and grudgingly accepted the job.

The trip back was uneventful. Whatever was happening in Vung Tau at this time of night was happening behind closed doors. Apart from the odd street light and a lit-up Shore Patrol or White Mice checkpoint, everything had gone underground. Pete told the driver to drop us off at the back of the Badcoe Club on the beach side. He'd heard it was easy to crawl under the wire there and get in unnoticed. Why such stupid rumours persist constantly amazes me, but I believed him at the time. The Lambro pulled up at the end of a wire enclosure that buttressed the sandy track. Wire fencing and concertina wire to the left, the beach on the right, searchlights and manned gun towers all the way to our gate, a kilometre up the track. Fucking marvellous. The driver wouldn't take us up the track, of course—wouldn't risk getting brassed up by the Korean guard posts, then the Yank ones, then our Aussie ones. He wanted his fare. His fee was through the roof, but Pete talked him down by almost shaking the life out of him after quiet negotiation and simple threats had failed. Two bucks from me and a kick up the arse from Pete was the stubborn bastard's final fee. We assessed the situation. Dead easy: hands above your head, sprint down the track yelling, 'Don't shoot, ya bastards. Aussies coming in. God Bless America, Korea very beautiful country'. Then someone called out, 'Over here, you two comedians!'. The barbed wire gates swung open and three MPs met us on the way through.

'Names?'

Gave them.

'Over here!'

Into a little office, couple of forms.

'Sign here! See you 7.30 am sharp. Orderly parade at the front gate. Know where it is?'

'Nuh.'

'Find it! Go to bed!'
We went for a swim first. Nice big pool with springboard and high tower. No one there—just a big sign on a tripod stand: NO SWIMMING. CLEANING IN PROGRESS. CHEMICALS ABOVE SAFE LEVEL. Kicked the sign down, leaped into deep cool water. Then Fuzz turned up from sleeping on the beach and we had a bombshell session from the high tower, until a smarmy blond-headed bastard in white shorts and beach singlet told us to get out.

'Fuck off!'—crashing in arse first off the tower. Fuzz tried to pull the prick in and Pete asked, 'Who the fuck are you?'.

'I'm the pool attendant. This pool is overdosed, it's unsafe.' He went to go on until Pete said, 'What do *you* know about unsafe? How the fuck do wankers like you get jobs like these? Get service medals too?'

Pete was looking nasty and I'd just copped a jolt of cold water. I always thought your arse was watertight but it isn't, it stings like hell. So we grabbed Pete and said we'd had enough anyway, which we had, and went and found our cots.

Next morning! Shit a brick! Pete's face was in front of me, calling me awake. Every bastard was talking like Donald Duck. The spirits served in this town were lethal! Fuzz crashed across the end of my bed, giving himself backache. I had a shower, got dressed, even looked in on breakfast (I must have been fit back then). The mess was a big asbestos-and-masonite-lined hall painted, you guessed it, pale green. I wish I was the salesman who signed up that deal. It had a food smell much like a ship I know. Took a sausage, half a cup of tea—it said coffee—had a quick gag just outside the door, and Pete and I were off to meet our buddies at the main gate. Had a look around, spotted a building near the gate and headed for it. Big Mick was leaning against the verandah lighting a fag.

'Hey, Mick, know where the MPs are?'
'Yes, here.'
'What are you doing here?'
'Just got in. Get this out of the way first.'
'What's this mob like?'
'Same as anywhere. Fuck, I wish they'd hurry up, I want to make breakfast.'

'Why?'

The MPs eventually rolled out on to the porch, sizing up the crowd of about twenty. Don't know what they made of the big Pommy bastard in the bowler hat and the Hawaiian-sunset shirt and the funny glasses and the vacuous grin propping up the verandah despite an order to shift, but we all got processed quickly. 'Name! Number! Rank! Unit! Next time, you're banned from coming here. Meantime, you're grounded to this area till noon—dismissed!'

Pete and I went for a look around. He'd heard the Yanks had a wild leisure centre on base. We found it right off; asked a Yank walking by. 'Straight in front of you', he directed. Just as well we asked. It was the last place we'd have looked, it was a bunker. A great thick-walled grey concrete bunker with a slot in the wall to allow you to enter through a steel turnstile. About the size of a small circus tent. Inside, the walls were about four metres high and laid out in a long octagon with a metre or so overhang coming in. Sheltered under this lip around six of the walls were one-armed bandits—fruit machines they called them—and some other crappy coin machines from way back. One told you about your star sign on small cardboard slips and dropped a stale-coloured sugar ball down the chute. Nothing in the middle of the floor, just three steps all around down to a bare concrete pad reflecting glaring sunlight. I walked up to a Yank marine playing one of the fruit machines.

'How do you play these?'

'You get tokens from the bar, like these.' He showed me some dull bronze pellets in the palm of his hand. I looked at his dull bronze eyes.

'There's a bar here? Where?'

'Oh, the candy bar over there, you can get tokens there. Oh . . . you thought I meant another type, didn't you. No, just soda.'

Pete and I each bought four slugs for a buck at the kiosk, and on the third wrench of the lever I got about fifteen slugs down. 'Hey, look at this, Pete. A winner. Let's cash up and fuck off.'

'Oh, those aren't redeemable,' called my Marine buddy across the way.

'What the fuck do you do with them?'

'Oh, you can play with them again.'

We admitted defeat and headed for the boozer at the Badcoe Club. Named after one Major Badcoe who'd been awarded a posthumous VC for bravery in the field over here. We sat it out until noon, too idle to plot an escape. The beer went down, the shouts went around, and I was just getting up for more beer when Dave said, 'Sit down, Barrie!'. He got up on the trestle, walked the length of it, bent over into the face of a total stranger and advised him his buy was past due. The stranger stood up and left without a word, joining another table across the way. After that little lesson on life we went out for another look at the town. This time sanely, and saw another Vung Tau. Dave suggested we change our MPC in town, rather than at the base exchange office—the rate was better.

South Vietnam's currency, piastra, or dong, had no international value. It was funny money, it only had value in-country. In order to pay troops like us a currency was established, with real dollar backing, called Military Payment Currency, or MPC, which we could convert to US dollars or Australian dollars as we left the country for R&R or when going home. MPC was naturally very desirable to well-connected Vietnamese because they could exchange it for US greenbacks. It gave them international buying power. MPC was designed by the US government to contain such currency movement. Street kids would roam the cities offering rates of, say, 400 piastra to the dollar when the rate through our exchanges was 300. You seldom got it, though, these raggedy-arsed little entrepreneurs of nine or ten could count it into your hand one note at a time and still swindle you, but you rarely got less than the official rate unless you were pissed or seen to be stupid. Bar bills or roots could be settled in MPC if no MPs were watching. The same joints would gladly exchange large sums at reasonable rates. About the only effective controls on currency manipulation were those imposed on soldiers. Aussie soldiers certainly, probably the Yanks too—field soldiers, I mean. We could only return home with as much money as we'd earned overseas, less what we'd drawn.

Life was dirt cheap in Vung Tau. The White Mice were the official police force but they were hampered with too many restrictions to be effective. They had only restraining powers over allied forces—once one of us was apprehended in a criminal act we had to be handed over to our own military police. They were encouraged by their own government to concentrate more on political rather than criminal acts, which was great because they could screw the criminal element for money without fear. Traffic pretty well looked after itself—not many road rules to enforce, big goes first, that was about it. During the day time it was safe enough if you stayed on the main roads of the city and didn't go alone, or go stupid. The hardest part was finding something to do that didn't involve whores, drinking Yank beer or bathtub spirits, getting clipped in shonky money exchanges, buying drugs, or getting run over by a Lambro.

Barbers operated from chairs on every footpath and thoroughfare in the centre. Big heavy wooden padded ancient chairs. Must have been a bastard to lug home each night. A chest of wooden drawers with combs, handshears, razors and mirrors sitting on top, a leather strop hanging from the side. In the drawers were the styptics, the haircreams, and the ear-cleaning brushes. Pete and I watched the barbers clean the ears of the customers, mainly locals but with some thrill-seeking Yanks among them. Dave had left us by now, seeking pleasures elsewhere, and missed this bit. The barbers used brushes made of twisted wire with bristles woven through the ends, like bottlebrushes. The brushes varied in diameter but were all about eight centimetres long. It was scary how far into the ear they went, in and out like a sewing machine arm, a blur. The bristles were stained like they'd been used to clean pipes, all a dark tar-brown. They were sanitised by putting them back in the drawer so the flies couldn't get at them. The cheeks of my arse were starting to cramp up with tension after a few minutes, so we moved on.

We went looking for shops after that, but there weren't many. I found a tailor's shop Big Mick'd been to. It had two suits in the window, dinner suits. One of white linen overlaid with black lace and what could laughably be described as black satin lapels; black trousers with the same satin stripe down the seam. The other was red. I bought the red one. Never wore it, of course, it shrieked fucking idiot if you put it on and I didn't move in those circles. Gave it to a car salesman when I got back—he wore it a lot. We walked along a commercial street from the tailor's shop and spotted a brand new Fiat 124S. White, with red upholstery. It was incredibly rare to see a car in this country, let alone a new-release model. Pete and I were both keen to own one. A bit pricey for us, about $3500 at home. My gross yearly salary was $2800. Still, it didn't stop us looking and we were poring over it like a couple of mugs when a Yank voice behind said, 'Like the Fiats, uh?' We turned around and it wasn't a Yank at all, it was a local. He was Pete's size, big for a local, about forty, big face, dressed in a white suit definitely not locally tailored, button-down white shirt, silk patterned tie.

'Yeah, like to get one when I get back—bit expensive new, though,' said Pete.

'What do you pay for one in Australia?' He knew accents pretty well; we weren't waving flags. Pete told him.

'You know, I had to pay $180,000 US for this.'

'*How* fucking much?'

'That's right,' he nodded, and grinned as if to imply, 'isn't life shit'. '$180,000 US, and I had to wait, no priority. That's what war does to your economy. Anyway, look all you want fellers; gotta go, nice talking to you.' And he walked into a shabby two-storied concrete office block. There were no signs on the building and the windows were small and shaded, so we couldn't get a clue on what his line of business was. Whatever it was, Pete and I reckoned we were in the wrong one. $180,000 US in 1969 was real 'get fucked' money, and that was just for wheels.

We might have written it all off as bullshit but on our look around we caught a glimpse of the south end of the bay when we went for a Lambro ride. Away in the distance we could see villas nestling into the hills above the sea. Dozens of magnificent multistoried villas, not relics from French colonial days—mostly quite modern, distinctly big money. Source? Who knows. Vice and drugs, sure; whether they accounted for all of it we couldn't say. But they seemed to be the only industries around. And we couldn't imagine a country like this sustaining that level of opulent living.

In between these glimpses we toured a few bars, and had a quiet yap with some of the Yank servicemen in them. They were more amenable when there were only two of us and we'd got the wild-eyed look of the jungle out of our faces. A lot of Aussie servicemen with Vietnam experience write the Yanks off as undisciplined or junkheads or both. I'm sure many saw evidence to let them make that statement in full confidence. I saw something different when I met and spoke with them. On this day we talked with a lot of Yanks at two bars that were pretty much their domain. We were received easily into their conversation.

They were a divided army; no question of that. The hardcore old hands, staff sergeants and above—the pros—didn't mix much in this quarter; they had their own setups. I saw mainly the draftees and the younger guys. A number of them were field soldiers but the overwhelming majority were service personnel, not fighting men. There were a few roughheads among them but they were quite tractable compared to my lot.

They were on the backfoot. Most of them had no idea what they were doing here—and I'm describing their daily tasks. Almost every sentence started with 'Oh', until you settled them down. 'Oh, I do things in the stores.' 'Oh, I'm a typist, I stay in an office mostly.' The bigger issues, like why they were here and what they were doing here, they couldn't put into words. Most of them were quick to say they had a noncombatant role. Their ratio of support troops to actual field troops was much higher than ours, and God knows ours was high enough. They didn't appear in the least gungho about winning this war—just doing their time, waiting to go home.

They saw all Aussies as a physical threat. We were different to them. From school age we'd experienced a rough grading into pecking order by strength or merit, *then* birthright. And although some of it was bullshit, that's how we saw ourselves—as good as the next bastard and tough enough to prove it. The Yanks on average were taller than us, they spoke well with good vocabularies and they were superficially better educated. Many had college diplomas in marketing, applied sales, technical trades, and had jobs waiting for them in a shoe department or a supermarket when they got back, maybe.

When I think back to them now I'm eerily reminded of our own youth today. A lot's been said about the Yanks' drug-taking and it was quite true. It was as available as you wanted it to be, any kind. These were young Americans in '69, so what do you expect? They were just typical of that nation's youth. When journalists see a man in a soldier's uniform drugged out of his skull, they report a soldier as in 'fighting soldier' when they often mean a serviceman. I'm not surprised if a lot of their infantry took dope into the field; their training could have given them little confidence and I'm not just referring to infantry training—education and upbringing played their part.

Were most Aussies clean? How would I know? My own company were usually red-eyed and sometimes paranoid from anxiety, fear, lack of sleep, exhaustion, news from home, and the odd hangover. It makes it hard to judge. I do know somebody smoked dope in my company—I did once. This isn't really the point. It was very quiet among us, that's all.

Enough of opining. Take a last look at the palaces on the hill overlooking the bay. We've got to be back in the base by 4.30 pm, to defend those who live in those houses. Forget I said that. We're due back at the Dat for dinner, and the boozer's open for a while. And I haven't properly introduced you to Fuzz yet. He's a funny bastard, a platoon radio operator, good in the field, steady—and just when you think it's safe he turns wild, and he encourages others too. He looks like Father Christmas: short, solid, potbellied and silver-haired, with a moustache that doubles as sideboards, and a beard but he has a pink shaven patch around the chin. He gets away with this, it's his particular eccentricity, but no one else would. In the company photo taken just before embarkation you see a stocky 22-year old colt, blond-haired with a moustache, fresh attractive smiling face. Has this country aged Fuzz! He was a Telecom technician before being called up. Good heart. Now you know Fuzz. Or enough to go on with.

At the boozer Big Mick begins filling his bowler hat with beer and those of us around him help him with it—it looks like fun. Then we have to drink it. He's won the punchout of course; we have to humour the big bastard. 'Here, Crowls' . . . and I'm holding a sweaty bowler filled with beer while its owner wipes the foam from his jaw. Hard getting your mouth around the rim. Fuzzy like a peach, too; sets your teeth on edge. The hat gets drained finally—it's bigger than it looks—then Mick clamps it back on and gives us a song. I leave just before last can call, 30 minutes late relieving the radio picquet. I have a bastard of a time waking the next on the list, which is Peaches, until I find where he hides his beer and open a can. Finally get to bed about 2 am.

Which brings me back to Peaches. After he'd left the field, refusing to kill any more, Peaches became the new company blowfly. It was a fair enough job if you liked shit work! War on waste in its basic sense. The dickhead who previously held the job had shot himself in the foot on a TAOR patrol. A foot wound is very nasty—a sensible man reserves that for avoiding combat, not local patrols. Being the blowfly meant that Peaches didn't go into the field except on TAORs. Actually, the job itself was an utter mongrel. Cleaning shithouses, shower blocks and piss-o-phones, killing pests and bugs, keeping the mess drains unblocked. Carrying out slop bins, cleaning them. Clawing the cooks' disasters out of grease pits with bare hands, waistdeep in grey, gooey slime. Enough gun picquets and radio watches to keep you from the boozer. Peaches had no choice but to accept the job. He meant to see the tour out with us, that was pretty obvious. He took to drinking subliminally. Every night he went to bed with a stack of cans of beer under his bed. Every morning they were gone. Well, Pete drank them! Peaches certainly couldn't have—he'd slept all night! Pete used to raid the mess fridges too. But Peaches privately accepted the blame for that. He didn't want Pete's reputation destroyed over a few minor personal quirks. And also, although Pete wasn't back at base too often, the fridges got raided nightly.

A weird culture formed within the company around this time. It was driven by a profound question: 'Why the fuck am I here?' I can't recall anyone who wholeheartedly believed we should be here. There must have been some; certainly, when we arrived it was a commonly held belief, though not universal. Time had changed many, though the officers held to the official line, at least in our hearing. It would be easy to say they were paid to hold firm, but so were we. We hung in together but broke into groups where differences of opinion were negated by friendship. It saved a lot of bloodshed.

The boozer was neutral ground. Woofer came by the Nugget one day and asked, 'How's the Schnerder Nine going?'. I said, 'Fine, how's Woofer going?' I knew what the bastard meant. So did Dave, sat next to me gazing languidly at a *Playboy*. We weren't taking the war seriously, not by Woofer's standards. Who was? He wouldn't stop for a beer, of course, in case he was distracted from his course of action, which was not only to stay alive, but to keep the rest of us the same. A bit tricky for him, in his position, but he was a crack scout and stuck with it. He had a problem which I could well sympathise with—as his problem. Mine was my own problem, very different to his—not only staying alive, but being alive. A problem which I shared with Dave, Pete, Brian, Peaches, Pigpen, Les, Ronnie and Tank. Also Fuzz, one or two others. And whoever poured the piss behind the bar. These last weren't a part of the true fear but some had felt it, and they fulfilled a vital service. That presumably was what Woofer referred to as the Schnerder Nine, the party people.

You could tack Support Section on as Schnerders. Boy, did that section become a popular little club! Still very much a field unit, but they never led the company in the field and did less patrolling than the platoon sections did. Any edge, however slight, still counted—Griffo never had so many friends, always off somewhere or other being courted over the next vacancy. There were other clubs, of course, but few wanted to join them; they were just in them, as far as I could see. I'm referring to other sections, other platoons. *They* should grumble, I came down from a nice safe haven in BHQ! Platoonies were applying for any jobs going. RPs, drivers, storemen; one lead scout scored a clerk's job under Fuck-Knuckle, our clerk, and against extreme competition.

What accelerated this migratory culture and the few going apeshit was a number of changes within the company. Quite a few Diggers had gone home with what looked like tolerable wounds, when you balanced it against possible death. Some went home crook, but if they were cured they got sent back. Loonies never returned unless they went home with a wound as well, in which case their state of mind was ignored. Still more were about to go home because their National Service term was expiring. Having what you had always considered a lifetime mate sitting across the table at breakfast saying, 'Seven and a wakie and I'm fucking out of here—how long you got?' was a real downer when you had seven months to go compared to his seven days, and he knew it. And he knew it because he'd asked the same gloating question every day for the last fortnight.

Then there was the matter of leadership. Above the company level it was bedlam, typical bureaucracy. It got safer up there, so senior officers could afford to be more daring in their strategies—it didn't affect their personal safety or comfort, only their career path. Ideas and grand plans came and went at a whim for them. Within the company, too, we had troubles with our officers. There was some doubt whether many of them could think. If they did, it didn't show often. Theirs was a career path; issues could be suppressed. Duntroon, for some of us, was tolerable, he could smell advancement and generally towed OC's line, as long as he was being watched. At least he'd wander around and talk to the blokes occasionally, and was prepared to debate a reasonable issue.

One of our platoons had a change of leadership about now. They drew the Prick. Second Lieutenant Prick was a squat, unattractive, hardnosed bastard driven by a craving for recognition. He was recognised by most of us as an utter cunt—but he craved more. Fuck knows why, you can't do worse than that. The Prick wanted to kill every Viet Cong in Vietnam. Sometimes his men wondered if he had a contorted deathwish, but they were his troops issued fair and square and if he wanted them dead it was for a good cause. He was in no hurry to go home—he liked his job, that's what mattered. If the troops wanted an opinion let them become officers, otherwise shut the fuck up. He knew he wouldn't rise up the ranks through good connections, so he sought the warrior's tag. That was his particular stupidity. Not many warriors make it to the top.

What made it harder on this platoon was that there'd been a hiatus of a couple of months between their original platoon commander's demise, brought about by his ability to display leadership at the highest level of pratfall humour, and Prick's appointment. The La The La, the platoon sergeant, had assumed command during this time.

The La The La. The stuttering sergeant. 'The la the la purpose of this exercise is to . . .' went his normal conversation. In times of really stressful situations the stutter disappeared. I never could figure that out. He was a short, nuggety lifer of about thirty, another of our Borneo veterans. A blue-collar type through and through. He'd debate an issue, brawl if debate failed, and could be compassionate with a genuine case. He performed with credit in his time as a platoon commander, but there was no future for him as a leader. You couldn't have him sitting beside the brigadier's wife describing how he'd fixed the wife's washing machine, and then asking her to 'Pass us the la the la tomato sauce will ya luv'. Social conventions must be given full weight. So our officers were selected from a shallow pool.

The third platoon was commanded by the company narcissus. His story is much like that of any other of that type, and has no place here.

Anyway, they weren't really my problem. I only had to deal with OC and CSM, so I had nothing to grumble about. Especially when one afternoon shortly after Vungers I was told I'd be missing the next Op. I was advised I was being detached to a Civil Aid team for a month or so as their interpreter. It suited me: seemed a good time for a change of scenery. I did another TAOR that night and was packed and ready to go by breakfast time.

Chapter 8

WELL, THAT'S VUNGERS AND A BIT OF THE DAT behind us. What are we looking at now? A stint at Long Hai with an Aussie Civil Aid team, lodging with the Green Berets, is my next venture. You're coming along too? Good. What happens to my company? They start getting pushed down near the villages. It's around April '69 and our higher command believe the jungle action gets a bit light on for people to shoot at around then, so the allied troops, meaning our mob, get shunted down to the more populated areas—in the hope that someone gets windy or correctly reads the spirit of his orders like Lieutenant Calley and gives a village a good thumping. The company loses no members, I don't think there's any wounded, monotony bites deep, and the boys rest up to some extent in between fruitless ambushes, stand-tos, patrols, cordons, digging rifle pits and walking or APC'ing to one new location after another near a village where hopefully they'll meet someone they don't like. The kill rate goes down dramatically. Nil while we're away.

Anyway, that's them. Forget those we've met to date, we start afresh. Forget old acquaintances, because they may not be there when we get back. We're not vitally interested in anything but our own destination. Ah, destiny. We're going to take a look at the elite, and do a bit of PR. Hearts and Minds, that's what Civil Aid is all about, isn't it?

I've no idea how I got the job but I got to the right place on time, so I assume CSM briefed me in detail—something like: 'Get your kit, you're to go to Long Hai where some Pioneers from Support Company are fixing up a school the VC blew up. You're their interpreter, about four weeks. Bugger off!' I met up with a Pioneer lance corporal driving his own issued Landrover and we drove off. I will call him Lance Jack from here on because I can't remember his name and the rank typifies his mentality. Lance Jack was an intellectual runt. He had all the words necessary to make his world function: 'If you're not my boss get the fuck out of my way because I'm licking the wrong arse.' He was a dehydrated dark-skinned yes-man with a lantern jaw, bug eyes and shrivelled wiry frame of average height. His hair was long on top, cropped at the sides, black and brilliantined. He perpetually squinted, which drew his lips back like a bucktoothed moron. Apart from that he was a nice enough creature. A Kiwi of about thirty and a Reg. His main concern with my presence in his patch was that I outranked him by a hook and, as I knew nothing whatever about building, and as these troops were his blokes normally, common sense dictated I should look after myself and let him control the rest.

So his logic ran. I was desolated at this prospect. Having spent the last four months or more dragging arse all over the countryside, ducking shit and growing up fucking fast, I craved nothing better than spending a month working sixteen-hour days supervising a construction team on a site that the VC appeared to like thudding rockets and mortars into at idle moments. All this glory because I had one more tick on my sleeve than he did. But he finally succeeded in persuading me to stick to interpreting. So by the time we drove out the gate of the company area I was considering how to spend the twenty-three hours and fifty minutes leisure time available to me each day, sweating over whether I'd brought enough money and cursing the fact that I hadn't thought to bring my music and more books.

I have no idea what route we took. Highway 2 due south on to Route 44 maybe, it's hard to say. The highways and main roads here didn't have reflective signposts, off-ramps and lights; they had deeply rutted dirt with huge potholes in it. We chugged and thumped along a road, getting out of the way of bigger military vehicles coming the other way, and pushing the odd ox cart off the side. The road's verge was a better driving surface than the road itself and virtually all military vehicles were four-wheel-drive anyway—but bugger it, let the Nogs shunt and turn a cranky pair of oxen; we were on business here and they didn't count. The road ran through open country, drab grey sand with blue-grey scraggly scrub. In the distance some signs of agriculture. After we'd passed a couple of small villages near the Dat, I don't recall seeing any more until we hit Long Hai. The road was guarded every few kilometres by little corrugated iron forts like those described earlier. Cheerless hopeless rat holes. Up close you could see the bullet holes and rents from shrapnel and rocket hits in the outer skin, the sand-packing drizzling out slowly but surely. A tattered faded flag or two, a few scrawny grey ducks waddling around looking for somewhere nice to shit. Usually two or three disconsolate ARVN or Provincial militiamen aimlessly guarding from the parapet. Occasionally, a glimpse of one of the garrison wives hanging raggedy-arsed washing on a string line out the back or tending a small dusty kitchen garden, watered from a greasy well.

The only sign of cheer was the odd group of little barefoot kids in tattered T-shirts and baggy shorts standing by the gate giving us a wave and a cheer. They could have been saying anything but they smiled, so I took them at face value and waved back. We'd been told a lot of bullshit about how dangerous the VC kids were. Thinking back now, I wonder how they dared say it. Our officers, I mean. When you think of war you never imagine kids being right in it, do you. But it's incredible how you adjust, how you put it out of your mind. Which is why you don't imagine kids being right in it. The human mind can become an exclusive circle within a circle.

The further we went the better the view became. A mountain range began to rise above the flat land on the horizon to our left—the Long Hai mountain range. Never close enough to see clearly, but the hills formed a green and pleasant backdrop to a dreary landscape. We were moving toward the wet season, rain was scarce, but the skies were continually overcast and threatening. After about an hour and a half's journey Lance Jack said, 'Here we are,' in a cheerful way, so I looked around for something good.

'What the fuck's that?'

'That's home for now, Green Berets' headquarters. Good blokes.'

All I could see was what appeared to be a Gestapo prisoner-of-war camp stretching endlessly along the left-hand side of the road. High barbed wire fence, guard towers, big expanses of flat grey sand and rows of barracks made of weather-greyed clapboard with asbestos or galvanised iron roofs. We turned into the gateway guarded by a strikingly uniformed Green Beret and a couple of surly, similarly dressed Nogs, and I saw a cluster of five or six buildings of similar construction to the others we'd passed, only painted—pastel green. These were the Green Berets' quarters. The other ones, separated by a hundred metres or so of sand and a few scrubby trees, were for the Nogs.

At the boomgate the Beret listened as Lance Jack explained my presence. Then, with an 'OK', the boom went up and we drove up the grey gravel path to the doorway of one of the barracks straight on from the gate.

'I'll show you your room and you can stow your stuff. We've missed lunch so we'll go straight to the school—I've got a lot to sort out there,' Lance Jack advised worldwearily. It was a manner I was to come to know well, self-importance—he had no other. The army got all that dedicated service for one miserable hook. Shit, how's that for cunning staff management?

I looked in the door of my room, an eight-by-eight plywood-lined wooden-floored dark cell with an iron bed and a metal locker; checked the bare bulb, it worked; threw my shit under the cot and headed back to the Landrover.

'We have a room each here,' said Lance Jack as we drove off—like I should care. 'Hot showers, good tucker in the officers' mess and full bar facilities at the officers' bar.'

'What's the bar hours?'

'About 10 am till after midnight, I think.'

Think? What planet is this clown from? I now had a mission—to answer my own question.

Right, let's grab a quick glance at the school and get back to work. What a beautiful grey sandy place this is going to be, viewed from a comfy barstool through a swirling pink haze. I'm going to like it here.

Out the gate and down the road we drove. The road didn't get any better as it started going downhill toward a small river crossed by a low crumbling concrete bridge. Near the bridge it became boggy in patches and water lay stagnating in shallow clay culverts on either side. At the lip of the bridge at each end was a deep water-filled depression where vehicles hit the concrete step of the bridge with a teeth-cracking thump going one way and a jolting splash going the other. You'd think someone would fill them in but no one was allocated the job. The bridge marked the start of the village proper, so at each end of the bridge there was usually a melee of ducks, pigs, handcarts and the obligatory bogged water buffalo dray. Do you know what these carts carried?

People. Thousands of these carts all over the countryside and you never saw them carting anything, never. Apart from people. Some smart bastard answer that one.

Once over the bridge, on the left the village outskirts became visible. Thatch-roofed houses mainly, but hard to see the detail through the tall green trees and palms planted among them. Most of the village lay in that direction. Down the road on the right I could see the schoolhouse over uninterrupted level grassland. Beyond the school I could glimpse more dense housing and the tops of some imposing buildings.

'What're those buildings up ahead?'

'They're hotels. Six or seven of them, all built around the bay. This place used to be a resort town for the French—pretty flash, a little Riviera.'

'Let's take a look first.'

'Nah, can't. Berets won't allow it.'

'Fuck the Berets, let's take a look.'

'Listen, I'm not bullshittin' ya, this is VC country. The Yanks are responsible for it and for us. Don't fuck around or we're out of here. To the school and back, that's it for us.'

It occurred to me the schoolhouse wasn't all that safe if the VC had hit it recently, but we're not dealing with consistent logic here, and I'm not talking about Lance Jack. One day it's 'Don't tread in that field, it's full of mines!'. Next day it's 'Run over that field, I see some enemy!'. Who am I to buck the rules?

The schoolhouse had been hit alright. We pulled up at the near side: there were burnt patches of grass all over the area; ground churned up by mortar bombs; several large holes shot through the walls, carbon-blackened round the edges—that's rockets. Big patches of the thatching and roof timbers burnt away; smoke stains lapping the upper walls where the charred remains of latticework hinted at what was once a screen between walls and roof. Working among a pile of debris and timber beside the schoolhouse were six or seven bare-chested Diggers who downed hand tools and sauntered up to us as we drove in. I'd known a few Support Company blokes vaguely back in Australia, but not these. I'm pretty sure they were all Nashos and probably joined the battalion along with Dave's intake, that's when most joined us. Lance Jack introduced them to me by a quick point around and we shook hands.

They looked a good bunch, big fit bastards, trade backgrounds mainly, which is why they were in a Pioneer platoon, an infantry version of engineers. Out in the field they did the more complicated construction work of the BHQ support base. I don't recall most of them now, but I remember Geoff. Not his real name, but I'm disguising nothing—I've just forgotten his name. He was about my height but stocky with a round, friendly, open face, blue eyes, light brown hair. Know the type? They walk up, shake your hand and you know right off you like them, and you want to start knowing why. That's Geoff. Lance Jack of course had the burdens of the universe to deal with so Geoff said he'd give me a tour of the place. That was agreed, 'but don't wander off' because I had to meet the school's headmaster and start sorting out a work schedule once all Lance Jack's other pressing problems were fixed up.

'How do you get on with this dickhead?' I asked Geoff, not trying to disguise my own feelings for the man.

'Ah . . . he's goodhearted enough. The Yanks use him up scrounging for them most of the time and he gets materials for here against the odds, but he's . . . shit. You know his type—one hook and he has to run everything. What's your rank, by the way?'

'Corporal.'

'Sorry.'
'Forget it.'
'Suits me. So . . . you're here to sort out communications, eh? That'll be a start. Have a look at this lot though, we haven't got a fucking hope.'

He started me on the tour. The schoolhouse was a whitewashed U-shape with a small grassy tree-dotted quadrangle in the centre, stone-paved paths. A class of small children sat here around their teacher under a tree. The bottom of the U was the office and administration centre and the two wings were the classrooms, four large rooms to each. Most of the damage was concentrated in the wing facing the Berets' camp. There was some lesser damage here and there over the other side—that wing was operational, so we only had a brief look in case we disrupted the kids' lessons. The near wing, where the materials were stacked, had one classroom damaged but operating and another classroom was being brought up to usable standard at the moment. The remaining two rooms in this wing were gutted by fire.

I was seeing a pleasant, primitive, native-crafted hut-type building made of thick whitewashed mud walls with a thatched roof. Nothing to it—where's the problem? As we strolled around the outside I asked Geoff about himself. Born in country New South Wales, Tenterfield I'm sure he said, right up the north by the border. Came to Sydney to do his apprenticeship as a carpenter, and stayed on there until he was called up. Not *for* that, though, he thought he'd beat that. No, there was a young city woman keeping him out of the bush. And he dragraced an old FJ as a hobby. Single but with intentions is how he put it.

We stepped into one of the fire-damaged rooms. That is, Geoff did. I jolted hell out of my back when I entered—the floor was burnt right out by the door and I hadn't noticed the drop. While I waited for the dazzling black spots to flicker out and to get adjusted to the gloom, Geoff was pointing out the problems. I saw a mud-walled room with old badly burnt floorboards and some fire-eaten lattice tacked on top of the walls, a couple of tree trunks minus the bark standing upright supporting the roof timbers which looked like dressed limbs for the heavier supports, split hand-dressed beams for the lighter rafters, and cross-battens holding the thatched roof, or what was left of it. Rough as shit.

'What's the problem, Geoff?'

'Look at it Barrie! We haven't had craftsmen like these for a century—more! This is fucking perfect. Look, it's all wooden dowels, not a nail anywhere. Feel the supports, smooth as silk. That's not wear, that goes right up, it's all handsanded to satin finish. Look at the joinery, it's irregular because it's not been milled but you couldn't blow air through those joints. Look at the floorboards, handmated and jointed. Know where I can get a good thatcher? And look at what we've got to work with. Fucking look at it!' A pile of rough-milled four-by-two beams, some planks and a few bags of nails lay against a wall.

'This is the best bit—look at the lattice battens we've been given.' A small stack of warped milled softwood strips about the right size lay ready to replace the burnt lattice. It had been machined the wrong way and the grain curled up like bristles.

'See, we're fucked every way we turn. What am I gunna do with this shit? You could brush your fucking teeth with it. And making up lattice is about the only part of this job we could do as well as the locals originally did. I'm ashamed to work on this place; we'll fuck it up more than the rockets that hit it.'

Geoff completely changed my view on the capabilities of this country's people—or peasants, to quote the Western press. I started to see with a broader view.

'Just think Barrie, this is a country schoolhouse, built by ordinary everyday workmen. Most of this place isn't that old.'

There was nothing I could do to help Geoff with the problem of skills and materials, but by the time Lance Jack came to get me to meet the headmaster I had the communication bit figured out. Easiest problem I ever had to fix: get Lance Jack out of the picture. The headmaster had come around to the work site to find out what Lance Jack was up to next. I was introduced to him and we shook hands. A good handshake, firm and dry. The headmaster was a thin erect man of sixty or so. Quietly spoken, dignified, not snobby. His hair was greying, his eyes almost black. Dressed in clean white shirt and worn black pleated trousers. Polished black lace-up shoes. He spoke no English but when I advised him I had trouble with his words he offered fluent French, which would have been a great help if I hadn't fucked around in French classes at high school. More to the point, he understood *me* without difficulty. Geoff was within reach so I called him over and, in Vietnamese, began.

'This Geoff.' They shook hands.

'Geoff see you in morning, say, this room we work one day, two day, you move student, do good work.' The headmaster smiled, nodded to me and Geoff, shook hands and went about his business. A very intelligent man, this headmaster. Well, that's communication solved.

It wasn't all of the team's problems solved but they now had direct contact. Up to then Lance Jack was controlling everything and it was too much for him. He was off most of each day sourcing materials and the team were trying to work around lack of supplies, overcrowded classrooms and Lance Jack's program, which like his mind processes was self-centred. The headmaster had been obliged to communicate only through Lance Jack, with the result that the workplace resembled a madhouse run by a philosopher. At least after the meeting Geoff could plan his work with the cooperation of the headmaster, based on the materials he had to hand. They understood each other very well without words; must have, Geoff never called on my services again and we spent a lot of time together drinking of an evening. It seemed to suit Lance Jack too—he made better use of his time with other priorities and overlooked the fact that I was an interfering little prick. He still meddled on site; couldn't help himself, but it was manageable.

That first afternoon I'd effectively put myself out of a job, so naturally I gave some thought as to how best to rejoin my company. Pig's fucking arse I did. I hung around the Landrover bored shitless, while Lance Jack stuck his nose in every other bastard's business, until Geoff pointed out they were short of some essential product or other—probably patience—and there was no point in them sticking around. That did the trick and we were off up the road, over the bridge and through the boomgate. Where's this bar, then?

As luck would have it, and I had a lot of that here, the mess hall and its bar were directly across from my barrack door. Geoff pointed the way, but instinct would have got me there unerringly. He said he'd catch me for a beer after a quick shower. I didn't need one, I'd done little or nothing that day, so in I went in to meet a few of the guys. The mess wasn't exclusively an officers' mess, it was for all ranks—Green Beret ranks that is. It was staffed by Nogs behind the bar, in the kitchen, and of course doing the cleaning. This place had cleaners for your room, too. Bliss!

There were about forty to fifty Berets here, at a guess, ranging from buck sergeant (our equivalent of corporal) through to master sergeant (our warrant officer rank) and a handful of officers. I don't recall a lieutenant here but I'm probably wrong. Certainly there was a captain, and the commanding officer was a major. The officer ranks were on equal ranking with our own, although I suspect their company commanders in infantry units were captains while ours were majors. Unlike Aussies who usually dressed anonymously in unmarked greens and floppy giggle hats—apart from our SAS who enjoyed preening—the Berets wore their green berets with the snappy cloth badge, unit badges, and rank insignia on their dark green fatigues. They even wore lanyards on their shoulder and campaign ribbons on their chests in the mess most nights. Staggering sight to see a young bloke of twenty-two or three wearing three rows of ribbons on his left breast, with less time in-country than we did on one of our tours.

OK, I'm in the mess. Geoff's sunk a few beers with me. Shortly I'll discover how to give the nondrinkers the shits in a big way. I'll establish a sound friendship with the most hated officer in the Berets unit and I'll meet the second most obnoxious sergeant major in the world and mull over a plot to bring the cunt down to earth. How's that for a couple of hours work? Oh yes, and I'll alienate us from that group of young men leaning against the far wall. Stick around, I'm good in company.

Better give you some detail. You enter the mess through a flimsy flywire door. (There was a sturdy wooden one too, but it was never slammed in my face so I can't describe it.) Once you're inside, the hall's a basketball court. Varnished floorboards up to the bar, which itself isn't much—flimsy partitioning painted a light insipid green—long enough if the captain sits to drink, in which case there's no problem getting a stool.

A few tables and chairs scattered down the left-hand wall.

A pretty basic setup but luxurious compared to the Dat. Couple of Nogs behind the mirrored bar. Stocks are a bit sparse: a variety of glasses and ice buckets, one or two chrome cocktail shakers, and spirits measures. All good signs. Bar towels and coasters. I can see the dining area through a wide square entry to the left of the bar: trestles with tablecloths, buffet-style serve-yourself setup; a coffee urn, iced tea, a pile of crockery, some plastic divider-bins with cutlery in them and a white-shirted Nog coughing and hawking over the lot.

I front the bar, grab a stool that isn't being sat on from among the small seated group—some mouthy bastard's standing to emphasise his point—and order a beer. In Vietnamese. The Nog behind the bar looks at me as if I'm talking Urdu. I repeat the order again to his mate drying a glass at the sink just behind him. For Christ's sake, I even *look* like a beer drinker; I'm not that mysterious. No connection. Blank stares. I turn to the group on my right and grab the mouthy one on the shoulder and ask, 'What's up with this lot?' He gives me a look like he probably outranks me, but says, 'Thaay urr Caimboooodiens.'

That had me groping in the dark for a moment.

'What the fuck are they doing here?'

'We train Caimboooodien mercenaries here for the DMZ, son,' he says, and turns back to his group. I order two beers in English.

Geoff turns up at my shoulder. 'Met the colour sergeant, I see.'

This Beret was mesmerising. Nine banks of medal ribbons on his chest, every dressing and badge of rank he could cram on to a strutting middleweight frame clad in immaculate fatigues above polished boots. Grizzled grey-black hair, red horsey face, cleft chin, spit-gap between square teeth, big-lipped pugnacious mouth. Talked *laarrk thayat*. Wore a black whip coiled around his right shoulder. Called it his Black Snake, Geoff told me, then tittered. Geoff was a country boy and saw the joke better than I. This Beret cunt was a lunatic, of course. He'd been blowing arctic wind up his subordinates' arses for ten minutes, all the while quoting from some trashy thriller about the Green Berets' exploits that was currently being passed around among the incurably stupid. The sort of book Rambo and Chuck Norris infest.

'In that part whayer the guy sez, poot her down heah, Ah see gooks ever'where? *Ah* sayed thayat! And when the guy jumps out the chopper as it's still cumin' down and busts his layeg? *Ah* did thayat! And when the guy sez to his squad, Ah still got wun good layeg, that's better than any ten gooks, lets go? *Ah* sayed thayat!'

His underlings sat on their barstools around this fucking maniac, smiling desperately at this bullshit, hoping to Christ they picked the right moment to laugh. I didn't see the humour of it either, but they had to go out into the field with him. As Geoff and I sat there trying to ignore the scene another sergeant major shunted into the group. This one was fat. Real fat, like an overblown copper. About forty. Big square head, bashed-in temples and a small crown, cropped grey oiled hair, bull neck, piggy eyes, wide fat mouth crowded with discoloured teeth. He used it to pour beer into. When he wasn't doing that his beefy arms hung slackly at his sides. The whole time I was there he communicated in three words: *grunt* . . . *haw haw haw* . . . and *affirmative*. 'Grunt' was reserved for when junior soldiers spoke, 'haw haw haw' for when he didn't know what was being said, which was often, and 'affirmative' for when the major spoke to him, or when he'd just grunted. No way was this fuckup a field soldier, we weren't built like that.

Geoff and I got tired of the surrounding interference after a while. Normal conversation was impossible with 'Ah Sayed Thayat' getting hot on killing and interrogating and who had 'daahd' in the unit and how. I tried to find out what Geoff's girl looked like, in bed preferably, but of course we switched to cars right away. I spotted a captain down the other end of the bar enjoying his own company, and suggested we move over there. But Geoff had to catch up with a couple of his team, so I went over alone. Maybe the captain talked about girls.

'Can I buy you a drink? Name's Barrie.'

He shook my hand, pointed to the vacant stool, said his name, which I've forgotten—anyway I settled on Captain, that way you never fuck up in officious company.

'You can buy me a drink once I've bought you one, Barrie.' He ordered and we started talking. My education took another leap forward. This man was an expert on what was happening over here. Captain was a huge man. Built like Tank but a bit taller and older, packed an extra ten or fifteen pounds. White-blond hair cut short, open face, quiet light blue eyes, strong square hands. When he smiled it was warm and his laughter low and gentle.

He gave me the charming news that he was the most hated man in the company and that I was being foolish sitting next to him. I heard it from 'Ah Sayed Thayat' in much the same words a few days later. Frankly I couldn't see why either proposition was right and asked him to clarify.

'I'm the intelligence officer for the unit, and as such I'm considered a noncombatant.'

I knew this was bullshit. Every fighting unit had an intelligence officer and he came from its own ranks. That was the whole point of the position, having a fighting soldier there to evaluate what the boffins in Intelligence Corps were slapping together and issuing as gospel. It helped if you were intelligent to some degree—but if your name was called you did it. Captain had several tours to his credit, so he'd been in combat, and he was intelligent, which was a rarity.

We talked about all sorts of bullshit. Fine wine, painters, music, types of beer, literature, boxing, not sex, more's the pity; and of course the war, or more correctly war. He told me a little about his unit. The unit trained up Cambodian mercenaries in basic weapon-handling and field drills, then flew them to the DMZ to kill Gooks. When they became too depleted they flew what was left back to Long Hai, shipped in and signed up more temporary pay cheques, trained 'em and flew off back to the DMZ. DMZ means Demilitarised Zone, but what's in a name? It was a strip of land along the border between North and South Vietnam. Being demilitarised, it was where you threw all the crazies, the cruel, the expendable and the unfortunate. Then you counted the dead at intervals. The Koreans were there of course, the Cambodians, some Green Berets, massed air power, armour, Yank infantry units. Some units liked to interrogate prisoners in choppers. Take six up, chuck a couple out, then start asking questions. What with the noise, the panic of flying high and the realisation that your interrogators couldn't understand your language, not many, if any, landed with the helicopter. So, for this unit it was rednecks from Hooterville and a lot of scared kids and the major.

'Some of these guys like the life a little too much,' explained Captain. 'Don't know why—the Gooks up there are mainly NVA, North Vietnamese Army regular troops, who fight fire with fire. Fuck that.'

I was getting sick of Yank beer and suggested a change. 'How about a Scotch and soda, Captain?'

'Fine.'

'No got soda, sorry.'

No you aren't, ya vindictive Caimboooodien cunt. Then I saw the two-litre jug of tomato juice with another large can behind it, through the glass door of the bar fridge.

'How about a bloody mary then?'

'One of my favourites. Most of the guys like tomato juice for breakfast, so we tend to lay off.' A thought emerged and spread across his face, becoming a beam. 'Then again, we hardly ever got it till your building team leader started scrounging.'

'Bartender, two bloody marys! Doubles, in those big glasses there!'

Not a bad drink, but it makes your eyes burn like coals in the morning. Nothing like a nice cold drink of tomato juice to douse the flames. No chance of that, though, some selfish bastards drank it all with vodka the night before. Among the swirling conversation over every topic that came to mind, Captain dropped pointers, phrases, that meant little to me at the time.

'Stay back, they will seek you out.'

'Every bastard's looking for Ho Chi Minh, running around stirring up shit. We got some crazy in the village looking for ghosts. No idea.'

'The will to win comes from knowing what you're doing, what the outcome will be, believing in that outcome. We don't have that, not here.'

He was a fluent speaker, educated, and when making a point sometimes held out his left hand, upright, index finger extended, his eyes directly on you. Captain was not a man of opinion unless you asked outright; his was a world of observation and recounting.

CHAPTER 9

I WAS EATING WITH BUCK SERGEANT FLETCHER. It was a scrappy meal—they all were. Every one was buffet and all seemed the same. Salads with jugs of pink mayonnaise sauce, stews, maybe a vegetable, canned fruit, spongy sweet bread. Thrilling at breakfast! In the morning, they had fresher coffee, cereals with thin milk for the bubbies, once or twice tomato juice, spring onions. I'd met Fletcher during the first day. He was a friendly, vacuous draftee of 21 or so, close to six feet with short brown hair, clear tanned face, wide friendly smile and a weak jaw. Over dinner he suggested he show me the village the next day, and the base.

'You've got a date for the village, let's drink on it.'

Fletcher wasn't much of a drinker, but he wanted to show me his room before pointing me to mine. His room was in the next barrack hut to mine. Identical in structure, so I wondered what the interest was. In fact his room *was* different. Same size, but there were two tubular metal beds in his, and lying asleep on one was a little young Cambodian dressed in a pair of black nylon tarzan undies. His right hand nestled inside them cradling his knackers, little uncircumcised slug drooping out above the waistband.

'Who's this?'

'He's my bodyguard. Most of us have them here. Wouldn't sleep or move without him, Barrie.' He'd expected a different

response from me, but I hadn't been able to adequately conceal my thoughts. 'They protect us in the field.'
'Where'd you say my room was? Next one left, out the door?' I took off. I still can't figure that one. Went to bed wondering what the finest troops the US had to offer were up to.

I awoke early next morning, fitter than I deserved to be, which I put down to tomato juice in the diet, and found the showers. Open stalls, stainless steel washbasins, scratched tin-plate mirrors above them, running hot and cold water, flushing toilets. Sergeant Major Grunt grinding a cake of soap into his fat hairy arse to shake the cobwebs out of his mind. Said hello, then ignored him and enjoyed the hot water. Quick lukewarm breakfast, then off to claim Fletcher from another table. We headed towards the gate and another young buck sergeant approached me. No formal introduction, just 'Hi, how are you? Say, could I borrow your rifle for the day? Those SLRs you guys use are beautiful weapons. Look at this piece of shit I got.'

This was a bit tricky. Losing your weapon is on a par with shooting a senior officer. All I knew of this man was that he looked about 22, spoke in a soft flat voice, stood about six foot two and had dark hair and blue eyes. Fletcher stood dumbly to one side as though he barely knew the man. I swapped rifles. His was a BAR, a Browning Automatic Rifle. It was a heavy-barrelled rifle you could fire as a machine gun—it had two adjustable legs which folded down just behind the muzzle. He'd removed them from his. He was right, it was a pig of a weapon, a heavy bucking clunker. I'd fired one in Australia. It took the same round as the SLR and the magazines were interchangable, so we didn't have to swap ammo.

'I'll call by at the bar this afternoon and return it. Don't worry, I'll look after it, I love these beauties,' and off he went to the firing range. I couldn't care less about its condition as long as I got it back. Damage could be explained away, that's what your brain's for. True to his word, he brought it back as he'd promised, gleaming like brand new. From then on he had it whenever he wanted it; cleaning a rifle is like cleaning your bathroom—necessary but irksome. I didn't clean his.

Fletcher and I continued our walk, the rifle soon forgotten. Out the gate and down the muddy road toward the village. The area here was starting to green after the first soft rains, but this side of the bridge the land was still featureless and bleak. Ducks waddled everywhere. They weren't wild but I seldom saw them in enclosures. Must have been a bastard collecting the eggs, if that's what their purpose was. A few pigs roamed around, rolling in puddles, having a root—interesting if you were the lucky owner. At the bridge we stood back while an old wizened man with one big brown fang thrusting out of his mouth tried frantically to control his buffalo cart. The buffalo was in a shitty: skewing the cart in a wild circle within the fetid puddle by the bridge. Three kids clung to the rails of the cart enjoying a riotous ride. Old granddad was starting to get shitty too.

A current model cream Chevy or Chrysler came wallowing up the road from the direction of the camp, stopping just clear of the muddy water, the ducks, and the buffalo slobber whizzing in glistening strings through the air. I'd seen this car drive past the schoolhouse twice yesterday and thought it odd, but I'd been impatient to get back to camp and had forgotten to ask about it. You never saw private cars out here, not away from the big cities. It sat there idling for a moment, the horn honked a couple of times, which infuriated the buffalo enough to make it spiteful and to have a lunge at its old handler. The driver noticed Fletcher and me then, and stepped out of his car. It was the strangest sight I ever saw in country. He was an American of about 30, perfectly groomed. Light brown hair cut neatly but longer than military length, cream button-down linen shirt with a brown knitted tie, light brown tweed jacket with leather buttons and elbow patches, fawn seersucker slacks and brown leather shoes. The outfit, the physique and the face were straight out of a *Playboy* magazine—the type used then for advertising quality Scotch or American Express cards. Ivy League look it used to be called—John Kennedy was of the type. The American didn't come over to us. He called Fletcher over and they talked briefly. I didn't hear much—the buffalo had latched on to the poor old bugger by now and there was a vicious struggle going on, kids and all having a whack at the demented animal with split bamboo staves. By the time this war of attrition had played itself out and the cart got creaking on over the bridge, the American had the driver's door open and was about to get back in. He looked over to me, waved and with a smile called, 'Hey, hope to catch up with you soon. Enjoy your walk.'

Off he drove through the wallow and on into the village.
'Who the fuck is that?' I asked Fletcher.
'He runs the hotel in town, invited us over for a meal. Interested?'
'Try stopping me. You're not kidding are you, it's open?'
'Sure, we go there from time to time. Good food, cracked crab, steaks, all kinds of things. We can go tomorrow night if you want.'
'Shit yeah, I'm in.' I couldn't imagine what sort of lunatic would own and operate a hotel in this village. There were no tourists, no Westerners at all except the Berets. Who made it pay? Not the locals that's for sure. And I knew enough by now to know the wealthy in Saigon wouldn't come out here, even with an army for an escort. Still, he'd said cracked crab, and the Berets went there. That'd do me. Fletcher and I walked over the bridge and I was just starting to get a glimpse of the village when he said, 'Hey, man, I think we'd better be getting back. I'll show you the base'.
I didn't argue, I was in his hands—but the *base*? Who gives a fuck? I'd been looking forward to having a nosey around the village. Fletcher was starting to act like the flake he was. We went back to base and he showed me around. It was a big camp and more boring up close than it had been from the road coming in. I saw one of their small-arms firing ranges. A half dozen or so Berets firing at half-man targets set at ground level about seventy-five metres distance. My rifle-swapping buddy was giving the targets a hammering, enjoying himself. I watched for a while. He refused a couple of requests from his mates to borrow my rifle, which was comforting, considering he didn't know I was watching. He shot well, as truly as any of our better Diggers. Aimed nice and low, some of the shots kicking up dust just in front of the target so the shot really ripped in on impact—none of this neat grouping wank you do in normal target shooting. We left and had a look from a distance at the Cambodian barracks. Quite a few of the men were squatting around in the dirt outside their barracks, yakking, having a smoke. Bit of washing strung up outside windows. Depressing panorama, nothing much happening.
'Let's have a beer, Fletch.'
'Oh, I'd like to, got a few things to do though—by all

means go ahead.' I wanted to talk, not drink, and he knew it. It was about 10 am by now and the day was buggered. Lance Jack was off foraging somewhere or other and Geoff and the boys were at the school. It was a case of lie on the bunk in my gloomy cell, hang around outside and get sunburnt, or hit the bar. What would you do? Of course you would. Let's go.

There was a small group already seated at one of the side tables, buck sergeants and sergeants, the younger brigade. I said 'Hi' as I walked past and they replied, but there was no welcome there, so I sat at the bar drinking and practising my spooky glare on the bartender, and then in the bar mirror when he couldn't face me anymore. In walked a sergeant major, younger than the other two I'd seen and maybe one stripe their junior, and joined the crowd. He was the biggest man I'd ever seen except for that one black SP at the Grand Hotel. He was a fucking monster! Six foot six, not uncommon now but it was then, among white people anyway; 130 kilos alive and lethal. Within seconds he'd livened up the self-absorbed group and got them laughing. He came over to the bar, ordered a round, then another for me, and I was dragged into the scene. That was Moose. Told me he'd played college football on account of his size and then a few seasons as a pro till his knee got mashed up—and so here he was. Someone in the group said 'Sometimes', so he answered my unspoken question.

'It's a standing joke with these clowns. I'm on my fourth tour here but it's still really my first. I got wounded the first two tours and got shipped back home early. Then I went for a beer in a bar in Vung Tau and sat next to these two Aussies—well one was, the other was a Kiwi, the one next to me. No, he was a Maori, that's right. These two bastards were playing that game where one punches the other when you need a fresh beer. You know, if you punch your buddy off the stool he buys, otherwise you buy?'

'I've heard of it, but I thought it was a myth.'

'Shit no, I played it more'n once with you guys. Anyway, they play for four, five beers and the puncher always buys. Then this Maori turns and says "Wanna play, Yank?". He's a big fucker, 'bout my size so, I say OK and he hits me *crash* on the jaw. I'm OK but I'm going down fast, barstool and all. I've got my foot slung under the crossbar. Hit the floor, *crack*, I've broke my fucking leg. I tell ya, you Aussies are fucking tough bastards.'

I went to correct him, to say he meant Maoris, then the penny dropped. Moose was a heartening sight in that team. He was the only NCO there who laughed without restraint; didn't give a fuck who was around. He had confidence in himself as a person. It was very rare among the Yanks here and it had nothing to do with his size. He must have been crazy. I didn't see much of him because he was actively involved with training. He certainly couldn't hide from my gaze in a crowd.

Next day I went off with the Diggers to the school for a change of pace. We got there early like building workers tend to do for some stupid reason, and I hung around waiting to wake up while they fiddled around with tools and bits of wood and kept asking me to shift out of the way. I took the hint and wandered back up the road a bit for a look around, just as the kids started heading to school.

It was a strange sight. As a child, I'd attended small outer suburban schools where local kids would ride their bike, walk or sometimes catch a bus to school. On rare occasions you would see parents drive their kids, but not often. We'd straggle in any time up to the bell and play unsupervised in the grounds if we were early. Not here. As I looked I could see in the distance small packs of kids jogging down each of the two or three roads towards the school, steadily growing in number as they passed houses along the way. By the time they went past me they were one tightly packed swarm of about 180 laughing, screaming, bickering, waving kids, dressed predominantly in white shortsleeved shirts and dark blue shorts, ranging from about six to twelve years old. As they passed, many waved and smiled. I did the same. The boys were more boisterous and cheeky than the girls, and I started to notice the missing limbs and the burns and other scars. I noticed more among the boys than among the girls. Fifteen or so were maimed: mainly leg injuries, an arm or two, several extensive face and upper body burns.

One little boy at the back of the column lives in my memory. Ragged cheeky-faced little bugger, looked more Mongol or moonfaced Chinese than Vietnamese. He would have been nine, I guess. Big front teeth and a smile like a beaver's. Right leg gone, he thundered along on two homemade crutches. Christ, he could shift, I'd need to jog fast to keep up. He passed and shot me a big grin which said, 'Not bad eh? I can keep up'. I wondered then how many of their number were gone through need of medical attention. Medicine was pretty honest here—no money in it and the risks were high. You walk into minefields and risk your own arse often, just to get to the patient, then you probably don't get paid. Not in money, anyway. A mug's game. Leave it to the district nurse.

I strolled back after them to the site looking for something to do. There wasn't much. It was skilled work and materials were in short supply, so there wasn't even much fetching and carrying to do. And the team weren't keen to give me any of this—the army rank structure is a stupid thing, it doesn't allow you to set rank aside easily and join in with the flow. Except out in the field. I went for a look around the school, trying to get an idea of how they taught these kids. For most of the country kids it was five or six years of primary schooling, then off to work. No high schools out here, university not even a dream. Yet they produced soldiers who wrote poetry and who carried books in their packs when they were out in the field; not just the odd one either, most of them. It had me puzzled. My company were pretty literate on average but most never dreamt of reading a poem, let alone writing one. I didn't get far in answering my own question. The teachers, all women—only the headmaster was male here—used simple, well-worn blackboards. The students wrote on little wood-framed slates. The teachers read from books. I saw no books in the kids' hands. Some of the lessons were conducted with chants, the way we used to chant our basic maths tables. That was all I saw, nothing special. How did this system help them to stand up against the most powerful military force in the world? I concluded the kids were being conditioned to continue their own learning process as they went through life. But of course I only had a view of it all through open doorways, or from a distance as a young woman read a story to a young class beneath a tree in the courtyard. I wasn't about to tramp into a classroom armed and uniformed after seeing the kids coming to school that morning. I'm not an invader.

When I got back to the team, Geoff said the boys had run out of timber and were packing up shortly.

'Want a quick look at the bay while they clear up here?'

'Shit yeah.'

'It'll have to be quick, the Berets really are fucking schizo about roaming around, but bugger it, let's go.'

We roared off out of the schoolground and followed the main road to the beach, or at least to the palm-lined street that separated the village from the beach. As we got out of the Landrover, on our right was a multistoried, pale green palace set in acres of lush gardens. After months of nothing but jungle, forest, small basic villages and the slapped-up shanty town of Vung Tau, it mesmerised me. 'Look over there, Barrie.' Geoff was pointing to our left. I could see a sparkling green bay, a silver beach framed by palm trees, and across the road five or six magnificent French-style hotels. The pale green one was a dump by comparison. Each was different but they were all similar to my eyes. Pale blue, white, cream stucco walls, long broad sweeping fan-shaped stairways leading to ornate columned entrances. The hotels rose four to six stories or more. Beautiful lead-paned French doors fronted each suite, leading on to private balconies. I imagined gracious ladies and their daughters frothy in long white lace dresses carrying parasols as they promenaded, the occasional old man in a formal suit with a moustache, a few well-dressed young colts waiting to pounce, waiters in flunkies' clothes, horsedrawn carriages in the street, lamplight.

The grounds of each hotel were green with plants, lawns and tall palms. All seemed in good condition, the gardens well maintained—by whom I have no idea. No one seemed to be about; it was very quiet.

'Pity they're all shut, eh Barrie. Nice place for a holiday.'

'I'm told one's open. I'm supposed to be going with Fletcher tonight. Some Yank runs it, met him yesterday, drives that cream Yank tank.'

'That what he does? Seen him running back and forward all the time. Berets go very quiet when you ask about him. Runs a hotel, eh? Hardly a big fucking secret then, is it. I can't believe this country. Better get back now.'

We did, without more than a fleeting glimpse up a street into the village proper. Looked interesting—tree-lined street with some shops, some tables on a sidewalk, a few people walking around. A US jeep parked by the kerb but no Berets hanging about to spot us. We picked the boys up then went back to camp for a beer until Fletcher turned up to take me to dinner.

I had a great time before he did. Had a laugh with Geoff about Lance Jack's latest idea, spotted Captain—he told me he'd be at the bar about nine—and got a rundown on the best brews of beer in the world from Moose. Seemed Aussie beers were good but bland except for Sydney beers. Some European beers were superb but only when drunk locally. And 'five states of America brew traditional full-strength beer which is unbeatable—the rest of the fucking country brews swamp piss!'. At the time I disagreed with his views on Aussie piss but he proved to be right anyway, eventually.

Fletcher turns up and says, 'OK to go?'. We leave in his jeep, just on dark. The wildlife has chucked in hostilities for the day, so we have a clear run except for the state of the road itself. We pull up at the end of the road and turn hard right into a small empty carpark. What a pity, we're at the pale green hotel. Never mind, it looks like heaven, there are lights glowing in the windows and part of the gardens is illuminated. In through a side entrance Fletcher knows, down a drab corridor, and we cross the ornate tiled entrance hall and pass into a roofed balcony dining area. Apart from the lobby, which has an ornately patterned tiled floor and an impressive reception area of carved wood panelling, the rest of the place is a lot like the Grand Hotel. Not as luxurious inside as the outside promises. The walls inside are painted a lifeless light green, there's little in the way of ornamental ceilings or doors, the light fittings are functional rather than decorative. Good use has been made of indoor plants, particularly in the dining area. A dozen or so small round tables, covered in white linen tablecloths, are screened from each other by shoulder-height palms in terracotta pots. Electric lighting from round white pearl glass shades gives off a discreet grey glow. The chairs are maroon, vinyl cushioned chrome-tube kitchen chairs, almost a luxury compared to what I'm accustomed to. I have a look over the balcony at the bay but there was nothing to see. No street-lighting—no scheme power—and the night is overcast; just a faint glow from the moon behind the clouds. Not that it matters—I'm here to eat and drink, and Fletcher's the wrong gender for romance. And on the food and drink side things are looking good. There's no one else in the place, not a soul.

We sit and Fletcher calls out tentatively for service. A minute or so later the American cruises by looking preoccupied and without noticing us, until he reaches what looks like the entrance to the kitchens at the back. He's dressed in slacks and open-necked white shirt, as though not expecting to be mixing with guests.

'Hey, hello there! . . . Glad you could come. Have you ordered yet?'

'Nuh, you're the first person we've seen. Any chance of a drink?'

'Sure, I'll get the waiter. Just be a moment.' And he disappears through the doorway. Five minutes later a Vietnamese waiter turns up in black trousers, white shirt and cummerbund, with a white tea-towel over his arm. Real grumpy bastard. Head like a Phantom ring. No menu, no wine list, no order pad.

'What you want?'

'I'll have a dry martini—got any gin?'

'Uhh!' And a roll of the eyes.

Fletcher orders some fucking thing which sounds like it comes with a flower and a paper umbrella floating in it. Judging from the look on the waiter's face, I'm probably not too wide of the mark. He starts to move off and I ask if they have crab on the menu. He says 'Uhh'. I yell at his rapidly disappearing back that we'll order main courses later. We wait fifteen minutes and I'm well into the shitty stage by now. Fletcher has run out of reassurances about the quality of the food here and is starting to get jumpy. I'm getting accustomed to his nervous states and I ignore him. Then the American cruises by again from the same direction as before, but a lot quicker this time.

'How's dinner going, fellas?'

'Let you know when we get it. Chase that waiter up about our drinks, will ya, we're still fucking dry!'

'Sure thing, just hold on a moment. I'll sort things out.' He sounds like he means it.

Through the doorway he goes again. We wait a few minutes

more. I'm not bored any more, though, I'm watching Fletcher crumble emotionally before my eyes. The conversation isn't much.

'Hey, man, I don't like this. Hey . . . I don't like this at all. God, what's going on here?'

'Take a look then, you know the bloke. I've had a gutful!'

Fletcher does take a look. He stalks to the doorway, sticks his head in, rushes back and blurts out, *'Hey man. Let's get the fuck out of here!'* and he bounces up and down, willing me to move.

'What about dinner? A fucking drink!!'

'Forget it man, let's go!'

Fletcher's dropped his bundle all over the floor. He is fucking jibbering. No point in staying any longer, he's flipped it. Down the corridor, out to the jeep and fucking *off*. He could drive, I'll give him that; we're back inside the base in about thirty seconds. Won't tell me what he saw, won't say anything. Drops me at the mess and speeds off in a spray of gravel to some other destination on the base, in a bad state.

I didn't see Fletcher again that night. The American I never saw again. Neither him nor his car. The Berets warned me to stay clear of the village, that was all. One badly dead CIA agent I concluded. A businessman might buy a place like that on the working assumption that a revolution would fail—buy it cheap and mothball it. If things go the wrong way you've lost a little—write it off. But no businessman would take the commercial risk this American did. Think about it. Businessmen aren't a brave species. They don't like the numbers against them. Now, you take an idealist, a dickhead, an arsekisser, who believes he's serving King and country—you've got a hotelkeeper in a bad location.

Nothing for it that night but to go into the mess, to see if there was any dinner left. No luck, so I ate the three bowls of peanuts at the bar (hate those fucking things), met up with Captain and helped him drain the supply of tomato juice by ten, then hit chilled Mateus Rosé, at his suggestion. It was made of grapes—fuck it, I was starving and snapping at the food chain.

The next day was a drag. Lance Jack found me at the bar and told me he'd been to the Dat and had heard my company were playing his company at rugby the next day. I was having a beer with Fletcher, who'd shaken off the worst of his nerves at last. Fletcher was curious to know what sort of game it was, so I told him it was like gridiron without armour and had a few less rules. How would I know? Not my code. I assumed it was Australian and tough as old boots. Some things never change.

'Hey, how about we take in the game?'

'You want to go to the Dat?' I thought his adventurous days were way behind him but he looked keen.

'Sure, I got a couple of buddies there I'd like to see. We could go early, split up, meet at the game.'

Fair enough. I offered to let him meet some of my company at the boozer after the match. He seemed interested. I knew the blokes would like to have a yap with a Beret—they'd have a yap with a kelpie dog if one turned up, we were a very isolated group socially. God only knows who his buddies were, but he didn't elaborate and there was little point in asking. These guys either told you something outright or they didn't. Captain came by for a drink and gave me three bottles of Mateus Rosé to take with me for the trip. He ordered the barman to keep them chilled for me to collect at breakfast. Here at least a captain had influence.

Next morning Fletcher and I were off in his jeep, his little bodyguard bouncing around in the back like a sheepdog too shy to bark. We hit the Dat about ten. I showed him the oval where we were to meet at one o'clock, got him to drop me off on the main road just behind the Nugget, and snuck in the back way, bottles clinking in my kitbag. Why the stealth? Would you like to cop a radio picquet or be linesman for the game when all you wanted to do was drink piss with a friend? Always pays to check the area for traps first, we don't live in a democracy here. Made it to the Nugget unnoticed. Stepped in. Dave was sitting in a chair staring vacuously at the track down to Pete's tent. Young Mick was fiddling with some webbing.

'How're ya . . .' I got out.

'What ya got in the bag?'

'Wine.'

Dave swooped on two metal cups, and filled me in on happenings as I looked around for my pocket knife with the corkscrew on it. We found it in Dave's pocket. He put a funny value on some of the shit I used to leave lying around, but sometimes he picked up things of use. Then he denied having seen it. I'd go through all the bullshit, under the floorboards, through the sea chest, anywhere snakes and spiders lived, then he'd find what I was looking for. If it suited him. It took a long while but he taught me to be tidy eventually.

'Fuck, have *you* missed a fun time! We've been in and out like a lizard's tongue since you left. Out on the chopper, run around in the APCs, back in, out on the fucking chopper, dig a pit, fucking move out again. A day trip in APCs doing escort they said—we were scrub-bashing three days and hadn't taken rations! These cunts up top have come unhinged. Two days before we go out again's the word. We're not over fucking Vung Tau yet! Did I tell ya I got the clap? Dirty fuckin' harlot. Here, give me a go at that cork!'

We got the cork out in bits and pieces and filled the mugs. There was enough left in the bottle to give Young Mick a taste, which is all he wanted, luckily for him.

'Where're the others, Dave?'

'Fuck the others, this isn't a bad drop.'

We drained the three bottles, had a couple of beers to kill the sweet taste and lunched on ration-pack crud that Dave still had in his pack, then wandered off to the match. Dave was playing, so he peeled off and joined the huddle to meddle with the positions. I found Fletcher standing midway along the boundary line, waiting for the action to start. He was in idle conversation with a couple of blokes from my company.

'Where's your bodyguard?'

'Oh, he's staying with the jeep.'

Knowing this lot, I thought it was a smart move, so I left it at that. He wouldn't have fitted in here anyway. The umpires ran out on to the turf and pranced around like sheilas to make it look professional—where they'd come from I couldn't guess. The two teams lined up to shake hands and crush a few toes and I couldn't tell who was who till I spotted Tank in one line. None of them had any kit. Some wore big baggy army shorts, some normal jungle greens, all wore green shirts. Some had sandshoes; the cunning bastards wore standard GP boots. There was a whistle and an almighty crunch and half the field's on the deck, kicking and gouging. Once the umpire fought free of his assailants and found his whistle, people started to get friendlier and stand up.

Dave didn't—he stayed inert on the deck, flat on his back. 'Get up, ya weak cunt!' and 'Who picked this poofter?' were the pick of the jibes failing to rouse him. The ump ruled: 'If he won't fuckin' play, get the cunt off!'. Dave was dragged from the field between two of the team in the crucifix position, his head lolling on his chest, his toecaps dragging up lines of red dust.

Like a dickhead, I was concerned about him and met him at the boundary. 'Where'd you get hit, Dave?'

His head raised mechanically. He peered at me through glazed red eyes, trying to make out if I was real or not. He decided I was. 'I'm pissed, you stupid cunt.' He spewed on the ground between our boots and reeled to the shade of the nearest tree, and collapsed comatose.

The game was mayhem; must have been Union. Everyone getting trodden on, Pigpen punching chunks out of the first row, Tank receiving the pill and thundering home over the line, straightarming anyone suicidal enough to try to stop him. We were three tries in and maybe a straight kick at the sticks within ten minutes. Then the other mob got cunning. It was a good game after that, malicious as a family reunion.

Eventually somebody won, then the ump whistled 'time' and everyone fled back to the boozers. Even some of the other mob came over to ours for a while. I've never seen Dave move so fast. I went there in the jeep with Fletcher and his car minder, a forty-second drive. I still missed the first can, every other bastard was already on his second. I led Fletcher to the bar, bought him a beer, went back out and pressed a can of soft drink into the bodyguard's hand. I fronted in again and was about to introduce the Yank to Pigpen and one or two of the more placid Diggers . . . and Fletcher dropped his bundle again. Turned ashen, stammered out 'We . . . we . . . don't mix with the troops at base. Hey, man, I gotta go!'. And he did. Pigpen plucked his untouched can from his hand as he passed and started telling me what an arsy prick I was and how he was getting jacked off with management around this place. Then Dave had the crown and anchor game going and we drank out of Big Mick's bowler hat and sang some ribald old songs. Met Peaches, dragging Pigpen off my throat. Had a good time. Next thing the hatch was closing, Dave fighting maniacally to keep it up, Pigpen too, among a truly desperate pack. I reminded everyone that the Nugget was still kicking, and Pete, Peaches and I drank beer while Dave fleeced the gullible at poker.

He was hovering for the kill when one of the young platoonies crashed out of the banana trees from the wrong direction, demanding to see Dave on an urgent matter. I thought it was Pete he should be seeing. Dave suggested that too, but Pete said 'I can't do anything for whinging, what I've got isn't for that'. Dave went out. We'd heard it all before. Dave was a magnet for loonies. This time it was the 'my fiancee's fucking my best mate' routine—not much of a change. Sometimes it was debt.

'Well, tell her to fuck off! Easy isn't it? Go to bed, think about it!'

'But I'm gonna kill myself!'

'Shit mate, hold off, think about it. Give it half an hour. I'm sittin' on four kings in there. Fuck off!'

Everyone in the tent heard that! Dave tore them to pieces before the night was out, but not with a hand as good as that, and *he* hadn't dealt it. I passed out around three.

Woke up at dawn like death jumpstarted. Still dressed, so that was one hassle eliminated; just had to find my boots. My rifle was stuck to my back where I'd slept on it. This man's army was getting to me. Looked over to the cot by the entrance to the tent: there was Griffo flat out, holding his rifle in a firing position, shirtless, one sock on, observing the spirit of stand-to as best he could. Dave sat up, yawned like a flytrap, farted, remembered he'd cleaned up again last night and sprang to painful life. Asked what was holding up coffee, then his sense of smell woke up and he counselled caution. A can fizzed. Peaches was up so we joined him in a warm one while the air cleared enough to light the PE, then had coffee. We'd lost Young Mick again, don't know where. Couldn't handle breakfast. I'd already missed dinner—anything to spite the cooks—why let them get me now? Went for a quick shit. Dave joined me to help sort out my problem.

'How are ya gunna get out of this one, Barrie?'

'Fuck knows.'

'That about sums it up.'
And that was the problem. Fletcher had wanted to flee and I'd voted with my feet—stayed with the company. They were due out in the field today or tomorrow and if I was here I had to go too. That would be OK normally, but I had a cruisy number going for me that I hadn't stuck my hand up for. I'd won it fair and square—I'd learnt Vietnamese. Had a paper to prove it, somewhere. I couldn't front CSM and say, 'Get me a lift back to peace and quiet, my man!'. I went back to the Nugget and before I could start to mope, Peaches walked in, dragging Lance Jack along. 'Look who's looking for you.' Turned out he'd come up for the game and pulled a similar stunt to mine. I showed him the back way out and we were off.

The trip back was uneventful. We hit the Berets' gate about 9.30 am and I went to the bar. The place was jumping—everyone on deck and drinking.
'Hey . . . what's the occasion?'
'The VC mortared the base last night,' said a pasty-faced Fletcher.
The room two doors up from him had been obliterated, the unlucky bastard sleeping there missing and very definitely dead. Good cause for a party! Better fun than chasing the enemy unit that did it. Four or five Cambodians copped it too, but I don't remember who told me that—not that many of those present thought to mention it.
The following day I went scrounging with Lance Jack, off in his Landrover headed for Vungers just down the coast. We stopped mainly at junkyards and stores, drab territory down at the docks. In he would go through a hatchway or door, put the bite on the shonky bastard holding the keys, and come out with an armful of goods or a frown. We stopped at the pier and he said he'd visit a couple of ships. He claimed he'd been in the navy and knew a few blokes. Must have been the Aussie navy, the Kiwis never ran to more than a frigate and a few supply ships. And mean as cat's piss with their stores, I'd bet. He boarded a lowslung rusty grey navy coastal tramp and a few minutes later waved to me from a hatch to come aboard. We went into a gloomy, cramped grey-painted room and Lance Jack

said, 'Grab that carton of spirits, I've got to carry this'. The guy standing there looked just like the room, grey and depressing. 'This' was a side of veal. That's pretty well what we got that day, booze and food. And tomato juice. Four cans. Apparently these trips were official, to scrounge for building materials among the wider community, hence the name Civil Aid I suppose. The Berets saw the possibilities and exploited Lance Jack's time. Or maybe that was how the team paid its board. Lance Jack's version was that the Berets were virtually unsupported by the US military stores system. I smelt a buck, but the whole system over here was fucked in the head. He also brought back some nails and a can of paint for the school.

Next thing I knew it was Saturday night. Geoff and I were drinking at the bar almost alone and two gorgeous Vietnamese girls fluttered through the door and skimmed over the floor to the bar. These were not the drabs you met in the Vung Tau bars, these were flowers. Dressed in dark blue and emerald silk jackets with black silk pyjama pants. High-heeled shoes. Polished toes. Silken sleek black elbow-length hair reflecting blue-white light, dark-eyed ivory faces, slender gentle hands. The nearest girl sat two stools up from me—Geoff scored the peeper's seat. He muttered 'I'd like to fuck that!' then roared, 'Who do these belong to, anyone?'.

'That's the sarn't major's whoooers, brings 'em in special Sat'day night.'

Fuck, where'd we been the last two Saturdays? Well, you've gotta try your luck, even if it's just to practise. I was over in a blink, sitting next to them. Perfect timing, the girls had just received their drinks from the barman courtesy of their client's bar tab. I hit them with the smooth lines. 'Hair yours . . . er . . . beautiful . . . smell good you! Smile you nice.' In Vietnamese of course. In English I'm much more fluent, but not as effective. Flatters the arse off them every time. They were both nervous of the attention but the nearest one to me liked me, I could tell. I told her I would touch her hair, which was especially beautiful, then shove off back to my stool and behave. I stroked her hair and she giggled and turned slowly to look at me and everyone in the bar started to tense up except the girl, me and Geoff. The girl and I hadn't seen him enter. Geoff had—but he was just starting to enjoy himself, the bastard. There stood

Sergeant Major Ah Sayed Thayat, not real pleased with the scene he was scraping his bloodshot eyeballs on.
'What he saying to yoo!?'
'We very pretty.' Softly, after a long pause.
'Say nothing,' I said to the girl.
'What he saying! What he saying! Is that Vietnamese he's saying? He talked to yoo in Vietnamese?'
'Yes.'
'He talk good?'
'Yes, quite good.'
I loved her for that. That was too tough for this guy. He went for me on the touching charge—I hadn't paid to touch, so I was stealing from him. Technically he had me fucked there. I let him talk.
'You touch somethin' of mine don't belong to yoo, Ah am gonna whip yoo with ma *Black Ssnake*!' He stood there, legs apart, hands twitching. Did I tell you I was a State welterweight finalist in '66? No I didn't, because I wasn't, so get ready for the unexpected—me using my brains. This cunt's giving me a warning which I'll observe in future. If he goes for the whip, I'm at his throat, no fucking around. If he doesn't, I'll have another beer. I'm not a hero. Don't wait up for that, go home now.
Geoff'd been waiting patiently for an opportunity just like this to present itself. Up he stood.
'Hey! Dickhead! You! Call that a fucking whip? Where I come from we wouldn't whip a dog with that, and only cunts whip dogs. Touch that Black Snake and I'll shove it up your arse!'
Ah Sayed Thayat died in the arse. He turned and stared at Geoff, resolve and anger dribbling off him on to the floor. He'd met someone in his own mess who meant what he said, and I respect him for at least recognising the fact. He spun on his heel and marched wordlessly across the stark silent floor and through the far entrance. The girls waited for him to clear the door, then, with averted eyes, shimmered away—silent visions drawn tentatively after him. The room exhaled pent-up tension like a bellows.
'Fuck! Finally stuck it up the cunt! Whose shout, Bazz? We'll make it mine.'

And with that Geoff exits my story, more's the pity—we go back to normal soon. But, we had a lot to laugh about that night. We left a few days later. I shouldn't wonder, after that stunt.

Lance Jack collared me at breakfast and advised that as the work on the school was about to be wound up, the headmaster was putting on morning tea for the crew and I was invited. Before I could dream up an excuse he reminded me: 'If you're not there it'll just be a staring match.' He was too quick for me that day. Ah well, it was only a morning, I'd just have to drink quicker when I got back.

We fronted at ten, boots cleaned, greens pressed, black dress belts, all nine of us. The headmaster met us at the entrance and ushered us straight into the staff room, the first door on the left down a short dim hall. He'd dressed up too. Wore stretch-metal armbands on his shirtsleeves and a dark blue silk tie, enhanced by a strident orange and yellow dragon. He'd certainly bought that at the stalls in Vung Tau—either education didn't pay much or he was less discerning than I'd thought. It was an oblong room with bare whitewashed walls, and dark polished floorboards, dominated by a plain solid wood oval table and high-backed chairs. Light came from a large wooden-framed window at one end. I got caught up introducing everyone formally to the headmaster, and watched Lance Jack grab the best seat at the far end—assuming the headmaster sat at the head, that is. Just as well. Lance Jack didn't understand this man's language in any tongue. Geoff saved me a seat next to him halfway down the table, so I could watch the unfortunate bastards either side of the headmaster squirm throughout the ordeal.

A female teacher brought in little china cups with saucers on a tray and we passed these around; our unasked-for assistance flustered her a bit, but it gave us something to fiddle around with during the growing silences. She was nice. But past it, from our point of view. Late middle-age, tubby for a country Vietnamese, a mum type. She left and returned with a plate of pyramids wrapped in banana leaf and a floral decorated airpot. That's a big thermos with a tap that you pressurise with air, so it pours with the lid on. One of the Diggers muttered, 'Fuck, those things are rice cakes. I ate one once, pissed outa my brain—fucking foul.' I told him I'd seen one of Woofer's mates eat a hundred-year-old egg. 'These things are much worse. Filled with minced monkey shit.' He slumped into a watchful sulk. The headmaster poured the tea, jasmine, whatever. Not bad, especially if you'd got a case of the screaming dries after a heavy night on the piss like I'd just had. Managed to string a bit of conversation back and forth between the headmaster and the team. Nothing worth repeating here but it passed some time—trying to figure it out. The headmaster seemed happy, younger and less worried than last time I'd seen him.

Then he passed around the cakes, smiling earnestly, urging with his free left hand, insisting that no one missed out. I still don't know if he was trying to be vindictive or just being a generous host. We started unwrapping the heavy bundles. Inside was steamed rice blended with raw duck-egg yolk moulded into a pyramid. I took a bite, I'm no coward. I can't describe it, haven't the words or similar experience to draw from. I enjoy raw fish, offal, even lamb's brains if I have to, but not this. I snuck a peek at the headmaster. He was beaming at us all, urging us like a proud mum to enjoy, enjoy. It was hard going. Diggers were trying every way—big bites, nibbles, looking for ashtrays, a rug on the floor; eyes darting ferret-like for any place of concealment. Then I looked at Lance Jack. He was glaring at this alien object open in front of him, face blanching, teeth bared, head and shoulders swaying back and forth like a high jumper psyching up for the big one. The headmaster was staring at him now, so I cracked my pyramid wide open to *see* what was inside. Minced monkey shit, no doubt about that. A brown gooey pulsing gob of it, no bigger than a marble, but it was lethal—and my sense of smell's only fair.

I looked back at Lance Jack, just in time to see him make his move. He raised the object up in both paws, crammed it bodily into his mouth, clamped his jaws shut, and pumped flesh till his eyes bugged out on stalks. His cheeks blew out like a horn player's. Down it slid like a mammoth slug. I couldn't beat that one—he was going to hold on to it, I could tell. His stomach heaved for a minute or so, after that he just salivated nastily from time to time for the next three hours. I folded mine up, squashed it flat and threw it in with all the other dead skins. Bit of a thud as it landed, but no one noticed. We had another cup of tea which was cold, but we all needed a good mouth rinse. We left with the headmaster waving us on our way, his smiling face leaning out from the school verandah. I often wonder how they got on.

On our last morning, the major assembled the unit and presented each of us with a red, white and blue bandanna marked with the unit's detachment number, and a Zippo lighter with the same, plus our Christian name engraved on it. I've still got the lighter stashed in a box somewhere. The bandanna went missing at the Dat. Bit of a pity, it was just the right shape to buff boots. Dave told me recently he'd knocked it off, but I suspect that's bullshit. I never saw this Green Beret outfit in the field; maybe they were first-rate combat soldiers, but I was there over three weeks, the rest of the team more than seven, and in that time they never went out. That's a very long break for field soldiers in this war, and when you add R&R that's eight weeks minimum out of a six-month tour. Certainly, I retain tremendous personal respect for Captain to this day, the same for Moose—leadership like his is rare—some of the youngsters looked good. But I didn't like the feel of the unit. Senior NCOs acting the way some of these did is not the way crack ground troops behave. I became very leery of so-called elite units after this visit, and I still am today. With good reason.

But, that's just my opinion and not really any of my business. The Civil Aid system is fair game though—I was involved. We and the Yanks did a lot of this type of work here, fixing war damage, providing infrastructure in villages. Why? You can answer that! Where are we at in terms of your experience? Shit, we've met the Viet Cong. Not bad soldiers, thinkers, pretty hard to knock over.

Consider tactics for a minute. Why would a group of VC rocket a village schoolhouse, knowing they had a Green Beret fortress hard against their arse? Can't figure it? Go back and think again about my description of the damage if you need to, I haven't got forever. It just seems to me that, every time something got blown up, of course the VC were the ones who did it. Civil Aid was a patronising approach to a people's misfortunes in my view. The villagers were better equipped to restore the school than our soldiers were. Why didn't *they* get the job? The government in Saigon wasn't focused on these problems, that's one reason. Our command, in their arrogant stupidity, saw it as a golden opportunity to show the peasants what we really stood for—generous, caring benefactors. But charity on the cheap doesn't weigh very heavy when set against the other side of the ledger.

We're going back into the field for a while now, to see how the company's getting on, then we're off on R&R—rest and recreation. So squeeze in the Landrover beside me or stay with this mob. Caught in two minds? You have the answer? Dead right. You're stuck with me.

Chapter 10

WE'RE BACK AT THE DAT and about to crash for the night, red-eyed and jaded from both the drive back and the radio picquet we scored just for appearing at the gate. The company's out on an Op but Peaches says it's OK, nothing drastic's happening. We've seen a different slant on what's going on here now, so let's take a broader look—at a few people, at organisation of people, and what happens to people as a result of organisation. It is a recurring theme with me; so is the killing. Taking these together, a picture eventually emerges. Trust me. There's some more rooting in this trip along the way, so let's go!

Back a day and I'm giving Staff the shits in a big way. Getting Peaches on the piss before breakfast, he thinks, roaming around everywhere getting under foot. I'm on the next chopper out with the water and the mail.

Ever had a chopper ride? No? Get by me. Here it comes, but don't fret about the rotors, just duck and squint your eyes against the shit and grit and aim to be last on. That way you get to sit on the ledge, the edge of the floor right beside the door gunner. We never shut the doors, too risky. Your own gunner usually grabs the far ledge first so he can cover the flight. Sitting on the ledge with your legs dangling is the only way to fly. Once you block out the clatter of the rotors and the gun of the engine it's like gliding; there's nothing between you and the earth but air, and when the machine banks sharply for a look at the approach you're freefalling. I often keep my pack on out of expediency and to weigh me back from brutal reality, but it's really quite safe, I think. Most of the blokes don't like the seat on the edge, they prefer the cramped crossbench or the floor to huddle on.

'Pigpen, you're fucking crazy. You walk in front of me down there but you won't sit on the ledge and see.'

'In the air I take a break. Watch if ya want to.'

The world is different from above. Not from a plane cruising at 30,000 feet—I mean zooming overhead at treetop level, seeing the mountains and the trees loom up at you, tracks that actually go somewhere, people moving below, and recognising them if you're in luck. That is a wonderful sight. There's the company in under that copse of trees. CSM and Griffo, it looks like, out in the clearing, signalling us in with a wave—no need for a smoke grenade, it's clear vision. Pete's standing at the fringe of the LZ. Spotted him from way back, mimicking CSM; definitely some news waiting for me. I grab the mail and leap off, looking helpful. Jerrycans full of water are heavy, and mail's always welcome. I think I brought Brian's first solicitor's letter to him that day.

I clip my hootchie up to Pete's. 'OK, what's news?'

'Slack as shit. Brian's fucked, shitting his packs. Serves him right. Remember Vungers?'

'Vividly.'

'He copped syphilis. Dave's got NSU by the way. He's out getting final clearance from Chuck Baby. Any sores or discharges?'

'Nuh.'

'Me neither. Anyway . . . listen to this—hey, the water's boiling, Bazz. Brian thinks he's copped something and gets it checked right away. Report comes back negative, so he's off on R&R getting stuck into the bride. Comes back, it's all clearer now—the *Yanks* tested his sample, not us; if it's negative you've got it, not negative you haven't got it. He's waiting for news from home. Fuck knows why.'

I see Brian—he seeks me out actually—a few minutes later. Scuttles up like a leper in bad need of a cure.

'Hey, Bazz, what are you like with needles?'

'I don't faint when I get one. Why?' I've said one word too many.

'I'm on penicillin and Pete won't treat me. I'm giving *myself* injections since Dave flew out. Why's everything a joke with that mad cunt?'

I know what the poor bastard's going through. I help him aim the needle when he needs to, don't fuck around like Dave did. It isn't humorous, not unless you like hearing a tough man whimper. OC won't intervene; he privately sides with Pete, I'm certain. CSM thinks it's a fucking riot. He and Dave are very much alike in some matters. Pete's answer is, 'He's a married man, fuck him!' and I can't see a way around him.

Dave's view, expressed later, is pretty highminded.

'Hang on, Dave, *you're* married and *you've* got a dose.'

'Fuckin' hang on there, Barrie, I've got NSU. There's a big difference . . . and I haven't given it to my wife.' Smug bastard.

Brian flew out a few days later and was sent home on emergency leave to sort out his marriage. The solicitor's letter had been terse. So was mother-in-law when Brian tried to enter his own house.

'Fuck, I couldn't get past the old dragon!' he choked out a week or so later when he returned. 'Thought she was going to castrate me—threatened to, the old witch.'

'How's your wife taking it?'

'Didn't see her—only briefly the third time I called. Had a shouting match on the doorstep with the old dragon and my wife shrieked out from behind her, "I've called the cops, shove off!". Had a meeting with her lawyer, fuck did she get personal—and here I am. It's hopeless.'

Brian took a while to snap out of it, but the ongoing solicitor's letters eventually killed the last lingering embers of that romance.

I had a family problem too, and I blame Dave for bringing me that.

'Barrie, write to your fucking mother!'

'G'day Dave.'

'Hang on. I've just spent an hour back at BHQ getting my ears bashed by the fucking adjutant just because I said I knew you. He wouldn't take the hint, jabbered on like it was all my fucking fault. Write to your mother for Christ's sake. Now!'

Did I tell you about the lazy clerk and the cockup? I didn't exist—that was the cockup. My Mum's letters were being returned marked 'Not at this address' or 'Addressee not known'. I wasn't getting mail from home—so bugger them, why should I bother writing. Mum had every agency and bloodhound she could intimidate trying to find where the army had buried her son and she wasn't taking any shit. The adjutant had his placid little world of dull committees and even duller society erupt when the Salvos, the Red Cross, Amnesty International and several other pushy bastards got finally directed his way, to be sorted out.

Battalion records were useless, I didn't exist. That's why the letters were being returned home. Try company records, then. 'Yeah, he's here, out on an Op,' yawned Fuck-Knuckle.

'Send someone up, I have a message to be delivered.'

Dave got sent up. Lucky bastard.

I wrote Mum and Dad a long, arrogant letter stating I'd soon be a pilot, a lawyer or a choo-choo driver and then took a look around.

The Op was almost over, but it gave me the chance to see a funeral procession. Considering the demand for coffins over here, you'd think the streets would be swarming with wailing processions, but they were a rare sight to us. Must have been very expensive. I was sitting on top of an APC having a yap with Pete and the commander, keeping an eye on the road in the distance, and the sound of tinkling bells reached us. Down the road came an ox cart with a coffin on it draped in garlands of flowers; little bowls with floating flowers, brass holders with incense. Behind the wagon walked four or five Buddhist monks dressed in saffron robes, shaven heads facing straight ahead, self-absorbed. Behind them the family group of twenty or so dressed in dark peasant clothes, supporting one another through pangs of grief with an arm on a shoulder. At the rear a small band of musicians playing bells, cymbals, gongs. They ceased for a moment and we could hear the mourners lament, then the band started again at the dull clang of a gong, and tinkling bells and clashing cymbals filled the air once more. The flowers drew me. I can't picture flowers in Vietnam—this is the only time I remember seeing any.

The procession passed across our front and trailed out of

view. The vision of the Buddha in the forest came into my mind. I recalled that Buddhism is based around a circle, a cycle of life. Once wisdom is achieved and worldly passions extinguished, Nirvana is reached. Ascension occurs. It is a personal journey that benefits others by its very success. The Republic is catholic, capitalist, believing in rigid class structure. Service to an unseen God, and those who speak for him. Could this be the cause of the conflict in this troubled land? I didn't think so, but it formed part of it, of that I was certain.

For the last few days of the Op we were based a couple of kilometres from a village, setting small night ambushes along tracks. Military intelligence suggested that VC were using the village for food supplies and that we could expect to blast a group of porters coming or going. It didn't happen. We were out in open flat ground, so we'd dug shell scrapes for cover in case of attack. At night we slept in them with only our mosquito nets for cover. It was dry and the hootchies made a bold silhouette that could be spotted easily. The two nights we stopped there were invigorating. Every two hours I woke up and saw an armed figure stalking about above me peering around looking for something. It was the gun or radio picquet searching for his relief's pit, but in that first split second of awakening it wasn't apparent, not when your heart'd stopped and your rifle lying beside you felt like lead.

The first night I had the midnight till two radio watch. Went to look for my relief and got lost. Everywhere looked the same—there were no landmarks to be guided by, just open graves with shrouds over them. I stumbled over the radio set finally, and sat it out till dawn. Fucked if I was going to rouse people and ask directions, some of them might be twitchier than I was. Next night I swapped and did the four till stand-to shift. But *that* wasn't where CSM grabbed me.

We're back at the Dat.
'Corporal Crowley, report to me—company dismissed!'
'Yes, CSM.' Christ, what now?
'You're to go before the OCS selection board tomorrow. It's on at the air terminal here, starts 9.30 am. You can make your own way there, it's not far. Have you got decent greens?'
'Yeah, think so.'

'See Staff, you can't go looking like a bag of shit. OK?'
This was a bolt from the blue. Officer selection. I'd done testing way back in rookie training, got so far, then the selection committee re-read the forms and realised I was too young. I'd been told not to worry, they'd remember me in another year when I was old enough. I hadn't worried, I'd forgotten.

Kelsie ran around finding a good dress belt for me to wear, found a lanyard somewhere, helped me reblock my slouch hat into reasonable shape. It looked like it'd been crushed under a sea chest for months when I found it, under my sea chest. Passed Kelsie's inspection finally, and I was off down the road wondering what to expect. Interviews were being held in a room in the small terminal. I waited alone outside until called; I'd drawn first appointment. Eventually I was summoned by a captain who stuck his head round the door and led me in, pointed to a chair in the middle of the floor and said, 'Salute the board'. The board sat in judgement at a raised table covered in green baize. There were four, once the captain took his seat at one end of it. I saluted and sat, then peered up at them. Here then were the proven warriors sent from Australia to select the next generation of leaders of men. Fucking what? The head of the board was a grey-haired old darling from Psychology Corps. A colonel. He smiled and nodded—he was looking at a kid. On his right was a smirking major who parted his black hair in the middle. From the same Corps. Psychology was changing its thrust pretty quickly in that Corps. On his left was a captain from Education Corps, pushing forty with a face erupting with livid acne. The captain who acted as doorman left no impression on me. The major leant back in his chair, crossed his legs above the high table, and asked: 'Corporal Crowley . . . what do you think about our involvement in Vietnam?'

'I think a lot about our involvement, sir.'

'Please elaborate.' He hunched forward in anticipation.

'I believe we shouldn't be involved.'

He sat back then, he'd got his answer. The colonel was of the old school, less pragmatic than the major, more inquiring.

'What brings you to that conclusion, Corporal?'

'We're backing the wrong horse. Sir.'

That satisfied everyone, so I was dismissed. Not that my reply was original, but I'd quoted a real soldier. Fuck! What a mob! Wonder what they all did for a living—it wasn't soldiering. On the walk back I evaluated my actions. I'd thrown away any chance of an executive position. Because of my belief that this war was wrong? Not altogether. Because I knew in my heart I wasn't up to it? That's more to the point.

Let's look at leadership in the Army environment for a moment. Firstly, there is a physical distinction from the Other Ranks, as people like me are called. Rank and file. Frank and vile, my Dad used to say—he was a funny bastard. Officers wear a tailored uniform with subtle differences. Rank is worn on the shoulder and they wear a peaked cap, a Sam Brown belt, plus a sword on ceremonial occasions. That sort of bullshit. They stand out. They are higher paid, have more privileges, can go further in the organisation, don't clean shithouses or hump garbage, get called Mister or Sir, get saluted by people below them—and there are many below them. And in front of them when the shit hits the fan. They also get greater recognition. In return they must order men into battle to achieve objectives, be accountable for their men's well-being and be responsible for their men's actions. The difference between Army leadership and any other form of public leadership is only the tools of trade and the end product, death. The organisation is the same. There are countless applicants driven by ambition, greed, snobbery, arrogance, vanity—and now and again there's one with a desire to lead because they feel they're worthy.

That's not a bad checklist. I went through it myself—I was one short. A commander in the field must be close enough to his troops to appreciate their situation, far enough back so he doesn't get gunned down at the first contact, able to reach objectives issued to him even if he doesn't personally agree with them, and achieve them with the support of his men. Some cunt invades your country: not so hard, no moral dilemma. OK, death's a risk but what the fuck. If you don't do it you'll almost certainly die anyway, or live in misery. Someone sends you off to invade someone else's country: things get complicated. If that happens you can lie low and be too indispensable elsewhere to catch the boat. Or you can go and not concern yourself with the consequences of your actions. Chances are you'll keep the rank—once you've been chosen it's hard for people to say, 'Sorry. We picked the wrong one'.

Being that odd worthy one is the trick to leadership. That person who can lead where people should follow, no matter how hard or unjust the world around might seem. To be able to walk that thin sharp line and survive with honour, to do better later on. I saw one who fulfilled that role, a bucktoothed, knock-kneed prick called OC. After months observing him in the field I realised he never considered self-image. Decisions were his only concern, and backing them up. I met several other officers who were regarded by their men as worthy—only one was in my battalion. Some others were good, intelligent men. The overwhelming majority were there for their own benefit, prancing through the motions, much as in any other organisation.

I didn't consider at that time that with a bit of cunning I might have ended up in a nice bludging admin job. I was infantry, that's what I'd joined up for. I didn't believe time and training would make me one of the worthy, so I didn't try to bullshit my way through. If you haven't got what it takes, find someone who has.

Well, there's the chance of five days in Penang for the final selection process blown out your arse, through my big mouth. Never mind, there's a sniff of R&R in the air if we don't weaken. Keep up.

I was back at the Nugget before eleven, with nothing to do. 'Fuck that was quick.'

'Yes, Peaches, they didn't like me.'

'I don't fucking like you. Got a warm beer? This Yank told me a trick about petrol and burying a can and burning it and digging it out with a bayonet and it's chilled. Fucking magic. Come on, I'll show ya.'

We drank the first can so hot that the foam jetted through our nostrils as we clamped our mouths to the lip. The second can we drank straight out of the carton, with much the same result. Then we got cunning and hit the Nugget's cold supply. That brought Dave out, Pete got a whiff—we were on the piss again.

'Pete, what's NSU?'

'Give it a fucking break, Barrie!'

'Shut up, Dave! What is it? What?'

'Non-specific urethritis.'

'What?'

'Clap. Like gonorrhoea, only non-specific clap.'

'Speaking of which,' chimed in Peaches, 'there's a lonely hearts R&R going begging if anyone wants it.'

I went off and put my name down with Fuck-Knuckle and came back.

The crowd had built up a bit by now, so I asked for ideas on where to go. Some said Bangkok, Singapore got a few nods, Kelsie said Hong Kong for shopping and food and they had whores too. Dave said, 'Don't ask me, I've got a wife. What the fuck do I know about fun?'

'I wanna go to Hong Kong. Stick me down.'

Fuck-Knuckle shunted around on his swivel chair, looked at a chart on the wall, sighed, and crossed off a box with a blunt pencil stub.

'You're on for the flight in three days' time. All I've got open. Lodge your passport, paybook, medical card, pink thingummy and green whatsit with the counter at the airfield 2 pm that day. What do you want now?'

'Give me the stuff then.'

'You've got it.'

'No I haven't, I've only got my paybook.'

'Well I haven't got 'em.'

'Check with BHQ then.'

A roll of the eyes, a drumming of fingers. Finally he picked up the phone. 'Yeah, Crowley. Hummph. No, not here, he's a detachment . . . fair enough.' Click. 'They haven't got 'em.'

'Well how the fuck did I get here then? No dogtags, no fucking passport, none of that other shit you mentioned. Send me home, I shouldn't be here!'

'Dream on, you're stuck here.'

'So how do I go on R&R then, ya helpful cunt?'

'Sounds like a personal problem—try the padre.'

He was right of course, it was a personal problem. I never got that lot sorted out. Even some of my documents I'd lodged when I enlisted got lost by lazy bunglers like this fat cruiser. Lucky to have my paybook—that got me to Hong Kong.

I'm standing in the queue at the Dat's air terminal. The Caribou's warming up on the strip. I've got my paybook in my hand and all the other documents fanned out ready for the clerk to check off and give me my ticket. If he opens my passport I'm going nowhere—it's got Lenny's black face beaming out of it. He needs it back to get through customs at Hong Kong, but I'll deal with that when the time comes. Just don't get jittery and give me away or we're back out in the field getting shot at. The clerk just counts the colours and we're off in the Caribou, climbing up like an elevator. Hadn't seen much of Lenny on the tour. Couple of beers in the boozer, a wave or two in the field. We'd never socialised much, he was a bit quiet for my temperament then. But I'm glad he's coming with me. Good company once you work out he can enjoy himself without laughing like a drain and stirring up shit all the time. And he is reliable. Just the type to go with to a strange city on R&R.

Lenny's a formidable fighter. He fought a bit as a welterweight in the amateurs and a lot on the streets in his teens, but now he's a powerful middleweight, close to six feet, broad sloping hitter's shoulders and limbs like hardwood. Big Mick aside, anyone in the company would get a horrendous shock if they roused Lenny, but few know of this ability. He doesn't employ it without cause. It is a quality I greatly admire.

We're over Saigon's Tan Son Nhut airport within minutes and preparing to drop in as soon as our turn comes. Reputedly the busiest airport in the world. The sunray-crazed glimpses through the windows of the Caribou reveal little—a vast slab of concrete surrounded by shabby crowded urban sprawl. So, that's Saigon, what's all the fuss about? We land amidst the noise of planes landing and taking off, a shrieking, buffeting barrier. All sorts of craft. Jet fighters, Boeing 707s, smaller Air Vietnam passenger planes, swarms of light aircraft, choppers whizzing past us in a shimmering heat haze. We follow a Yank ground crew and enter a military mess. 'You can eat here; call for you when your plane's ready to board.' We're in a pale green mess similar to the Badcoe Club, getting peered at by Yank servicemen, but at least we're out of that bedlam for a while. Lenny and I sitting together eating attract some stares but it's more curiosity than anything else. The food's lukewarm and bland. The airman comes back for us and we're off!

On a PanAm 707, Lenny, me and a planeful of Yanks mostly wearing the dress uniforms of marines. We're dressed in civvy shit. The plane is dry and so are the hostesses. All past fifty, steel-grey hair, scrawny legs, hatchet-faced. They'll be out of a job come war's end, nothing surer. Hong Kong glitters into sight as night falls and we land on the sparkling pier of the airstrip jutting from the mainland into the bay. All around, towering skyscrapers of crystal light, from the sea to the hills in the far distance. We start to get excited—home doesn't look like this.

We take the bus to the terminal a mile away and I begin to agonise on how to get cleared. Lenny goes through OK but the Chinese guard at customs can't figure out how I'd gotten here. I explain, but he's worked out already that I've flown in. No passport—of course, that's what puzzles him. He leads me over to a long desk with two Chinese customs officers behind it and a middle-aged Indian man on my side wailing theatrically about his need to get through. One of the officers prises himself free from this tortuous tale and takes my paybook from the puzzled guard.

'What's this?'

'All I've got. And five hundred bucks.'

'How did you get here?'

'Beat the system.'

'You're here for R&R?'

'Yep, then straight back again.'

I watch him silently appraise the paybook, then me, for a full minute. 'OK, pass. Get into trouble—deep shit.'

'Thanks mate.' Whew! I settle the nerves down, then catch up with Lenny on the other side of the barrier.

We're not on the streets yet, though. Got to get briefed. We trail in with three hundred Yanks into a bare room and there's three suits with smiling crewcuts waiting for us. The first one gives us the bullshit about military secrets, the second one craps on about condoms and alternative fun things to do on R&R, the third gives us a rundown on where to shop for fair deals and what to pay. The first two are idiots who've scored cushy jobs, the third is a tout. The tout finally finishes his pitch and starts allocating hotels. They're block-booked for the military at selected hotels, probably by this slimy bastard. You can't just cruise out and suit yourself. The Hilton, we are advised, is exclusively for officers. This is news to me. Jomo, the mad Kenyan who's Lenny's second scout, told me to make sure I went there. He'd just been, and he said 'It's a great place to go fucking mental in'. Maybe his stay brought about the new policy. Lenny and I are at the back of the queue and we score the Grand Hotel in the centre of the Kowloon action. It turns out to be a bit depressing, much like the Grand in Vungers except that it's a dowdy dark brown and you get your own bathroom. We check in, then out the door for a look around and it's on.

We both come from Perth where service, when you can grab some lazy bastard's attention, usually runs to 'Nah, we don't stock your size' or 'We're out of stock. Nah, dunno when we're gettin' any more'. Here it's different. Even in Vung Tau, apart from the street kids, most of the traders don't hassle you—pretty laconic traders for the most part. Here they're at you nonstop. Pause in front of a tailor's shop, you get dragged in. Look in a camera shop window, some shark cruises out to sell you something. You're having a piss and the stranger next to you slips you a cheap jeweller's card and tells you about a good bar. You go into a bar and the radio's playing 'Born Free' or 'My Girl' till you want to strangle the arsehole who recorded it.

Then this mind-crunching little Chinese playgirl is sitting on my lap telling me I can possess her for a while, real cheap. That's what this part of the story's all about, Lenny and whores. I'll get on to them first, but I'll have my say too; I get fascinated by other things.

Lenny and I've made about 200 metres of ground up the crowded shop-lined thoroughfare by the time we know we've had enough and lunge into the bar on our right. We meet a Lancashire Fusilier—a crack Pommy infantry regiment who fought and died to the last man at least twice. Big black bastard who speaks with a Yorkshire accent. Tells me he's a clerk—fuck this dying shit. I can see Lenny going off him real quick, so we drag arse up the street again. The Fusilier follows us and pats my shoulder and says 'And that's *the* best tailor in Hong Kong'. We fight clear of the rabid gang of tailors, Indian this time, and limp across the road into a bar. And that's how Suzie Wong with the big tits comes to be sitting on my lap, writhing on a rising column of expectation. I glance across at Lenny. He's being looked after well enough to have him laughing, so at the signal we bolt back to our own rooms. We have to tip the lift attendant first. A few bucks turns a slut into a lady in this town. Then we drive ourselves up, the lift attendant only attending to business. I make it to my room after brushing the floor porter away from in front of the door. 'Nah, call you if I need you.' Need him straight away. 'I haven't got a towel', Suzie says. Fair enough. 'Porter, another towel!'

'Where old one?'

'I mean *another* towel.'

'Got a towel.' Sulky muttering cunt.

'He want tip.'

'Another towel, ah, extla towel, yes.'

We get the sheets changed—Suzie says they've been slept in. Then I send for some booze, figuring I'm already fucked. The only thing I've taken off is my wallet, it's in Suzie's playful hands. She's curled up invitingly on the clean bed. Now we're talking her money. The week costs so much and she'll take care of me; a single night works out much dearer over the course of the week. I tell her to take the day rate. She plucks that out right away and undresses down to black bra and bikini briefs, then pulls more notes out and smilingly fans her body with them. 'And this is for me, for so good.'

I'm not arguing, I've read the books. I'm looking for experience, delight, erotic adventure, and she's just the answer. Christ, I'm taking her bra off and her breasts are round and warm and heavy in my hands. She's lying down and sliding off her panties, hips gently thrusting, welcoming, smiling shyly, beckoning me with outstretched arms. My strides come off. Nirvana next stop.

I have a fuck. And get screwed. After that she starts up at me about places to shop, places to eat at, places to shop again—I'm back on the street! I turn a deaf ear to her parroting so she gets me to call the porter, for an extra pillow. Shove it under her arse for the next fuck, then we both get some sleep. Shake her off before breakfast—I offer it, but ladies who are sluts can't eat in the dining room. Tough shit! Am I glad to see Lenny's face, sitting slurping over a bowl of cereal.

'How'd it go Lenny?'

'Great, how about you?'

'Ah, mine gave me an earache.'
'Yeah? Shit, you're a funny bastard, Barrie.'
We walk out the front door and two Yanks are waiting for us, both in light buff dress uniforms brilliant with service ribbons and badges. One is an affable young blond draftee from Omaha or somewhere bland, the other a big weird-looking black geezer.
'Hey, hi there! You staying here too?' This from the white kid.
Let's look at the possibles here, then the improbables. Luke is lively. Tall, skinny, good-looking. He's courteous, thinks Lenny and I look cool together. 'Aussies are so cool. You guys . . . you don't give a shit.' Luke is an idealist, a dickhead. I look at Lenny. His horseblanket tweed sports coat is hardly cool but he's proud of it, otherwise he wouldn't wear it. He's better dressed than me, though, so it's not fashion that makes us cool. The big black bugger is Glen. He has a physique like Ali had when he was called Clay. Except Glen has a face like a voodoo priest, long and spooky. Might be the front tooth. He does have another one—his name is Glen, not Fang—but one of them bears a star of gold with a diamond embedded in it. It sure draws your attention. He sounds friendly enough.
'Well, hi to you too, can we catch you here later? Good.'
And we're off into the unknown.
'Lenny, let's go to Victoria Island.'
'Where the fuck's that?'
'On the ferry.'
We force our way on foot out of the shopping street we're in and catch a cab to the quay. The city that morning reminds me of Melbourne on a winter's day when I was very young. Granite buildings, grey skies, deciduous trees, old Morris cars, wet black streets, smoke, drizzle, umbrellas. The smells of old-fashioned vinyl and bakelite in the taxicab. We buy tickets at the terminus gate, pass through the barriers and go down the wide steep walkway to the piers. The structure is painted light green, so are the many ferries. *That* salesman's been here too. Relentless bastard.
The covered windy quays are too crowded with purposeful black-headed people to be picky, so Lenny and I jump on the first available ferry. How far can they go? Who cares? And we shove off at the same time that six or seven others do, and it's

a race, a regatta, once we clear the jetties and join the full fleet. It is fabulous. The sea swelling and chopping, white spray misting off wavetips churned to light green with air and sand. Huge ferries passing and falling behind, pitching and leaning, looming high above, then plunging below our view. Lenny and I stand at the rail, all the others sit in rows awaiting the trip's end. Seen it all too many times, I suppose. At the end, a concrete pier with a turnstile. Beyond it a rickshaw driver resting between the shafts.

'Let's have a ride, Lenny.'

'Nah, can't see the point.'

'Where's your sense of romance? Far East, British Raj, Somerset Maugham.'

'Who?'

I get my way. Costs us about a day's pay. The rickshaw operator is middle-aged, strong, with massive calf muscles, hates his job. We climb on. Sit there for an eternity while he psyches up for the ordeal. Then with an almighty lunge we're inching our way imperceptibly from the terminal. The crowd of locals watch balefully as the poor downtrodden man struggles against impossible odds to wheel two heartless foreigners off on their pursuit of pleasure. Progress is agonising. We limp about 500 metres up the docks, bland grey warehouses lining either side without break, then he's had enough. He manages to wheel us round, pulls a hamstring, and limps us back towards the terminal, wheezing and farting alarmingly at every shuffling, pain-filled step.

'Fuck this, Barrie, this is embarrassing. Let's get off before this cunt croaks.'

I feel embarrassed too, but for a different reason. We've been had again. The old swindler gets us back OK, gives us a cunning, spiteful glare, then totally ignores us. This town isn't much on service—let's check out the shops. Straight back on the ferry.

The shops here have it down to a fine art. Everything that's portable. Perfumes, clothing, footwear, cameras, jewellery, electrical goods. A fair few shops run by Indians, too, fat ones. Everything seems to be a matter of bargaining. Alright if you like arguing greed all day with a shifty trader. I want a camera and a suit, at the right price. Ever heard your mates crap on about getting incredible deals through smart bargaining? Fucking bullshit!

Lenny and I go into a camera shop.
'How much this camera?'
'Ninety dollar US.'
'Give ya ten!'
Bicker bicker. Settles for fifty.
'Back in five, hold the deal.'
Up the road to a fixed price shop. The camera's $72 US.
'I can get that for fifty down the road.'
'No you can't. For fifty you buy *this* one, see, smaller lens, less features, older model.'
Back to the bargainer. 'Give you fifty for this one.'
'No no, this one hundled-twenty.'
'I can get it for seventy-two up the road, marked price.'
'OK. Seventy I can do, vely special.'
'Stick it up ya arse!'

I go back and pay the two bucks extra for integrity. I've still got the camera, it works fine. Bargaining is bullshit. It's finding out how big a dickhead the buyer is, and on his time. After this the mystery of Hong Kong evaporates for me and it has to stand on its merits. I have to hand it to them, though, the goods are mostly first-rate and the tailoring is superb if you don't haggle too much. What you save on price comes off the finish otherwise.

We went back to the hotel. Our two Yanks were in the lobby. We organised a drink. Luke was a medic with a combat unit, first and hopefully last tour half done—he was a draftee. He'd become a medic because he didn't have to carry a weapon in the field, and didn't. Glen was in infantry, and much smarter. He was a typist and didn't know what the field looked like—he thought he had a gun somewheres maybe. He also claimed to have written the lyrics to one of the Supreme's hits, and a couple of others that only charted on the black R&B scene. He was a Reg; apparently writing lyrics didn't pay too well! We got a bit sick of being asked to explain why we were so cool, and suggested lunch. Glen had a date with his tailor, to pick up some stuff he'd ordered by mail. He'd been here before and knew his way around. Luke tagged along with us, so we went to find a restaurant. When in Hong Kong—what the hell, let's eat Russian. That's what the sign said. It was a Frenchified steakhouse but the food was excellent. Luke ordered frog's legs.

'Why would you go to a restaurant and eat a frog?' Lenny wanted to know later, as we left the movie theatre.

'Why did we pay to sit through that crock of shit?'

'Better than paying for frogs.'

Debatable. We'd shaken Luke off and gone to see a movie. The house was huge, 2000 seats or more. I was the only blond head in the audience, or on the screen for that matter. Jim Brown and Raquel Welch in *A Whole Load of Bullshit*. Hollywood remake it forty times a year.

Back at the hotel was a sign saying: Happy Hour in The Basement 4-6 pm daily. Went for a look. The dim, quiet bar served Lowenbrau on tap from wooden barrels—into chilled stone steins. Half-price. There was a jazz trio—piano, drums, double bass—playing 'Fly Me To The Moon' in the corner. We had the place to ourselves. The beer was wonderful, the tuxedo'd Chinese trio were good. Played all my requests except one, 'Raggedy Waltz'—the drummer said he wasn't Joe Merillo. At the break I offered them a drink. 'No thanks, the management gives us coffee. We are amateur; this is just our hobby, our relaxation,' explained the pianist, a quiet, elderly man in his sixties. Something of value given freely—in this town! We went back each day. Had the place to ourselves. Didn't ask what the musicians did for a living. It might have shattered the illusion.

Speaking of which, we met Glen in the foyer and he said, 'Hey, you guys like music? I'll take you to a real Brothers club tonight, great R&B. I'll get out of this shit and be right down.' And off he went to change out of uniform.

Just take a look at this idiot, will you? He steps out of the lift like a gold bat. Gold high-heeled boots, gold satin suit, gold satin cape spread wide by his outstretched arms—like a chorus boy prancing on to centre stage. Quite an entrance.

'What do you think? . . . Huh? Ain't it *the* very thing. I'll give you my tailor's card.'

'Give it to Lenny, I've already been fitted.'

I let Lenny squirm out of that one as we made our way to the club. It wasn't far from the hotel; upstairs from a bar. Walked into the room past the squat black pinheaded tuxedo'd doorman and we were in a Brothers club, alright. Could have been in Detroit or Chicago. On stage a ten-piece band with blaring brass, five black women singers giving it shit. The room reeled. It was fucking wild. Pity, that described the crowd too. All the men were black servicemen. Some on the dance floor jiving solo to the music, some dancing with bargirls tottering perilously on high, spiked heels. The rest were glaring at us. I ignored the looks and tried to concentrate on the music, but a burly brother with a snarling face was at Glen's throat before we settled.

'Whatchew doin', man, bringin' these muthers here? Whatchew thinkin'?'

Glen's 'They're cool, man' wasn't going over well and the crowd was moving in to see more. Lenny guarded my back on the way out.

They didn't like him either. Seemed we all had a long way to go.

We went on a bar crawl after that, letting Glen frighten the locals with his costume, listened to 'My Girl' thirty times, then finally went up to Glen's room to see what was so shit-hot about this special aged bourbon he had. Glen and I were debating music over the drink when Lenny started leaning forward, peering in fascination at Glen.

'You've got a star on your tooth! Right there.'

Lenny's powers of observation astounded you at times. With that he said he'd had enough and went to his room. I sat finishing my drink and talked a bit about the war, about Vietnam. I hadn't seen much except what we'd shot, but of course Glen didn't know what I was talking about. He described life in his own hometown of Detroit and that didn't sound much better, so I asked him about his music. Glen drew a crumpled scrap of paper out of his pants pocket and said, 'This is my next one'.

No, it wasn't a classic. It was 'No Man is an Island'. Not much of a ring to it. He'd only got about four lines down, so it hadn't been much of a waste of time yet.

Glen ran out of ideas then, lay back on his bed, loosened his tie, undid a few shirt buttons, wanted to pin a blossom on me. Gave my shoulder a cuddle. Fuck! Perfect end to a patchy day.

'Ya can knock that shit off, ya big fairy!' I'm on my feet

and pointing. If this big prick can punch his weight, I'm buggered. To my undying relief he snaps right out of it and becomes apologetic.

'Hey, no offence, I thought you'd be cool. It's not rare, you know.'

'It fucking is in my tribe!'

What tribe? Must check with Lenny.

Glen seemed crushed by the encounter, puzzled at having got it wrong, so I brazened it out and had a beer with him before going. To hear *him* talk, it was a pretty common preference among the Yanks. I didn't know what to make of it at all. I liked Glen, he was goodhearted, but he wasn't going anywhere that I could see. At least Luke had vague ideals to be guided by.

I met up with Lenny at breakfast.

'When'd you pull the pin, Barrie?'

'Soon as I found out he was queer.'

'I figured that. How'd you find out?'

'Asking.'

'Pass the sugar, will ya.'

'Get fucked!'

Let's not dwell on five days of this shit, I'm telling you what you already know, and there's something on my mind.

Lenny and I flew out in the evening with three hundred quiet Yanks. The skyline we saw as we rose still dazzles my senses—you never get blasé to the magical glitter of it all. The visit to Hong Kong had been a revelation, and no regrets. I'd seen God. His name was Dollar Bill but you had to call him Jehovah. It means God so almighty I dare not say your name. Now there's cunning for you. And I'd got the sex bullshit sorted out. No more whores, I'm on the lookout for a woman. Could have turned it in there and then and become a monk, but if you're stubborn you never know—there's plenty out there.

While I was mulling this over Lenny was squeezing his forehead. He'd worked up an interesting grimace so I switched on.

Pop!

'Shit . . . look at this, Barrie. Looks like a grain of rice. Fuck, this land's getting to me.'

When we got back to the Dat, Kelsie started going through and over my stuff, asking what I'd paid for each item. Finally he was satisfied I'd done pretty well. All the while I'd been getting audited, a black hole had been flickering and clicking incessantly by the stoop of the tent.

'Put the bloody thing down, Dave, before ya break it!'

'Automatic umbrella! Who dreams these fucking things up? Shit I've had a gutsful. Here you go, it'll be handy in the scrub. When do we get to the raping, looting and pillaging? That's what I wanna know . . . Get any stick books?'

Peaches came roaring up the track just then and he wasn't being chased. Full alert.

'Hi, Barrie . . . Hey, don't use the crapper!'

We'd been rained out last night after I returned and the earth at the back of our crapper had caved in. Peaches had gone down into it to investigate—maybe the slab had become unstable.

'Fuck, I was outa there like a rocket. There's old grenades, M72s, all sorts a shit. Rusted to fuck. Not going down there again.'

We still used it though. The tropics gave you a different perspective. And there was no reason to suppose that the comedians who dumped the stuff would stop at just one crapper. Anyway, it was convenient. We still used it; just cut short on the yap a bit. And definitely no reading on the thunderbox.

I know I go on about reading, it's in my blood. Books are very precious to me. I love to lend them to people in the hope they'll see what I see. I discovered books at about the age of nine—real books, not picture books. Mum and Dad often had their noses stuck in them of an evening, and always belonged to a lending library wherever we lived. As a kid I often had time alone. It helped that we shifted a lot, there was always the period of breaking the ice, not knowing the local culture and its pecking order. But I would have sought time alone in any case, it's my nature. Books filled that time. I started with Homer's *Iliad*—the kids version, no rooting. I got ambitious and had a crack at the poetry version but it was too long, weighed a tonne. Read all I could on ancient Greece, Rome, the Incas, all sorts of ancient societies. Then in my early teens I moved on to novels. Hemingway, Alec Waugh, Golding, Monsarrat.

Paperbacks with young women with big tits on the cover and TORRID! printed on the back. And Steinbeck. Books hold a magic for me—every time you pick one up it contains the same words but over time the meaning can change. Some books turn out to be utter shit; others continue to grow, to illuminate more at every glance.

Let me show you.

I was reading *Cannery Row*, a small Steinbeck work. I'd read it four or five times and loved it because of the off-the-wall characters. There were whores and pimps and a madam, and a bouncer who'd hit some cunt too hard and lost his nerve. There was a neurotic artist who fucked heaps of women and lived in a yacht he'd built in the hills because the sight of water frightened shit out of him. There was a Chinese shopkeeper who wanted to swindle but had a kind heart, so he traded with swindlers. There was a bunch of bums with valuable skills and opposing character traits led by Mac, a supposed philosopher. And there was Doc, who was a marine biologist. The community loved and respected Doc because he was wise and learned, yet he lived among them by choice and was one of them. They decided, at Mac's instigation, to throw a surprise party in Doc's honour at the laboratory, which was also Doc's home—leaving Mac to organise it. The first effort was an absolute disaster. Doc returned home to clean up the carnage, and punched Mac in the mouth for offering to help. The community had another go and this party worked. It was a horrendous disaster too, but at least Doc was there to help fuck it up. At the party Doc recited a poem—which I'd always skipped, because I found it too profound to understand. As I read the party scene again I wondered why it was there. It was about a man recalling the love of a young woman now dead, the wonder of that time, and the beauty of the world around him. And it referred to men he had met. Mighty, rich and learned men, who could not know what he had known, because they could not see what he saw.

There was an asterisk at the end of the last line of the poem and I looked below and saw: 'Black Marigolds', translated from the Sanskrit by E. Powys Mathers. What's Sanskrit? An old language, isn't it?

'Anyone got a dictionary?'

Sanskrit: classic language of ancient India, member of the Aryan family of languages.

What's Aryan? Flick, flick . . . Early race of pure Hindu, forebears of the white Teutonic races.

Fuck! We're standing still as people. For all our arrogance and technology we're getting nowhere—deluding ourselves. The story isn't about a party at all. That to me is the magic of books. They are a mirror to the world. A touchstone among all the bullshit.

Chapter 11

A LOT OF SIGNIFICANT CHANGES were taking place at the Dat. OC wasn't washing his socks in the little zinc basin on top of the rickety wooden stand beside his tent—he'd found a batman who'd actually do the job, as opposed to simply taking advantage of his better nature. And about twenty of our oldest Nasho intake were due to return home any day now. Good Diggers. Gunners, scouts, gun group commanders. We were reluctantly bedding in the Reos taking their places. At the arse end. Must have got 'em cheap as a job lot. Funny-looking crew. The two big ones looked fucking slow, the rest runts—looked too young to be here. A few unusual breeds too, Ceylonese, Greek, a couple of other Meds, not the usual haul. My position as shortarse of the company was up for grabs now, no argument. I'd have to project a personality real quick or get forgotten.

Some of the lucky arseholes due to fly out were giving us a shafting. One went too far. A big Digger from the outgoing group was talking to a bunch of the new runts several tents away from me. I could sense unease spreading among the new boys. Banjo joined the group and said something. The Digger replied—and got dropped by the harshest straight right I've ever seen. There was a crash as he landed and his body convulsed, head and heels drumming against the hard clay. I took an uncharacteristic interest in tidying up my tent—this was section commander business. I didn't know Banjo could hit, I just thought he could think.

Talking of thinking, Dave stuffed up a good thing, at least I blame him. Yeah, OC's arseholed us out of the Nugget. Put us across the road next to one of the platoons, not far from his own tent. It had rifle pits, which was a bastard, we now had to observe stand-to properly like every other prick. No place for a beer garden, no cover. We couldn't use the old one because there was no reason to go up the track—nobody lived there anymore. Dave was now Support Section commander, Griffo had gone home, against his will. Top End Mick had gone to a platoon, experienced gunners were getting scarce. Peaches was getting sidelong glances from a few recruiters. Two of Support Section were flying home, their tour done. Dave's special gifts with loonies were being exploited to the full. He got replacements from the platoons to fill the gaps. One forward scout who'd had far more than he should handle but who was still too proud to howl at the moon. A tough rifleman who'd overcome a small wound but ducked a few more, until ducking became virtually all he could do. A third who betrayed no hint of his particular grief, or himself. That would be Ronnie. He used to be great company. How we got him remains a mystery, he was still front on, just a lot quieter. I suspect Dave drove that deal because we'd lost Young Mick permanently; he'd followed his heart and returned to a platoon.

I liked Zarbo, the wise ex-scout. A Dirk Bogarde lookalike. He still had his shit together, no bad habits. But Erik-the-real-fucking-quick gave me the heebies more than once. Now you see him, now you . . . no, I was just thinking he was here a minute ago, silly really. Still, he wasn't threatening, as it turned out. Played League footy, a brilliant defender, wouldn't have believed it if I hadn't seen it with my own eyes.

Nobody came to gamble at the new tent, we referred to it as the Tent. The Nugget was probably buggered anyway, after Dave had the last big night there and cleaned out four dickheads playing Slippery Sam. Ever heard of it? No? Don't play it! Whoever starts with the most money wins. Dave had just made a killing on that night's crown and anchor. Took Fuck-Knuckle for a year's pay in about an hour, and he wasn't that pissed. Dave did a sensitive deal on account of his wife and small family, but Fuck-Knuckle's probably still not listed in the telephone directory. Never came good. We still lost the Nugget.

Then OC's radio operator was transferred out. He was a Lance Jack, newly married with a kid on the way. A Reg of about 25. Not my type socially, a bit tight-lipped. His idea of abrasive social behaviour was: 'Pass the salt please, this one's empty'. Or if really upset: ' No. I didn't hear that. Sorry'. Which made him an ideal command radio operator. They hear nearly as much of the shit coming down the line as the commanding officer does, so you can't have a yapper in the job, not unless you want the troops bolting for home without firing a shot. He went to BHQ as a sig, working at the fire support base out in the field. Nice cruisy job, safe. Even the brigadier visited the fire support base now and again, briefly. OC had pushed hard for the bloke to get the job—he'd done seven months fucking tough and there was an extra hook in it. A week into the next Op he was dead. Killed by a mortar bomb going back to his pit from a radio watch in the command bunker. The odds on all of that happening are spot on. Fate cuts through the best of defences, and there's no use screaming injustice.

The ducks I'd brought back for Staff died. Don't know why—they were thriving in the wet and getting known.

We were choppered out to the jungle not long after this. I was on the last of the flight; got the seat on the ledge. Things weren't looking too good—we were down a few proven colts and the last month or two'd been very slow. We'd got another new bloke a few days before, a corporal, a Reg of about twenty-five. Blond, a taller version of me but not as attractive and a damn sight less interesting. He'd been spending some time in the boozer getting known. He'd drawn my attention one afternoon by his manner, intense and emphatic. I'd overheard a bit of what he said but it left me cold. 'Who's that maniac?' I'd asked Pigpen, the right one as it turned out.

'He's from 2RAR, I think. Got shot in the guts last tour, about a year ago. Fuckin' zapped, isn't he, eh?'

'What's he doing here?'

'New section commander. That'll be fun for some, poor cunt's looped it.'

Pigpen had repeated to me some of what had been said earlier. The new boy had described holding a field cup to his gaping guts and drinking his own blood so he could survive until the contact ended and the medic could reach him. That was after describing the eighty-five raging battles he'd survived with great personal glory.

As we landed in the chopper, something about the feel of things seemed unnatural. It was a typical small circle of swirling grass, but CSM was doing all the shit work, manning the strip and directing traffic and stores. Part of that was Dave's work. Where was Dave? I hit the deck and followed the finger fast, and came to a standing halt under the tree cover, hard up against Brian.

'What the fuck's going on?'

'Don't know, nothing's happened. Usual shit. Here we are, that's it.'

I started out to catch up with Pete, and Pigpen came down the line.

'What's the holdup?'

'We're holdin' the last chopper. Cup o' Blood's up the track lyin' in a puddle of piss, blubbing. Trees freaked him. Fuckin' whoopee, eh? Dave's got a hold of the mad cunt.'

Who sent this poor bastard back? His trouble was obvious to all of us. No officer should have given him command. No medically qualified person should have sent him back. What the hell did they think we had to contend with here? Long lunches? Someone should have sent those cunts over for a while, out fucking *here*, to see how *they* liked trees. Anyway damn him, everybody else did. At least in a funny sort of way he still acted like a real soldier—got out before he became a lethal burden. Dave and a few of his section escorted him on to my chopper. He was cheering up a bit as he passed me but he had a long way to go, back through the fucking healers again. I'm staying here, the odds on survival are better.

We spent a few days patrolling through dense hilly forest. Nothing much seemed to be happening except wrenching endlessly through entangling undergrowth. Getting drained by the heat. The tactically minded among us figured we were part of a concerted mass trying to encircle a big body of enemy and drive them into an ambush. That proved correct as far as Task Force policy was concerned. On about the fourth day we harboured on a hill and dug in, not our usual manouevre in the jungle. But just fire pits, not covered. We were already tired out, water was scarce and we didn't go near creeks too much. Resupply was held off. Up went the hootchies and the blokes found a use for the length of camouflage netting we'd just been issued. Made brilliant hammocks!

Then I saw Pete busy with something. 'What the hell are you fucking around with?' He was tying bits of string to the bottom eyelets of our tent, bumping me in my hammock as he shuffled around the two pits beneath me, irritating the shit out of me.

'Apparently you get more water this way. Put your dixies and cups under them. It's gunna rain.' As though he had spoken on a direct line to the heavens, the rain thundered down. It had rained most days up to now anyway, but we'd been tramping through it, lately with empty canteens and sopping kit. The strings worked, became crystal rivers; we ran out of things to fill.

'Where'd you learn that trick?'

'Outside.'

He was referring to all the other tents with strings hanging from them, and Diggers soaping their hairy arses and washing socks and shirts. These guys knew how to capitalise on every opportunity that presented itself, regardless of what form it took. There's something about sitting snug and secure in a dry tent, with mates sprinting under for a yap and a coffee, while rain beats down all around you on to a silvery green landscape. Something that stays with you forever—whether it was a feeling of peace or excitement I can't recall, but I remember it.

This interlude didn't last long. No enemy came our way and we were choppered out next day into a bleak landscape. A glaring silver-grey plain lay ahead as far as you cared to see. A scraggly tree clung futilely to life here and there. We approached the plain over scrubby dry country and stopped at its edge to set up a company-strength ambush for the screaming hordes who were about to run past us to be killed. This was SAS intelligence we were acting on. Here for two weeks. You little fucking beauty!

It's a funny war. Want to know where the enemy is? Ask the Diggers. They don't spend months searching every inch of ground for signs, appraising the strengths and weaknesses of the enemy they meet, only to learn nothing. They get a crystal clear picture of their enemy, almost a personality profile. They know how to react at a given time with a given situation. The only problem with a Digger's intelligence is that to access it, you have to be a Digger. Can you see the catch?

That's why people like the SAS are used. God bless High Command's ignorance.

We have to dig two-man mortarproof pits. Pity we're in desert scrub, no wood here, nothing supplied. Out with the entrenching tool. That's the little fold-up shovel and pick hanging from the back of your pack. The handle's bruised your arse for months. Let's dig a U-shaped pit two metres deep so we can backfill a roof 500 mm thick. The sand's like silica and we've got punky deadfall to form the ceiling. If you put paper on top of the twigs the sand doesn't leak on you at night—if you've brought any paper that is.

But there's lots of pluses here as long as your pit doesn't cave in with you inside it. Pete's and mine doesn't, but many do—and few are as arrogant as us and actually sleep in them. Less mozzies down there. Pits aside, we have some shade. We have regular resupply. We can't patrol the area because it's an ambush—a secret—but choppers can land and drop food and water without being seen. Which is definitely true. There's no enemy *here*. What large body of trained men would cross this killing ground? Not our VC mates, they're not that stupid. Although if they were to march obligingly by with Pete or me on gun picquet a few might get away. We're placed in the killing ground and share a gun roster with one of the rifle sections. Support Section lies behind us in reserve, while Dave teaches them how to stop twitching. He sticks at it manfully but flees now and again for a breather, one time crunching in one side of our pit.

'Fuck! Ease up! That's our pit.'

'I know that. Ever met a mob you don't want to lead?'

'Yeah.'

'So have I.' He gets out of the pit. 'Soon as we move from here I'm off on R&R. Fuck this shit. I'm even looking forward to it.'

This is one of the few places in the field I remember taking a crap. Come along. We go up this track and say hello to the gun picquet and ask how long he's got to go. If it's less than five minutes, we wait for the picquet to change. It's OK, he'll be there until we get back, let's move on out to the trench. Here we are in no-man's land—yep, there's the flies droning, we're here. Squat astride that and let it all hang down, but I'd keep a sharp look around, you're on your own out here and a shit isn't the end of the world. You can manage on three quick ones a month with these rations. OK, throw a bit of sand on it and let's get back.

The gun picquet at night here was freaky. A sandy silvery plain and bright moon all night. Music. Most of a grunt's memory of music comes from the field, from a pissant little mono earphone screwed into your earhole. Every picquet looked deaf. During the day it was pop stuff. Night time started around eight when the company sig handed over the radio to the watch—most of the important traffic was done by then. Eight o'clock was still day shit. At ten, country music came in, till midnight—some good, Buck Owens, Hank Williams, hang on . . . Round midnight it got better—Creedence, Morrison, later Steppenwolf, some Zappa, Led Zepp, leading into who knows who, jazz-fusion, blues, some hardcore jazz. Then around dawn the Doors creeped out. Ever heard Creedence by moonlight? It's the only way, they put down some good shit. If anyone captured the feel of Vietnam it was them.

We got all this from American Forces Radio Vietnam. AFVN wasn't its own boss though. Sixteen days straight we got the sob on General Eisenhower croaking. Sixteen days by twenty-four hours. The general who had never fired an angry shot, never led a small unit into battle. Let the civilians mourn the cunt, we're soldiers. But of course AFVN catered to the Americans. Still, they were about a year in front of Australian radio musically. I was back home a year still saying, 'What new release? Heard that one a year ago.'

We were ahead of our civilian counterparts in other ways, too. In this hiatus, in the sobriety imposed by the field, we were led to self-questioning, in admitting those questions to trusted friends around us.

What if I die?
What if I kill?
What if I am forgotten?

What if I am separated from the company and lost?
What if I fail, cause others to suffer?
What if I am injured, become useless and ugly?

This little rest in the field, courtesy of typically bad intelligence, served us well—time to address these and other questions. What's so unique about these questions? To us they were not academic. And they all came at once.

We had plenty of water here, stored in jerrycans. I saw our youngest member—no pun intended, but remember the bite on the dick?—drink straight out of one. Saw the size of the spider hanging out of his mouth. Big black nasty bugger—only four legs covering the kid's face, the rest was in his gob. Stretched his lower lip when he dragged it out. Fucking *aaahhh*.

'Last time I did that it was a bullfrog. Better find me cup.'

Let's go, nothing here to kill. We chopper back into the jungle. Dave's back from R&R, OC's just gone, Tizzy's acting as OC, his first gallop in months. Duntroon's right beside him—he's got the knowledge, he's barely missed a day in the field. The two of them make up OC group. Everything's quiet. We should be able to manage until OC gets back.

We're walking along a brown muddy track on the left bank of a swift green river. On through a tunnel of saplings and low boughs which some have to stoop under, the river well below the bank we follow. *Brrraatt! Ping ping.* Everyone drops down. An experienced section commander's appraisal is ignored, a crack scout's vivid description of what lies ahead is not listened to. A minute or two at the halt, and we're off again; no signals: no feedback. One of our platoons leaves us to set up an ambush further along the river. The rest of us turn hard left and we're walking up the hill following another track. It's steep but the day is beautiful. Above us a high canopy, saplings all around us waiting their turn to grow, golden shafts of sunlight everywhere. Pete's back is in front of me. We've just passed a body and two blood trails down at the ford, but few are aware that they exist. Fewer still that they had been sunning themselves, unarmed, a short stroll from home. The body had been turfed out of sight into the concealing brush; we follow the trail.

Dust and dirt shower down on me, Pete's flicking at his neck—'Fucking ants above'—and the wall of sound crashes all around us. Pete's gone, I've got his hat, webbing and pack. Who's here? My stocky engineer mate from the first big bunker find, Dave's section below me, one platoon behind them. In front, the rest of CHQ, one platoon ahead of them, and the VC throwing everything they have at us. Pete's up there somewhere, among the real shit. I'm on the deck, watching my arc. Then Sharkey's gun hits back. There's rockets sparking and whooshing everywhere, the light's turned yellow and tinder's sparkling in the air.

Commanders are on the blower and CHQ scuttle further up the hill, settling just below the brow. Support Section link with me and we push up to form a rearguard umbrella as the rear platoon fan out left to sweep and then link up in support of the contact platoon. They have to cross a gully to get up in support, but it isn't a gully it's a fire lane, withering gunfire pouring down it at the sight of a limb or a hat.

We're fucked. It's late afternoon and we're pinned down along the line of a big bunker system. We've reached the Hill. OC group are planning to assault through it, but you can't. It takes numbers and support—tanks, artillery, air strikes. When in doubt, dither is the order. Meantime the lead platoon's getting the shit shot out of them, some of the walking wounded are finding their way down near me. One sits quietly with a bandaged head wound, he's OK, he knows it. There's rounds and rockets roaring overhead hard and fast, but you can almost stand here, and the shrapnel's thinning and half spent. Sharkey's second number two comes lurching down and collapses a couple of metres away from me, lying against the low bank. He looks likes one of the big blokes from the last batch. I see his hands cupped close in front of his chest, they're embedded with a few bits of gun link. Must have copped a round in the belt. He's dressed in rags and looking all in but he's OK, no real bleeding. He asks for water so I lob a canteen beside him and watch my front again. Then I hear him whimpering and look back around. He's holding out his hands signalling 'Can't do' and coming unravelled. The stocky sapper beside me crawls over and cradles him round the shoulder while he holds the bottle to his lips. Then he's stuck with the job of pacifying him. I feel a real cunt—I reckon I should have done that. Anyway, I go back to watching my arc.

'Bazz! Where's Brian?' Shit, Pete's back.
'Went up straight after you—he's not with CHQ, look.'
'Fuck! Must have missed him, can't see fuck-all up there. Look what they did to me bag.'
His medical hipkit is hanging in a sodden tattered bundle against his waist; morphine, iodine and goo oozing from it. I don't tell him about the six or seven bullet holes in his torn flapping shirt. 'Gotta go, see ya'—but the Sapper is worried about the man he's minding. He's going into shock, whimpering and shuddering.
'Take a look will ya, Pete?'
Pete looks from where he crouches beside me. 'Fuck him, he's OK.' And Pete's gone again.
I feel better about my reaction towards the man's wounds then—but *I* only have hurt feelings. And lead platoon are still in the killing ground and getting nowhere. Sharkey's gun's roaring out nonstop, he's on his third number two by now. The badly wounded are being dragged clear and plugged up, lying low just in front of CHQ until they can be moved without getting hit again. Duntroon summons Dave, has a quick briefing, then Dave's back and briefing Support Section. While they drop everything that might slow them down, Dave comes over to me.
'Looks like this might be it, old son. We're going up.'
'Me too?' It's a question, not a request.
'Nah, you're rear defence—look after this fucking lot.' He describes a 180 degree arc with his arm for my benefit. Then he's off with his section at a crouch, Zarbo leading. They look bloody good.
They don't get right into the thick of it, staying on the edge waiting for the order to go and seeing what they can. The assault can't succeed in any aim other than the total annihilation of the company, so it has to stop. But lead platoon have a fallen scout out in front—he'd gone down in the first burst when he walked straight into a bull's horn of gun bunkers, metres from the muzzles. Sharkey has come this far and isn't stopping for any cunt until his scout is retrieved. The platoon isn't going to leave Sharkey. Orders are at a stalemate. Pete makes it to the fallen scout, confirms what he knows already—instantaneous death—and gives the order. 'Fuck off! He's dead. He's fucking

dead! I'm going.' The scout's body is left behind as what's left of the platoon withdraw the few precious metres down the rise and regroup in front of CHQ, standing only to carry the wounded back under protective covering fire. The other platoon then breaks off contact and eventually forms a defence around us. Silence falls, a muffled roar. I am able to concentrate more now on what OC group, about ten metres in front of me, are doing. Duntroon's on the blower, giving details to Fire Support Base. First a more coherent description of enemy position, likely strength, and type of country, so that air and artillery support can be sent in. Then a description of what has happened, plus number of casualties, dustoff and resupply requirements, and position of the LZ. I'm mystified to hear him say, 'And I also sustained a small wound, but will remain in the field'. He looks fine to me.

CSM, Dave, Support Section and some platoonies go back down the hill to secure the LZ by the river, as Pete and Brian start directing the wounded down, in order of urgency. I hear Tizzy start to talk quietly to Duntroon, then without warning he blurts out 'I've failed, I've failed totally'. And begins to cry, burying his face into the earth. We're all still on the deck watching for counterattack—it isn't over yet. Duntroon talks him around, advises him there's little else anyone could have done. Fair enough, considering that Duntroon's input in the proceedings has been considerably more than token, and not in keeping with OC's policy.

The next thing I know Lieutenant Prick had mustered some of his platoon in a tight semi-circle before him, not ten metres from me and OC group. This platoon had struck the fire lane in the gully. 'When I give an order, it will be *obeyed*! Do you *understand*?' Prick's glaring face scanned his men as he snarled out his message. There stood men that I knew—in deathly silence, heads bowed, eyes averted; being accused, it seemed, of letting their mates down in order to save their own lives; when their welfare was merely incidental to *his* agenda. No effective order had been given. Communication had been impossible in the bedlam swirling around them. The platoon had been reduced to individual action during the entire conflict.

Tizzy summoned Prick over to him. A short, sharp, muttered statement from Tizzy followed, then Prick was walking down the hill while his platoon settled down—perhaps to reflect upon his own actions.

Just then the clatter of the choppers shattered the quiet and I could see them dropping down through the canopy, where they hovered half over the river until their cargo of wounded was hauled on. Then they reappeared briefly before tilting, banking and clattering off again. Shortly afterwards came a chopper laden with ammo and other equipment, hoisted off by Peaches who'd come out for a look around. He waved but didn't get off. It set his mind thinking, though.

Duntroon collared Pete, who was headed back my way, his job done for the moment.

'Take a look at this, Pete. I've been wounded slightly, it may need treatment.'

'Where is it?'

'Here, on my hand.' I saw him hold out his left hand and point with his right.

'Where? Ah that. That's a nick from a bit of bamboo or something.'

'It's a wound, bit of shrapnel. I've reported it.'

'Look, it's a fucking nick. See!' Pete picked at the wound with his hand and held out his finger to Duntroon with something stuck on it. Then he wiped his finger on his shirt and went to walk away. Duntroon made to speak again.

'It's just a fucking nick. Want a fucking Bandaid, ask Brian. My bag's fucked.' And he stomped over and sat with me.

'D'you know what that cunt's saying to me?'

'I heard it, heard some mention of it on the radio report.'

'Fuck, I don't know.' Pete couldn't settle, and soon wandered off elsewhere to check a couple of the blokes out.

A few minutes later Dave's beside me. 'You seen Pete? He's fuckin' ropable.'

'Duntroon, yeah. How'd the dustoff go?'

'Pretty good, some of 'em shaken up. One poor cunt's got his hip all smashed up. Why do I always get 'em? He's crying his eyes out about dying. I'm telling him, "You're not going to die, you're going home, cheer up, think of us poor cunts, we're not out of it yet." There's no pleasing some people, Barrie.'

Soon after that, the gunships arrived and the rockets and miniguns started ripping through the canopy and thumping into the bunker system. Long before they'd finished, darkness fell and they switched on arc lamps and continued in shifts until our ears became deadened to the shockwaves. They finally withdrew and the artillery began. Salvo after salvo crashed in, whistling in the eerie personal way of all incoming shells, seeming to come straight at your own head. We were only metres from the fall of shot, but no injuries were sustained. Some shell casings whoof-whoof-whoofed through the air above us, but fell clear. It was a deafening, flashing, earth-trembling night, one I find difficult to picture clearly now. But it must still be vivid in the minds of those above us in the bunkers—those that survived it.

This encounter was the one most of us felt could have been our undoing. We'd hit bunker systems before, several as well defended as this. But OC had been in sole command. He used his platoons as intelligence, pawns to probe and assess the enemy numbers, then if the odds were against us, he'd withdraw them and call in the fire support. With him out of the picture, Duntroon's desire for recognition got entangled with Tizzy's command of the situation. A command that for months had wrestled exclusively with supply, administration and bureaucratic wrangling. Confronted with a large enemy force in extremely adverse terrain, and urged on by a second-in-command there supposedly to assist him, he took a while to get his balance. Our platoons were committed to an impossible position for too long. The leadership had been a bit rusty and top-heavy for a while.

So much for the officers. This day belonged to the little men. Sixty-odd men, and that's being truthful; twenty-odd new ones, inexperienced, young, poorly trained and vulnerable. Flung into the path of a war few had chosen, and commanded by a nice guy and by a kid who was keen for glory. We, you and I, lie in a vortex and watch men do what they don't wish to do. And do they do it! Forget Big Mick, Pigpen, Sharkey, Tank, and Pete for the moment. I'm talking about every other average member. None of the men engulfed in the mayhem metres above me beyond the low ridge withdrew—they stuck it out. Those whose wounds rendered them useless were dragged out. By the time the company harboured around me for the night they were utterly spent. Eyes like zombies. Pete had ordered an end to this madness and I believe he saved the lives of more than just those he dragged clear and tended. I witnessed just about every form of heroism imaginable that afternoon, and hope I never have to see the like again.

But when first you look up and see that wide red river roaring past and golden suns bursting everywhere and everything upside down, and realise this could be it . . . it is fucking orgasmic!

At first light The La The La and Dave crept out to locate the scout's body, then came back to organise a bigger party to secure the area so it could be retrieved. Tank and Dave had tried the previous night under cover of pouring rain, darkness and shellfire, but without success. This time I tagged along as Pete's offsider. I had to see this killing ground. We walked the thirty metres or so up the rise to the lip where the ground flattened out, and there was no missing it—it was a ball park. There was no vegetation left. Pete and I could see one of our sentries across the clearing, fifty metres away, leaning against what remained of a bunker. A few metres back towards us The La The La and Dave were kneeling over the body of the outstretched scout, quietly talking. In the early grey light the area had the appearance of a Japanese garden, raked grey gravel bordered by twisted, strangely pruned trees. The gravel was ankledeep grey punk, plants and saplings ground to powder by constant gunfire. People had lived through this; moved through it; survived, hidden in the blinding swirl, deafening noise, and the fear of the storm the guns stirred up. And not a single spent cartridge to be seen. The Viet Cong had collected them during the night, all the while under artillery bombardment, to recharge for future battles.

The scout lay face down with his arms stretched out before him. He was clothed but his webbing, weapon, pack and wristwatch were gone. So were his dogtags. There were no rings. Much as we would leave him if he were our kill. Except his boots had been taken, I suppose they were a rare prize for a ragged army. Maybe we'd bury him, we usually held the ground. Pete said, 'Let's get him on the litter and fuck off. He can't go back like that and I'm not doing it here.' The body was carried back to CHQ and Pete went to work.

'Hey . . . any squeamish bastards turn away and hum.'

I watched Pete kneel over the body lying face up with the arms locked solid in the position of surrender.

'Hum!' . . . *Krrackk*.

'One to go.'

I turned away, but heard the second *Krrackk* before I could pick a tune. Then Pete covered the body with a hootchie and the bearers carried him towards the LZ.

They passed right by where I stood. My riflesight snagged on the hootchie and dragged it clear of the head. I saw a strong young face framed with wavy black hair, black arched brows and the most penetrating sapphire-blue eyes I have seen. Pete hadn't closed them. I had never seen his face before; perhaps he was a new member. I put the covering back in place and the body was carried down to the chopper. Wait on, I did know him! He was one of Dave's intake. Not well, didn't see much of him, but I knew him. He just didn't look the same in death.

After that was over and done with, we linked up very warily with our third platoon, who'd been separated from us overnight, upstream in ambush. Keeping in constant radio contact until we sighted them. Then we circled around the bunker system and came in from the far side. Time to check out the spoils, but I'd dropped well back with Pete, Brian, OC's batman and a radio operator. Plus three or four platoonies who needed to settle their jitters down a bit before they pointed a rifle again. It was a very long day, sitting in the heat waiting for everything to be found. There was a blast of gunfire nearby. 'Hello, there's another woopsy,' said the radio operator. 'Hang on . . . it's OK, nobody hit.'

Finally we got the call for my group to enter the company night harbour, about a kilometre away. Thank God for that. OK, who's the scout? Stupid question. It was my turn. These blokes were all-in. So we headed off on the given bearing, through burnt-out country, with smouldering ashen trees overhead, an occasional glimpse of green foliage in the far distance, a wisp of smoke curling from a knothole in the trunk of a small fallen tree. I could describe every inch of that journey right up to seeing the pink-tinged faces of the gun picquet through the dense cover—just after they'd seen me. I counted the group in and truly appreciated then just a little of the pressure a scout contended with daily.

It was a big bunker system we'd encountered, and mercifully everyone had fled, taking the dead and dying with them. We got credited with some kills, but the exercise killed Tizzy's career. Duntroon succeeded him.

OK on the ledge, are you? Move this way a bit, you're blocking the door gunner's arc. God, I love choppers! Big clattering freedom birds hoisting you up. Up out of the callous caste that relentless fear culls you herdlike into, glazing over your humanity; free momentarily from all the bone-grinding, mindless, futile toil. Look at the forest down there. Trees in a new guise, soaring up at you from the mountains. There's a stream, green and rushing. Is that where we've just been, do you think? Does it matter? Does it change anything? Of course it doesn't. But it changes a few perspectives.

All you could gain from this action was recognition. Sharkey was recognised with a Military Medal, below a Victoria Cross. Everyone knew that what he'd done was special. One of lead platoon's section commanders won one too, though his name wasn't being talked about. A few of the company cynics suggested that his earlier acceptance into officer training might have influenced the decision, but I wasn't one of them. I had no idea how he got named.

Duntroon, for all his connivance, didn't even get an MiD— a Mentioned in Despatches, the lowest award for valour or distinguished service, and not a medal, but a little bronze cluster worn on the ribbon of the service medal for the tour you won it on. Pete went unrecognised too—for dragging Diggers out of a withering storm of gunfire and rockets, and seeing them right, for reaching the fallen scout so that the men would snap out of battle frenzy and respect an order. No one made him do any of this. Medics are not ordered, they do their job. No one tells them what to do. But Pete had said 'It's just a fucking nick', and an officer who'd had a scheme to have a probable MiD bumped up to a Military Cross all silver and blue, through bravely soldiering on while wounded, got a fart in the face instead.

We didn't acknowledge Pete's actions to his face. You don't stroke your friends—that's what awards are for. Many of us assumed he'd get the VC in the normal run of events. Pete never mentioned the day. I gnawed away at this day for years. Over what people said out of context, straight off the shoulder. 'He shouldn't have left the gun, wounded or not. He could at least have flung the fucking bolt into the scrub.' Who Big Mick was referring to as 'he' I didn't find out. I overheard it while not included in the conversation. We had lost a machine gun to the enemy that day. Soldiers *must* retrieve weapons; the enemy can kill you with them. I thought it might be a reference to Pete—that maybe I'd become confused; that the dead man Pete reached was actually the gunner, and he'd failed to retrieve the weapon. 'Nah. it was the scout—Ray,' said Lenny. 'Used to pester me to teach him the tricks. He *started out* a gunner, a good gunner. I told that stupid cunt we shoudn't a been there.'

'Who? Ray?'

'Nah, that Lieuy! Fuckin' Godsgift! I told him what was up there. Just looked at me. I said, "Take a look, that's where you hootchied the other night!" but he couldn't see.'

Couldn't see we'd been there some days before, left a couple of bodies floating downstream and on closer inspection seen there was something big above us.

Duntroon knew that.

Why were we there, without proper support in place, if we knew what we were heading into? Think it through for yourself. I don't tell you things just to hear the sound of my own voice.

Here we go, the Dat coming into view. Shower, clean clothes, a meal—hit the piss with friends—heaven. You know, you may have to do this for real one day, or maybe your kids will. And it's likely you will not want to kill. For a variety of reasons: fear, moral reasons, maybe just too hard a life, no opportunity to get on. The job of medic is often suggested as a good option—honourable, caring, don't have to kill anyone. Be very sure you're up to it. I couldn't do it, haven't got either the guts or the unquestioning love of our species. It's way out of my reach.

Right, quick muster in front of the Q Store and we're clear. CSM says: 'CO's parade at the parade ground 8.30 tomorrow morning. Parade here 8 am, pressed greens, boots polished, dress belts, lanyards, rank on, for inspection. Dismissed!'

What now? Somehow we get enough bits together in the morning to pass muster, and off we march in column of three over to the footy field. Who're all these bastards? Shit, it's the rest of the battalion, they look different. Ah, there's Bert sticking his tongue out at me; some things never change. We're towards the back and settled, at ease. Up steps our fearless leader.

'Battalion, yarp yarp yarp current brigadier yarp yarp excellent leadership yarp yarp ending tour of duty yarp yarp new brigadier yarp yarp kiss kiss yarp wants to see how an infantry battalion deploys in the field yarp . . .'

'He should *fucking well know* what a battalion looks like! He's a brigadier, isn't he?' Big Mick voices the weak point in the argument. Everyone below sergeant howls with laughter, of course, but Mick didn't intend it to be funny. CSM cruises by and quietly suggests he save the wisdom for those who don't understand, but doesn't push the issue. CO hides behind his dark shades like a squat blowfly until the ranks die down to sporadic titters and then finishes reciting his exciting little scheme. 'We have volunteered to deploy in the field in full defensive position for four days from tomorrow yarp yarp yarp . . .'

Fucking arselicker. We went, don't worry about that. Dug covered pits, patrolled our perimeters, the whole bullshit, waiting for our leader to come out and see what we did for a living. The prick never turned up in our lines, we wouldn't know what he looked like. The only good thing about the whole laughable exercise was that we were in a very safe area. No chance of spotting enemy where we were sent to give him his demo. There were two other battalions currently out in the field, engaged in legitimate Ops, who could have shown him what he needed to see. Real shooting, and bodies too if he chose to stay long enough.

The new Brigadier's nickname was Blackjack. Maybe it described an affliction. Can't say, I never saw his shadow, any more than I'd seen his predecessor's. Ah well, let's take a break and I'll tell you about a certain TAOR. Know your own way around the boozer now, do you? Good. I'm getting pissed out of my brain with Pete and Dave tonight; need the company of people I'm closest to. You'll be okay. Drink with Peaches if you're smart, he's been through all this shit before. See you!

Chapter 12

AND HOW ARE YOU FEELING THIS TIME . . . It's not a question, I know the answer. Like you want to croak. It's not my fault you didn't drink goffers—that's what you have to ask for if you want a soft drink here. 'Can I please have an orange goffer . . .?' But where's the fun in that? You didn't seem to mind, you drank out of Big Mick's hat. Don't bullshit, I was right next to you. Pigpen went at you with his strangler's hands, thought you were me—or took a softer option, but I doubt that. Want to know what you did then? Okay, my lips are sealed. Don't get edgy, every bastard got a bit wrung out last night. Woofer had another crack at 'toe the line' with Big Mick; did pretty well for a while, too. Patto slept in a pit. Fell down the fucking thing through a different form of stupidity this time. Dave fell asleep in the chair on radio picquet, again. Slept through Pete's shift so Pete woke me up for mine, the prick. Big Mick's on a charge. Fell asleep in his cot with a fag in his mouth, set fire to his mattress. Cunning bastard charged himself straight off. Now he'll be prosecutor as well as defence counsel, so he should beat the charge.

It's now the morning after the morning after and I wish it was still yesterday, I give you the tip. I'm in deep shit. We're standing in a line in front of a flimsy little prefab hut. I'm about ninth in line and certainly in no hurry to be next. This is Task

Force Headquarters and I'm here to explain why I fucked up. Oh good, the line's moved up one. See the little black krait with the red and yellow bands around it, up ahead? Too late. Well, at least you can hear my story before it becomes official.

We'd just got back from the brigadier's little look around in the dark, dark jungle, and I was warned out for the next night's TAOR patrol. That's why I sought Pete out. I'd had a gutful of being fucked around—like the rest of the crew—and Pete was safe company if you knew how to handle him. I was to lead this patrol. You know that a TAOR is a tactical area of responsibility. Phuoc Tuy province is carved up into six or more little boxes so the brass can stick coloured pins in a map and decide which colour to support on a bad day. But to an infantryman a TAOR is a defensive patrol made outside the Dat to see that no one's out there waiting to get in here and start shooting at us. We have a funny way of going about it, but you should be used to that by now. Hang on, here comes a jeep.

Two sergeant majors bounce out of it in tigersuits, carrying over-and-under guns, barge past the queue and go straight in the door of the prefab hut to have their say. These guys wait for no one. Don't know whether they're being briefed or debriefed, this lot. They're SAS. You can tell with us—if we're being briefed we're in clean greens, if being debriefed we're covered in shit and all raggedy-arsed from weeks in the field. SAS are harder to pick.

Many of their Ops were overnighters: into the chopper, land, walk 500 metres. Whoops!! Is that Nog carrying a gun? Chopper out. 'Go get 'em grunts!' So then *we'd* go out. To do this reconnaissance work the SAS had to have camouflaged clothing, and weapons like the over-and-under—an Armalite with an M79 grenade launcher fitted to it. The M79 was a little cannon mounted up similar to a short shotgun. It fired a grenade about the size of a hen's egg. We used it too, but we slung it over our back as a second weapon. Our job was to stay in contact with the enemy till we killed them, so of course we had all the time in the world to scrabble around behind our necks for the M79, while the shit flew all around. Priority radio bands and hot and cold running choppers to get them out 'right fucking *now!*' completed the SAS boys' back-up support. It was tense work being out in the field in a group of five to ten men, looking for signs of enemy, so time back at base was generous for this lot. They were given only thirty metres of the Dat's outer perimeter to guard; one gun picquet was all they needed. One squadron at a time was based here, so it wasn't a hard life—plenty of hands to man the gun. They didn't do TAORs as we did. What they did were called Ops or Missions, and they seemed to find enemy on them easily enough. We did TAORs on our own time and only saw villagers.

The SAS were bloody good soldiers, no question. They were all volunteers, most had previous experience in other fighting Corps, mainly infantry. Regs. And they had to pass a tough selection course, the emphasis on physical capabilities. Their training was superintensive and protracted. They didn't have to accept whoever the draft dragged up willing or not, as infantry did. They didn't storm bunker systems after dragging arse for weeks and weeks through the scrub either. They didn't have it too hard—don't let their own headlines fool you. What would you rather do: find the enemy and piss off, or come in after them and deal with the situation?

Scared about patrolling in small numbers? Many infantry platoons numbered eighteen or nineteen for months at a time; three sections of six men each. And they patrolled *as sections*, and carried less firepower. It's a matter of what you view as elite, I suppose. You walk a damn sight less in SAS, don't get shot at nearly as much, have much more time in base, and everyone thinks you're a hero. Take your choice.

I'm here because I led the TAOR . . . we jumped off the truck and I gave the boys the orders for the night. Briefed them on where we were to go, and what we were to do. Cave-in was there, the rest were platoonies; Fuzz was radio operator. We were to patrol 7000 metres towards the foothills, set up an ambush, then call in artillery fire to our front and walk it back towards us in steps until it was hitting 200 metres in front of us. Then a bigger barrage would drop in. This ploy was intended to flush the enemy towards you so you could brass up the fleeing survivors.

That was the theory. Sometimes it might have worked. The briefing didn't go down too well with the boys. It was no surprise to me, that's why I'd held off briefing them until we were out there. Seven thousand metres was seven hours careful patrolling in daytime. We'd got seven thousand on the return trip too, that's fourteen hours. There was twelve hours of dark, and the barrage was set to be fired at 10 pm. It was 6.30 pm now. The likelihood of marching into an enemy ambush out here was remote, remote by our standards anyway, but a possibility. What was quite likely was that some smart bastard'd put a few mines down or set some other sort of trap. Worse, there were other patrols out there—you'd get a clerk navigating for a patrol of base wallahs at night and you might meet up with them without recognising them. Then there were the ARVN recruits operating trial runs out of Heavyweight. Some of those kids wouldn't have a fucking clue.

'What are you going to do then?' Fuzz asked.

'Sort out a plan.'

And we did. Fuzz, the scout and I agreed on a spot on the map 2500 metres away in the direction we'd been ordered, and which we knew to be a fair defensive position, and we struck out for it. Got there just after nine, set up ambush, checked that no one stuck out too much, then Fuzz and I radioed in and told base where we were and got the artillery organised. On cue, in it thumps, big red flashes, and I walk it down to where they wanted it. It was a buzz once you got used to the sound of the shells whistling overhead. Apart from the fact that they were dropping 4000 metres away from our location—when we should have been right near the point of impact—the exercise went off beautifully. After that we went into fifty-fifty watch and pulled the pin about 5.30 am, so we could meet the truck back at the spot we'd been dropped at.

So, I'm standing in line now, waiting to explain why I didn't reach my objective. Why I disobeyed a lawful command. I could have lied about it, called in a shonky location, said I was in position when I wasn't. But there's an issue at stake here and I mean to fix it.

Here we go, my turn. Some pale indifferent corporal's directing me to the debrief room and closing the door on me. Not much to see. Bare room, ten by ten, grey metal desk, what's in the drawers? Fuck all. No view, the one small window overlooks a bare wall. Two chairs, a straightbacked metal one and a padded swivel chair the other side of the desk. Tempting.

OK, play the silly game out. I wish I'd brought a book. After an eternity a sergeant walks in and sits down.

'How are you, Corporal Crowley?'

Things are looking up. This bloke used to be a sergeant in my company when I first joined the battalion; fair type. So this is where he ended up.

'You didn't make the position last night. Why?'

'Seven thousand metres is too much. Company policy is we don't move at night.' This was true, but we broke the policy frequently, when OC was there to direct it.

The sergeant comes back with: 'Policies change. Another patrol went out last night—they covered a similar distance. Any other reason?'

'Tell 'em to get fucked.'

That finishes the interview. The sergeant doesn't take it in a personal way.

'Well, leave it at that for now. Report back to your unit.'

That's what you get when dickheads who know nothing about field work get to command. This is Blackjack's doing: new broom, new ideas, not a fucking clue. This chief could prove worse than the last mongrel.

I found out who'd led the other patrol, the successful one—good old Lance Jack from Long Hai. One of his patrol came out to our boozer that night to see me.

'Did you cut the TAOR? That fuckwit Kiwi cunt had us running like maniacs to get there. Fuck, I should have shot him . . . What's happening with you?'

'Dunno yet, still waiting for the other boot to drop.'

I was shocked at how quickly the story had reached him. I'd been ducking for cover and being real quiet about it. But nothing happened, no one mentioned it to me again. I didn't lead another TAOR, but I went out on a few and they were never 7000 metres, rest assured.

That's the advantage if you're in an elite unit like SAS—you don't have to stick your neck out to complain about abuse, you're elite, you're covered, it just doesn't happen. When you're down the bottom like me, it's a bastard to stick up for what's fair, and I'm still surprised I did it. I don't like trouble. But sometimes you have to get disagreeable.

You don't want to go through another TAOR, do you?

Pretty simple stuff. The best part of them is coming in at first light. The countryside is lovely out from our sector. Undulating golden fields right up to the low mountain range in the distance—the one we just shelled. The sun has a warm golden glow then. You watch the villagers come to life and start out on their day's journey in spindly ox carts. A water buffalo pulling a heavy dray, or heading for the paddies with a small boy perched on its neck, steering it. A copse of leafy trees by the road, a small forest away in the distance. Vietnam is a beautiful country, definitely worth fighting for. Don't let the old black and white footage fool you, it's not that grim.

Funny . . . the word grim's just jogged my memory. About this time, Lenny took the chiefs on. Not like me—lodge a complaint and hope for the best—I mean *took them on*. Let's take another look at Lenny. I call him a blackfella because he is, there's no escaping it. He's very Australian. I should know—I'm an outsider and very observant. This bastard is straight up. Brave, amusing if you like Aussie humour, loyal, resilient, tough as an old boot come crunch time; and holds an unshakeable belief in justice for its own sake. Lenny's Aboriginality just gives it all a keener edge, an intangible solidity, a spirituality that you don't often feel from others. Here's some of my memories of Lenny.

Take the day at Corps training when our platoon were staring blankly at an empty, flat, windswept grassy field. Lenny saw five 'enemy' riflemen hiding in various parts of it—in shallow gullies, behind rocks, in folds in the ground. In fact there were six, we found out—we walked right through the field.

Then there was the night Lenny decked a bunch of Palmer Street hoons. What a night *that* was. I'd gone up to the Cross in Sydney with a mate of mine, Robbie, for a look around. Robbie was a smooth bastard with the women. Anglo-Indian— the son of a wealthy general, Indian Army. Usually we went to restaurants, jazz clubs or good nightclubs on our leave nights. This particular night he wanted to check out Palmer Street just out of Kings Cross, Australia's equivalent of the Reeperbahn. It was a narrow road lined with two-storied terrace houses packed with whores intimating that they accommodated every perversion. The downstairs windows were lined with the proof

—flashing thighs and tits, pouting faces, gyrating buttocks, all the bullshit come-ons. The upstairs windows were curtained for action. Robbie spots this *fucking* big mama, and I mean big. Two front teeth missing, tits like watermelons, thighs like a Sumo wrestler's. 'I feel like a bit of flesh tonight,' he said, and he was at it like a mad rat. I was left standing aghast and alone in the street—and it was crowded. Yank servicemen, some of our lot, the rest mostly twisted cunts, thugs and thrillseekers. One of our platoon jostled past saying, 'Lenny's in a blue'. Good luck, Lenny. 'Hey, Robbie! Finished yet? Lenny's in a fight.'

Robbie came machining down the stairs. Thumper followed him halfway down—he must have made an impression. Mutt on her like a Persian cat glaring through her gaping wrap. But we were already off through the gawking crowd.

We got to the scene just in time to see Lenny's head bobbing between two big coppers, then into the wagon he went, and off. Crowd milling everywhere, excitement still buzzing all around. Alan, a hardcase Sydneysider from our platoon, was waving to us so we headed over. 'Did ya fucking see that? Jesus, that bugger can hit. Look . . . look at the cunts!' I counted eight hoons stretched out on the road and the pavement, whores trying to revive them, to help them inside. They were needed, they were the whore's protectors. Lenny walked into barracks late next morning, calm, unmarked, and had a nap. The Army had claimed him quick smart. Otherwise he'd have been fucked. The cops wouldn't let you beat up common paying criminals and get away with it, especially if you were a blackfella.

Fuzz came to my tent at the Dat one morning, accompanied by a couple of other platoonies. It'd been drizzling non-stop so there wasn't much work going on. Wouldn't stop for a beer, just wanted to see me.

'Lenny's in the compound, want to come and see him?'

I'd seen Lenny two or three times since Hong Kong. A beer at the boozer, a quick nod out in the field. Hadn't kept up. Like every other bastard, too tied up.

'Why the compound?' I asked.

'Dunno. He's been accused of brassing up monkeys, says his eyes are fucked.'

Fuzz was walking with downcast eyes. The red muddy road was slippery. When we reached the compound, not far up the road from us, I saw Lenny standing in a gap in the bamboo that grew around the barbed wire fence, watching us approach. I'd come unprepared. Fuzz and the others had cigarettes, gossip; I'd only brought myself. All I remember of the conversation is Lenny saying, 'They're shipping me out soon'.

He was calm, relaxed. Didn't need us to bring anything else, he was OK. Across the compound, leaning inside the gate, was the big fat RP who had thrown the apple at the little kid on our way to the Dat. Smirking. I hoped to Christ he'd try the cop act on Lenny, right then. I'd have shot the cunt, after Lenny'd decked him. The fury I felt! Then I saw RP Hipslops standing quietly outside the fence and for once the sight of a good cop depressed me. Raise the red haze of insanity, Barrie. We shook hands with Lenny through the wire, he said, 'Take care,' and we walked back towards our lines, to whatever came next.

What had happened here? The best visual scout in the country didn't like to shoot people. *There's* a problem. Scouts are hitters, they don't fuck around, but in truth Lenny did. He could have led us to fifty personal kills and not risked the company. Just didn't see the point in it all—he'd seen through this war straight off. He could shoot as truly as any we had. He'd see you before you cleared the grass, know where you'd be because you were living off the land, but he didn't shoot to kill unless he had to. He always saw first, fired a burst over their heads; gave them a chance. That's what brassing up monkeys means. Giving comfort to the enemy. He was charged with an AD, an accidental discharge. 'Bullshit!' said Lenny. 'That's where I aimed.' I suspect that's where the bad vision story crept in, but what we're talking about here is lack of reception. Once it reached that point, OC was backed into a corner. He had to hand the case up. Lenny offered no deals, no crazy stunts. He'd said 'Get fucked. That's as far as I go'.

Lenny went to the compound, then went home and got his career trashed. Copped the whole Boong Act. But initially he retained pride in the service he'd given his country—he felt he'd served it truly—until in a rage he threw his medals at the organiser of the Anzac Day parade in his home town, and walked away from it all. Why? Because the organiser refused to recognise him. Lenny was made out to be a lead scout who wouldn't kill unless he had to. Hang that title on *me* baby, and my bed would never be cold or my fridge empty. My attitude's no different to that of most field soldiers. I wonder what that prick of an organiser learnt from *his* time in Vietnam? Not what it takes to be a soldier—you can quote me on that.

On our way back to the company lines a massive flight of B52s passed overhead, bearing west into the sunset.

'Where are they going?'

'Cambodia, Barrie.'

'What for?'

'To bomb it.'

Fuzz was the only one kind enough to tell me what every other bastard in the country knew. The Yanks were blasting allies into ashes. Ten years later, in '79, the news broke worldwide. Did I feel like a real shithead! I thought everyone knew Cambodia had been bombed back into the stone age and just didn't care. How do you get away with pulling a stunt like that? Suppressing any hint of such a massive, protracted operation—when we had the free press crawling all over the place looking for news. Go ask a fucking journalist! I can't answer you.

Fuzz also told me something about Lenny. He described a day Lenny had called a halt to his platoon's progress. The platoon commander and one or two other Diggers had gone ahead to try and verify what Lenny had seen.

'What's up, Lenny?'

'Big crowd went through here, we'll catch 'em soon if we don't watch out. Too many for us.'

'Where? What d'you see?'

'See the bent stems, leaves. Blokes picked things on the way through, dropped some, damp side of that leaf showing; big party to have so many useless bastards.'

'Bazz, I fuckin' saw it. Everything he said. Like a battalion'd gone through. I turned round to tell the next bloke in the line, turned back, and I couldn't see any of it! I'd lost the lot.'

I already knew about this ability of Lenny's, but Fuzz describes it better than I do.

I felt utterly alone for the first time in my life as I headed back to the tent. Not because of the obliteration of Cambodia currently taking place. I couldn't imagine then that the Yanks would go as far as they did. Who could? Not me, I didn't have the imagination or personal experience. Nor because of what awaited Lenny—tough as it was going to be for him, he had made his decision, he knew in his heart what was coming. And again, I plead ignorance. I'm not a blackfella. No, it was because I realised with a dreadful certainty that none of us here counted at all. It seemed to me that there were only two classes of people on earth: cunts and the shit. And I didn't want to be either. And I didn't want them around me.

I met Lenny about eighteen months later, one night in a city street in Perth. I was out of the army now and on the town with two old schoolmates.

'How the fuck are ya, Barrie?' Lenny's lurching full tilt across the street, one leg in a hip-high plaster cast, a front tooth missing from his dazzling grin. We collided in a bearhug at the kerb, nearly went arse up over his cast. As we settled down I told him 'Yep, I'm out too'. He told me he'd been injured in a car accident. 'Some cunt ran me over and fucked off.' We started making plans for a beer. Then we noticed our mates, standing off. The atmosphere crackled with static, the crowd gathering interest. We realised where we were. He shook my hand and we parted, promising to catch up soon, and I watched him hobble away into the crowd with his friends.

'Where do you know him from?'

'Old army mate.'

It was only recently I met Lenny again, but from that day on when people talked about 'boongs' in my presence I said, 'I knew one in the army, called Lenny. He is a leader to his people.' I had no cause to say it, no supporting argument, didn't do it to shut them up, I just said it. Time takes care of the heart . . .

I didn't feel like going back to the tent just then, after all. Dave was off somewhere and the other two who shared the tent I didn't know well. I sat up at the old Nugget for a bit, propped on a crate that was probably once my bedside table. Some bed frames and the locker were still there. I just sat for a while and let my head spin. But the advantage of going the full tour is that you get answers to some of your questions over time—if you're patient, and take people for what they are.

There was another face in that scene at the compound with

Lenny, a bloke called Makka. He'd been standing next to Hipslops, with a funny look on his face. Makka was one of Dave's intake, a Nasho. Hefty bastard, Scots origin way back, came from somewhere near Lenny's hometown—a small country town in Western Australia. He'd been a section platoonie with Pigpen's platoon when we arrived in country, had gone through all the same shit, gave it away shortly after Peaches threw the gun down; took a job as an RP. Claimed he had a back problem. Fair enough, we all had that. Promotion went with the new job, up to Lance Jack. Coppers always do better, otherwise what's the point? I wrote him off as a cunt! In fact, most of the company cooled towards him. Not because he left the field, but because he became an RP. It was he who drove down and arrested Lenny. Fuck me, he was a close friend of Lenny's! There's an RP for you! And in one sense that's true—why favour your mates? But through his involvement I came to get a clear view of what I could only guess at, sitting alone at the Nugget.

Lenny had been sent up to the RPs with a chit. Quite a few of our field troops ended up in the compounds during the tour for jacking up, not wanting to continue. They were branded cowards, weak cunts, and no doubt some of them were; but many were like Lenny and Peaches, driven by other motives. Didn't matter to our system. Our system was to court martial them, and if they wouldn't respond to counselling and punishment they were scrapped, then discharged, branded useless. Unofficially, the RPs had a duty to treat these people like garbage, and they did, right from the start. Wake-up call was a blast from a firehose and a good kicking if you didn't like it. Humiliation, brutality, all the tricks of the trade.

'This man's been beaten up, Corporal?'

'Sorry sir, he went apeshit, had to restrain him. Snow's got a sore thumb from the bastard.'

'Hmm . . . Lay your charge then, I'll deal with it.'

Coppers! When Makka drove out of our company lines with Lenny sitting quietly beside him, Lenny held a chit in his hand, issued by OC and almost certainly seconded by CSM. A chit meant 'Guilty as charged, we send him to you for processing, but we still recognise him. Don't fuck with him!' Chits were rare, a sign of respect.

And that's why Makka had that funny look on his face. He was glad that Lenny had the chit, of course, because it made his job easier on his mind. But he was a bit pissed off too. He'd secretly harboured the hope of seeing Lenny ripping these arseholes apart when they tried the cunt act on him. I never did hear if Lenny used the chit or not, but personally I doubt it.

Well, I feel game to go back to the tent now. Our leadership's still strong, I guess it'll hold out.

It was also around this time Peaches thought about taking up the gun again. He hadn't touched one since the time he'd left the Op. He'd only ever carried a rifle on TAORs. He had to do two or three of these a week when we were out on Ops. There was no way of avoiding them. Not that it mattered, there was little chance of having to shoot anyone. After coming out on the chopper at the Hill his resolve was starting to weaken. I guess he felt angry at seeing the company sliced up, and guilty that he hadn't been on deck to help. Gunners like him were rare.

He didn't go into OC yelling, 'I wanna fuckin' *kill* again, let me at the cunts!' but he *was* thinking about it. Yet he delved too deep. As a mate, he became a cranky bastard some days, seeming to want you to punch him in the head. And all this over whether he should go back in the field again or stay out. This was Peaches' real crazy period. Who would consider going out at this stage of the tour unless ordered to? I suspect that's the main reason Peaches stayed a blowfly until the end; not even a dickhead wanted to be beside a bloke who thought he actually wanted to be out there. Definitely not healthy. And we were fast running out of dickheads, given the ruthless rate at which Ronnie and a few other headkickers were operating.

I was drinking in the tent with Dave one day. The slides Kelsie had taken for me with my camera last time we were in had come back in the mail. Dave asked me to 'hurry up and open the fucking thing!' because there might be one of him in it. We sat over a beer looking at the slides through a hand viewer. All taken at the boozer; every bastard pissed. Pigpen strangling me, Dave leering across the crown and anchor table,

Big Mick singing, a blurred shot of someone's elbow, the usual thing.

'Who are *these* cunts?' Dave wanted to know.

'Let's have a look . . . They're the job lot, last batch of Reos.'

'I don't know these cunts, never set eyes on 'em. Look like a bunch of poofters.'

'Gimme another look . . . Yeah, you shovelled half this lot on to the choppers a week or so ago, they were RTA'd.'

Dave was right, though, they did look like a bunch of poofters, some of them, anyway. The group of about sixteen sat all huddled together in the boozer. It'd been hard for them to settle in at the Dat. Nearly everyone around was bigger and six to eight months crazier than them, and looked it too.

'Look at this Dave! Bottom right corner.'

There at the edge of the bench sat one of the Diggers, his arm intertwined with that of another Digger sitting on the floor at his feet. Gazing tenderly at one another. Not the sort of form we were used to seeing.

'I'll be fucked. There's some among us!'

Dave stared hard for a moment, then carried on looking for a better shot of himself, but there wasn't one.

We'd never seen evidence of homosexuals at the front. Sure, some blokes liked to get a look at Horse's slug when he showered. We shrugged it off as jealous curiosity. I'd have liked to've seen it too, given some of the stories I was told about it. If anyone *had* been caught in the act we'd have heard—it was a pretty small community, with not a lot to talk about. Yet here they were, doing the job, taking the risks along with us. That changed my view a bit on who's who.

Dave and I go off to a village for a while now, on a mini training team. Want to come along? You won't miss much here at the Dat—the next Op isn't too exciting, just unrelenting hard slog and a few shots at enemy, usually running too fast to be hit. Come and hide with us. Dave's OK, I think. Anyway, he's fun. Have you learnt anything yet? It's just that, if you haven't, you won't make much of the rest of the trip.

Chapter 13

PHUOC LOI OPENED IT ALL UP for me to see. It wasn't Captain discussing it with me, it wasn't Dave thinking ahead on good intelligence, it wasn't Peaches, who was well informed, describing it to me. It was *me* out here. With no one able to tell me not to go somewhere. Scary place Phuoc Loi, in some ways, but I got around a lot, mostly against my will. Good way to see a country, but I don't recommend it. I'm timid, I like to stand under trees and watch out for cunts cruising by.

Phuoc Loi was down near the coast, just north of Vung Tau, reached by typical roads and drab countryside. When you were driven there by Dave, all in a shitty because in his view the two dickheads driving the Landrover in front were CMF and couldn't drive their finger up their own arse, you worried. Actually, there was nothing wrong with the driving; it was the leadership he was shitty with.

When Phuoc Loi bounced into view I thought: How beautiful the land on the far side of the village seems. And it's true. Past the village, the green paddy fields explode into facets of jade all the way to the green, pyramid-shaped mountain in the distance. The village is another vision entirely. Grey dusty road. Chooks—grey scraggly bantams and bald scaly-red bigger ones. Government adobe-style office on the left as you come in, raked with bullet holes, and shut. A structure of kiosk-like appearance on the right that looks modern. Fuck, here's another pothole. A few shacks. Then the camp gates are at the right—nothing special. A huge dusty crater stretching right under the gate, which consists of two high wooden frames stretched with strands of barbed wire. Two Nogs guarding it—they look like ARVN—and one in the gun bunker alongside. Two idlers picking their nose with the long nail they grow on their little finger just for that purpose.

A short, stocky bastard struts out of the weathered wooden shed on the left—his home it turns out—and the garrison commandant's ordering our entry. A bump and we're in, two Landrovers and a truck full of shit going back empty along with one of the Landrovers. We're dropped off smack in the middle of the compound.

Who's we? And what for? Glad you asked those questions. Told you you'd learn. Wish I could answer them for you. But I'll try.

Dave and I are part of a team of eight soldiers sent to the village to teach infantry skills to the Nogs and to give 'em a bit of discipline. This garrison's become a bit slack and it's in our territory. Our personnel include two sergeants, both CMF, which if you're not Australian means home guard, hobby soldiers. They head the mission. Head the mission! These two dreamers are over here for a bit of a look around for two or three months, then it'll be back to the quiet life, waiting for the medal in the mail. Below Dave and me there are four Diggers—two gunners and two number twos. They've been with us several months, which can mean two seconds or a fucking lifetime depending on how you view the Hill and one or two other shootouts. I'm supposed to act also as mission interpreter. We have a radio set and very restricted call times. It's going to be a bludge—just have to get these two sergeants sorted out. That is the extent of your briefing.

We're given the task of unpacking the shit and the sergeants are off with the Commandant sorting communications out. He can speak English slightly better than I can speak Vietnamese, which is a help. We've got an eight-man tent and camp stretchers, which pinch skin off your knuckles when you're getting them sprung but are heaven to sleep on. Gasoline pressure lanterns, we know them to be good. Aussie ten-man rations, they're more like the stuff you buy off the shelves. If you're infantry, they're good—put it that way. Sixty feet of bare, level dirt. No radio picquet, no gun picquet. Feet up, Barrie, have a fag! Brought some books and plenty of MPC. Life's been tougher than this.

The two sergeants represent their chosen fields, I suppose. The younger one is about 28: neat black hair, neat black moustache, average height. Clerk, bank johnny or beancounter. I see him in long socks and a scout hat. Doesn't speak much. The older one is mid-thirties: prune-headed, mouse-grey crewcut. Fucking hates me. Tradesman I guess, government worker probably; seems too slow to earn a dollar. Of the Diggers, I remember one vividly, a gunner. Same stamp as Peaches but of Irish descent. Don't know what his name is and what he did for a living, but I pick him as our best bet.

Dave breaks up the chain of command. Sergeants on one side, us survivors on the other. We get the Irish gunner and his mate—never play cards with Dave!—and all this while I'm flat on my back reading. Dave's off finding a cook when I fall asleep.

Next morning I wake with a morning glory, a bursting bladder, and nowhere to go. No crapper. I hit the wire perimeter and hose the dirt hard enough to test the mines. Quick fart. Where the fuck are we? Get a brew on, someone needs a shit, the sergeants go to talk with the commandant, and Dave and I get to organise the crapper. We are to sink a 44-gallon drum with a hole in the top into the turf, half surround it with a hessian screen, and dump in a bit of creosote. Fuck you two! We're going for a look around. Dave briefs the Diggers.

Opposite the commandant's shed is a big hut; oiled timber planks, corrugated tin roof. In front of that a ground-level well where the garrison draws water with a weighted bucket. This is the hub. In the mornings and at dusk the local troops squat around the well in thongs and khaki boxers, shooting the breeze, brushing their teeth, the backs of their throats, their tongues, and hawking, all without hurking their guts up. Good trick. The women draw water and go back inside the hut to cook. There are few children here, mainly toddlers. Have a quick peek inside. Open plan, hammocks strung up, a rug strung out here and there for privacy—seems you can fuck in a hammock. A few women tending little charcoal cooking stoves or little kids, a couple of off-duty soldiers swinging in hammocks. Better pull your head out. Dave reckon's there's a good sort in there, but I'm not going to comment, not going to give Dave any encouragement. Out at the gate we pull a face at the guards so they'll recognise us if we come back fucking fast, shooting and terrified, and off we go up the street for a look around.

The village is bigger than it looks. There are dusty lanes branching off here and there from the main road, houses half hidden among the vegetation. All the housing is traditional: weathered silver-grey wood and thatch, elevated on low pylons. No tin shanties anywhere. That means something over here. Tin shanties mean people fleeing to a safe haven, under Republic and Yank protection, theoretically.

This village is protected by a garrison of Provincial forces, locals trained in soldiering and positioned in a fort at the outskirts. The little kiosk is the village aid post. A medic—a Civil Aid rep or whoever—lobs into town now and again, dispenses a bit of help, then flees the place before nightfall. The garrison we are here to train are mainly local farmboys. The commandant is a lieutenant, late thirties, probably ARVN, switched on. They are properly uniformed, armed with US M1 carbines and the odd hunting rifle—but that's not too bad, not far below ARVN standard anyway. They have two or three machine guns around the perimeter of the fort, which are light enough to patrol with, but I can't guess what breed the guns are. Provincial Forces are widely regarded as being very poorly trained, undisciplined and slack.

Here we are, at the end of the village. The fort's just back up the road on our right, ricefields and mountains lie to our front, and the village store is on our left. This is a small rendered-brick shop with family accommodation behind it and a tacked-on wooden verandah at the front. It has a table and two chairs. It sells beer and has a view of all we need. Headquarters has been established!

Go up two wooden steps, across the verandah, push through the plastic fly curtain, and Asia smacks you in the face. Not much to the store, considering it's the only show in town. A small floor area for customers, a scored and battered wooden counter round three sides, rickety shelving right up to the ceiling behind. Our side of the counter is cluttered with kerosene and cooking oil drums, one of each with a handpump leaning in it, plus a couple of hessian bags full of dried beans or rice. On the counter there's an open barrel of salted fish, surrounded by bits and pieces, a spool of twine, scissors. On the shelves, all manner of goods. Small crude tin oil lamps, bolts of cloth, packets of tea in palm-leaf wrappers, tiny cans of mackerel in tomato sauce, packaged noodles, spices, coloured paper cubes of balms and quack remedies, iron woks, pots, chocolates, cigarettes—mainly Yank ration pack varieties—and garlic and chillies on strings. Around the counter there are two middle-aged adults, three old people, eight or nine kids ranging from 15 down. All fat, all ethnic Chinese, all smiling at a new opportunity. 'You want, we got, we open.'

Boom times had just hit the merchants of Phuoc Loi. They sold beer, local brew, Thirty Three brand. If you wanted it cold they poured it into a glass filled with chunks of ice. They sold noodles in spiced soup too—what more could you want? We sat on our terrace, at our table, quite a lot while we were here. Served by the eldest child, a 15-year-old slab of a girl; like the rest of the family, never destined to bloom. No conversation, just served. Suited us. No one bothered us much. This store was lucky to take twelve customers a day, and few brought a bag. Packet of cigarettes, fill a can of lamp oil, two salted fish and some tea, one soda. That was a fair afternoon. Most custom came from the garrison—they drew wages. Two dozen beers a day, prepared food, table service was a real bonanza.

We were very welcome, but no toilet was provided. That was a hassle. The camp was a couple of hundred metres away and you never knew, if you cruised in to take a piss some bastard might want you to do some work, especially this day. The crapper might not be finished. We had a look around at the back of the store. Not even a shrub for cover. Then we smelt the ammonia. It came from a hip-height enclosure, attached to the side of the store, containing a pig—a sow actually, judging by its long flaccid dugs—lying back farting quietly into its own slop. We initiated the custom of pissing on the pig. It was days before we noticed the gaggle of large-eyed faces staring at us from a small window high up in the wall of the store. Too late by then to concern ourselves with modesty. Anyway, these people out here had no TV, radio or newspaper—nothing but gossip to amuse them. No power, no school that I saw, no medical clinic, no fuck all. Just ricefields as far as you could see. The local village communities were not spenders. They supplemented their kitchen garden produce by swapping any surplus at roadside markets.

Get ten people squatting on the side of the road in the shade with some matting, some baskets of vegetables, eggs and poultry, and there's a market. Each village had one. The village women caught the bus down to the next village to exchange what they had for what others grew. The produce looked stunted and mean, compared to our own. Little tomatoes, shallots, chillies, mangoes, a green leaf vegetable I didn't know, bright yellow small bananas. But the fragrance from the wooden huts each evening was enticing.

We walked back to the fort around three, half pissed and drowsy. The crapper *wasn't* finished yet. There were the crew, the two sergeants included, sweating and heaving, shovelling and swearing. Fuck that. We slunk into the tent and got a bit of siesta. About five o'clock some bastard was shaking me awake. 'The Nogs are shitting in our crapper!'

'Really! Who gives a fuck?' I unglued the eyes, prised the tongue off the roof of the mouth; Dave was struggling off his cot to go take a look.

'Get your arse off there, ya little yella cunt!' Typical Queenslander, Dave. There was diplomacy out the fucking door straight off. What had we got left? The crapper was outside the wire, dug into a paddy bund. You had to walk out to it on a narrow wooden pier. The hessian modesty screen had been erected so close to the thunderbox you had to face towards the camp with your back to the fields. Brilliant. Ever had a shit with a cold thrill of fear arcing up and down your entrails the whole time?

No question, he was having a shit, squatting Asian-style, arse pointed our way. Three of his mates were scratching around outside, waiting for a go. None of them spoke English but they knew exactly what Dave had said. Didn't like it either. Still, it reflected the feelings of the rest of our group pretty well; they were ready to defend it. The rest of the camp was getting interested. I suggested we let it lie and walked away. Everyone settled down to a quiet seethe, our man finished his shit and they left. By next morning the drum had popped out of the ground—the groundwater level was too high. We had to three-quarter fill the thing with sand to get it back down. The locals didn't use it again, they had better—but the episode could have got lethal, just over a shit.

The two sergeants had organised a night ambush exercise with the garrison, out on fallow ground south of the village. Good idea that. Take unknown troops out into the field first, then see if they can fight. Dave went, and so did a gunner and his number two. The sergeants found a good spot, got the troops deployed, started to sprinkle our blokes out among them; typical training manual procedure. Dave suggested the method was inappropriate.

'Butt out!'

'Listen, shithead, you don't know these little cunts. I don't know these little cunts, but I know we're sticking together—fuck the manual. You lot, in here!'

The Diggers harboured together within the ambush, and when morning came they walked back to base alone. Every member of the garrison had slipped away in the night. Dave and I knew what the sergeants could not. They had only the official briefing to work from. They were not a part of the company, not really involved in this war, so they didn't one day hear Peaches say: 'That's the place those Kiwis went to a while back. Got brassed up in their beds. Three . . . four dead, the rest wounded. Something about the mountain . . . A regiment of Yank Rangers or Marines went up it, no one came down. Cunt of a place.' (That might have been when I gave Peaches the ring, to remember me by.) Dave had heard similar. The mountain certainly held a secret the Yanks didn't like. Every day a Yank fighter-bomber or a Cobra rocket ship, more often than not both, would fly by and thump fuck out of it with what they had and fly off again.

We took it easy after our first field exercise—we got some sense into the program and took the troops out in the daytime to go through basic training. First up I took a squad of about fifteen just outside the wire to show them how to use parachute flares.

'Know how to use these?' the older sergeant'd asked me.

'Yeah, sure.'

'Demo them one o'clock!'

Must be instructions on the box. Never used them before, of course, they weren't part of a grunt's kit. They were simple: a long aluminium cylinder, pull the cap off, put it on the other end, smack it with the heel of your hand, up went a beautiful sparkly flare that floated on a little parachute for a minute or two, trailing smoke. Immediate interest from the squad, hands up everywhere, wanting a go. Nine flares into fifteen troops is best left to fate. The winners smacked their flares off in turn and marvelled at the brightness. I felt sorry for the losers and offered them a crack at some M72 rockets that were also in the box, but no one was interested. One or two mimed the actions and someone else pointed out that there was no suitable target anyway, which was true; the flat land stretched to either nowhere or the mountain. This to me indicated good weapon knowledge. The Irish gunner picked up on it.

A couple of days later I took a much bigger squad, forty or so, out into the fallow ground for training on movement in various formations through open country. Arrowhead, column of two, pepperpot fire and movement, crawling, that sort of shit. I didn't know the Vietnamese terms for them, so I used hand signals. These little bastards knew it all: kept their spacing, changed formation without a jumble. Not easy in waist-high stubble with crumbling paddy bunds everywhere underfoot.

Two hours or so of this in the heat of the day and I've run out of variations, and it's getting tiring and boring. And a waste of time—these men are pretty well trained. No, better than that. The gunner's satisfied, he gets on my right, and we start back to the village in arrowhead, our backs to the mountain. Out of nowhere a big black Cobra drops from the sky in front of us, hovering. Christ, they're scary cunts! You never hear them till it's way too late. All you see is this narrow-gutted black body with its two huge rocket pods and the machine gun muzzles pointing at you, the rotor softly clipping the shimmering air above. The pilot's staring at us from behind dark shades. Young, strong, white; impassive. Can't see his co, he sits behind. I can see this bloke's hand on the tiller, that's where the button is.

We're at the halt, no signal. It's not my order, we await his judgement. He might be seeing an enemy force moving towards a friendly village, from the mountain behind. Three white faces in the crowd mean nothing out here. If he thinks he sees an enemy force, my gunner's got one burst, second guessing, or we're all dead. The pilot doesn't. He views the calm, disciplined troops; watches for an eternity, levitating just off the ground, arse end twitching; slowly raises a thumb. It's a close call. After a moment we crane our necks in time to see him plant his rockets into the mountain, then bank and head off. We do the same.

Some days later I was sitting on my arse having a brew with the sergeants, killing time until one o'clock, when Dave and I could get on the piss. Up came two of the garrison. They wanted me to go for a walk. A walk? I wasn't thrilled but the sergeants had things to do that didn't involve me, so I knew I'd have to lie to avoid the invitation. Their behaviour was totally out of character, we didn't fraternise with the garrison. Suppressing a host of conflicting emotions, I grabbed my webbing and crammed some canned rations in, found my rifle, and off we went. For a walk. Through the wire and out into the paddies. Everything was green and gold. In the paddies were people, mainly women—straw hats, black pants rolled up— fiddling around with the rice. Back in the distance, a hatless man in a rust-coloured shirt, bending to open and close sluices.

My guides introduced me to a man who lived in a hole in the side of a paddy bund. Stocky bastard with leathery skin, and brown teeth in a wide, creased smile. About 60 and greying. He offered me crabs and rice with tea, cooked on the bund, on a campfire set on a flat stone. The crabs were the size of bull ants, but had an exquisite flavour. The rice and the tea were good. He got me to lie in his bed. I'd said, 'Do you live there?' so he said, 'Sure, you try'. Then I gave him a pinch of my Drum. He rolled it into a soggy trumpet. I also gave him the canned shit I'd brought with me for lunch, and left before the taste of it soured his appreciation. A nod, a grin, a handshake.

'What was that about?' My guides didn't understand me.

Out of the ricefields and on to a road. A bus was stopping. The taller guide peered along the bus windows and then called us on board. A real old rattler: grating gears, worn leatherette seats with chrome grab-handles, windows clattering hard, pitted rust-patched chrome pillars down the aisle and straps on the rail above to hang on to. The suspension suspect, but made worse by the state of the road.

With the three of us it made about twenty-five on the bus. Five males in farm clothes, the rest women. Locals. Basket under an arm with a bunch of onions and some chillies in it, several with a dead chicken. One woman was standing in the aisle, talking to a mixed group at the rear. As we drove on she moved up the bus and spoke to two seated women, then came up the aisle and started talking to my tall escort. She was good-looking: tall, slender; angular face, golden complexion, not brown; wide deep eyes, white smile. She looked late twenties but was probably ten years older; women age well here if they're not worked to death. Dressed in black trousers, ornate batik print shirt, olive blue and maroon. She carried a flat basket.

This woman stood out—she wasn't from here. She spoke in high or northern Vietnamese. Compare an Oxford don to my speech, that's the difference. I knew it, that's the tone I'd been taught. You didn't hear this accent much, around these parts. I couldn't understand what was said, too deep. No military stuff, statistics or hello how are you, so I was shut out. They talked for five minutes and several times one or the other looked at me. She smiled at me twice; he grabbed my shoulder once and laughed. Finally she stopped talking, turned and came close to me and said something, what I don't know. She took a small green mango from her basket, put it in my right hand and squeezed my fingers around it.

'Keep . . . keep,' she said. Then she smiled and walked back down the bus. She glanced my way twice. I know, because I couldn't take my eyes off her.

The bus stopped at the next village and she got off, talking to a couple of the women. We got off too. We were going to lunch. The bus had dropped us in a shady tree-lined lane with a few shopfronts and with houses opening on to the pavement. A very pretty scene, dappled sunlight, yellowed leaves underfoot, but we walked only about ten paces and stopped at a cafe with two small metal tables on the sidewalk. The little guide ordered lunch—noodles and a bit of meat fried together. I still had the mango in my hand and asked, 'What's this mean?' but they just laughed, so I shut up and we ate. Soon the bus came grinding along the lane and we headed back. This time I was looking out the other side, and as we drove past a gap in the houses I caught a glimpse of the tops of stately buildings, and realised we were in Long Hai.

It's reasonable for you to ask me at this point: 'Well, what's the story? You speak the lingo, you're living among them. What's holding you back?' Let's add up what we have here. We are living among the enemy. Is the path you're walking safe? Is the figure in the distance carrying a scythe, or something else? Are the group of men passing you smiling at you, or among themselves? You cannot get it wrong twice.

Two Viet Cong from within the garrison have shown themselves to me, and given me a glimpse of their structure—the reasons for their doing so I must work out for myself. I conclude, correctly, that while I restrict myself to simple observation I am safe enough. But dispel any thoughts you may have that you can cruise around this countryside, talk to all and sundry, and get the story. All that will get you is an epitaph.

Dave dreamed up some bullshit excuse for us to go back to the Dat for a few hours, so we grabbed the gunner and his mate and headed off in the Landrover. About halfway we saw a massed body of troops spread out all over fallow ground on our right.

'Looks like our mob', said Dave, and stopped the vehicle. Sure enough, it was. The whole battalion sat around in companies. Fuzz and Top End Mick spotted us and came over.

'What the fuck's going on here? Looks like a Boy Scout's jamboree.'

'Might as well be,' said Fuzz. 'We've been fucked around for weeks. Cordons, mine clearance and shit, just like before. What're you bludging bastards up too?'

'Hiding. Don't tell anyone.'

'Sounds better than this fucking caper.'

'It is. Pop in for a beer, any time.' And we were off again.

I'm telling you this because if we'd all been the sort of soldiers that people have accused us of being, we would have reported straight to the CO and told him to come down our way if he was looking for enemy, we had hundreds of the bastards he could chase.

By simple observation of country life, any idiot could see

what was going on here; it just depended on what you considered war to be.

Let's cut through all the media-driven *official* bullshit. I owe you that much, you've come so far. This, we were told, was a war about a global communist conspiracy to destroy democracy as we know it. It was a war about the Devil leading the fiendish, godless Viet Cong against the simple gentle peasants of this peace-loving little land, and slaughtering them barbarously.

That is bullshit. This peaceful little land had been at war for two thousand years that we know about. If it wasn't a foreign invader, it was some arsehole of their own trying to grab the lot.

This was in fact about ordinary people working a fertile, beautiful land and paying 90 per cent of their efforts to absentee landlords in Saigon or elsewhere, and getting nothing in return, no enrichment of their land. This war was about ordinary people demanding a fairer go, and getting obliterated by the US war machine for daring to ask—because the Yanks thought there was something in this country that concerned *them*. None of the other issues, real as they seemed at the time to some, would have amounted to more than a farting match if the working people in this land had not had a gutful and said, 'Fuck you, you're out!'

This wasn't a political ideology tug-of-war, it was pure economics. And equity. These little bastards were up on their hind legs and the Yanks were bombing shit out of them for it.

That woman I met on the bus was a Viet Cong political cadre, moving around the villages keeping in touch with people, supporting them, working as a midwife, social worker, regional nympho maybe—a cover that explained frequent travel. I remember her because she was a northerner and because she made contact with me, but she wasn't in this alone. The women had *risen* in this war, not just suffered. Among the Viet Cong, this was very much a women's war also. True women, choosing their role in society. Tending the farms, raising the children, engaging in active political roles. Working as porters bringing equipment to their field troops, fighting as field troops.

Imagine our surprise, after storming a small bunker system, to find among the dead a heavily pregnant soldier. Consider for one moment what it took the woman to make that statement—

the risks it entailed, the price she paid. Yet it said clearly: 'Men and women side by side'.

The old bloke in the paddy bund was a letterbox, a link for the Viet Cong to communicate through. Jobs for the old, even! Not everyone out here, by far, was a communist sympathiser. Many people were just caught in the middle with nowhere to go—but the Republic didn't seem much of an option. That's why the Yanks couldn't Vietnamise the war later on when they wanted to pull out. It was already Vietnamised. The ordinary people were not truly united: many issues still separated them. But neither age nor gender were issues with these people. They were far better focused on the real issues than any other society claiming rights over this land.

Anyway, that's their problem. We reached the Dat, caught up with a few of the blokes, and checked for mail. Dave said, 'Grab a sports shirt, we're going native', and back we went to the training team. We hit the 'Piss On The Pig' the next day wearing our civvy shirts. This was a quiet road but every few days a Yank convoy passed through. Five or six big tarpaulined trucks with machine gun turrets mounted on the cab roofs, two or three Yanks in flak jackets and steel helmets guarding each of them. This time they stopped—don't know why. Two of the guards saw us on our terrace and came over, curious to know what we were doing here. Dave was already half pissed and gave them a load of bullshit about being rubber planters, and unconcerned about the VC because we just paid both sides off and got on with making a buck.

I wanted to know what the Yanks knew. They knew they were conscripts, they knew they were surrounded by VC, but they didn't know about the mountain. They knew when their hitch was up, they knew that was their truck starting up, and they knew we were planters. Dave had made his point.

They appeared to me to be decent, well-brought-up 21-year-olds who didn't know their arses were on fire. Realistically, how can you stop a country determining its own future by putting troops like this into the field! You can't. But while they're there you can bomb the place to cinders, can't you? Bodycounts work any way you want them to if you're cunning. These cunts were cunning.

The Yank field troops over here were written off as useless, gutless, undisciplined rabble. When people's hearts are not in their jobs they tend to appear that way. But their *fathers* were good soldiers, from what I've heard. Maybe it takes a cause to bring out the fighting qualities in people.

Let's have another look around, a party, and then shove off back to the Dat, eh?

'Where the fuck are we going, Dave?'

'Fishing!'

'Where's the tackle, Dave?'

'Grenades!' He's starting to sound like Pigpen.

We're hurtling down to Long Hai in the Landrover with all four Diggers. They're hanging on for grim death in the back. 'I've got the fuckin' keys' was Dave's appreciation of the situation.

We're into the last week of the mission and training is now dispensed with by mutual agreement. We're all relaxing and sleeping at night, not just me for a change.

'Piece o' piss. Two gunners, village full of Nogs, bit of a cast,' Dave informs us. We're almost there now, thumping along the ruts too fast to steer, the gunners hanging out the back watching our arse.

'Pass us the wheel, Dave, I can see where we're going.' That's the sort of gunner you need, but Dave gets shitty when you criticise his driving, and we plough into the beach by the time he's finished arguing the point and turns back to watch the road. Long Hai again, smack in front of the hotels.

It's about seven in the morning and a golden glow still pervades the air. Slight breeze, the sea coasting gently up the wide slanting beach fifteen metres from the low-water mark. Salt, breeze, sun and sound. Gulls crying excitement. The fishermen have quit for the morning; eight or nine wooden boats lean on their gunwales, tethered to stakes above the high-water mark. One boat still floats in the shallows, being worked on by the owner. The Diggers wander off up the palm-lined street, trying to find the opening times of the hotels. We don't wise them up. Dave walks up the beach a bit for a better view of things.

There are several thatch-roofed shade huts near me on the sand. Eight or nine women, dressed in black, are scattered about, working under them. Dave is watching a fisherman mend his net; the women interest me more. They're making the ricepapers they use to make spring rolls and wontons. Get a woven mat the size of a dinner plate, spread the rice paste thinly all over it with a spatula, add it to the drying stack. Fascinating to watch them. They seem happy enough, chatting away, and they let me look closely. One offers me a go, and I mess it right up. Then Dave calls me over his way. I can't understand why they're doing this on the beach. Then it strikes me. Boring job, but it's a lovely spot to work in.

'Hey, Barrie . . . check out the old bird pressing a darky. Not up there, ya dickhead—down there at the water.'

There she is, squatting with her pants clutched up round her knees, chewing her gums contentedly, waiting for a wave to wash her arse. Further up the beach a bloke is doing the same.

It doesn't take long to lose its novelty and Dave approaches the man in the boat to organise a trip out. He's bent over the engine, farting around with the carburettor as we lob in, arse pointed Dave's way, knackers hanging out the left leg of his shorts.

'Hey, you take us fishing!'

The bloke doesn't know what Dave's yelling at him. Dave holds up a grenade in each hand and points out to sea. The man catches on right away. The Diggers are straggling back with long faces by now and we climb into the old boat. It must weigh tonnes: solid wooden planking, huge cast iron donk, wide-beamed twenty-footer easy. We chug out 500 metres or so and the skipper starts a slow lazy circle, then gets all excited. 'Beaucoup, beaucoup.' He's pointing out to starboard.

The Diggers start plopping hand grenades over both sides— and I mean plopping, right next to the sides. Dave plops one either side and starts to grin.

'You fucking maniacs! *Chuck* the fucking things!' But it's too late for my advice to have any effect.

A pretty pedestrian result initially—eight or nine bloops, a few bubbles, a bit of smoke, the timbers vibrate a bit. Then the old girl lifts her skirts and we start to rise up. We lift up about a metre, pause, then start to drop, and drop, and drop. We hit the bottom of the trough and there's a four-metre wall of green water all around us. My arse is stuck to the seat like a plumber's plunger now, so if we sink I go with the boat. We rise up and level off eventually, wet as shags, starting to laugh like no one's been at all scared.

Around us the water is yellow with sand. Then the fish start to float to the top, ten or twelve flat yellow-finned silver ones, about the size of a baby's hand. The skipper's getting real excited, pointing and giggling. There's a fair crowd on the shore now, urging us on to higher lunacy. We agree it's time to head back in. The skipper drops us on the beach and goes straight back out and scoops the fish up with a little net. He never asked us for payment. How can he afford the fuel for that pissant catch?

There's no real point to this story. A day out, that's all it was—one that I remember.

Dave had taken a sudden interest in admin, sorting out resupply and other boring tasks. Next time the Landrover came down from the Dat with our stores three cartons of canned piss came with it marked 'Dave'. Funny that. VB they were, how could I forget it—I helped stack them in the tent, threw a tarp over them and put a book on top. Dave had planned to give the Diggers a pissup on the last night of our stint here, for seeing it through. They'd stayed sober throughout; you can put it down to youth. It was meant to be a surprise. But if Dave and I drained the local store beforehand the Diggers would be lucky to smell one, so it played both ways.

However, some other prick stuck his snout in—Senior Sergeant, who could talk, or would talk, more's the pity. Dave and I were sprawled on our camp stretchers peering glassy-eyed at a couple of bugs frying their arses on the pressure lamp's shroud. The Pig had been well pissed on that day. In came Senior Sergeant to advise that there was a feast being put on, to see us off.

'Know that?'

'Fucking whoopee. No! You tell me nothing.'

'Well there is, and it could be big, the whole garrison maybe. Big meal.'

'Good.'

'Yeah . . . well, we should contribute, buy the drinks.'

'The store sells it.' Dave's suddenly on the alert and homing in like a missile.

'True, but there's a problem. They're not flush—seems you characters drained 'em and you've got the only beer in town.'

'There's your problem right there,' said Dave. 'Sixty odd blokes and 72 cans—there'll be a bloodbath for the second round of beers!'

I opened my big mouth and said, 'Best hand it in, Dave,' and he's thought me a weak cunt ever since. But he knew in his heart it was inevitable.

Good in one way that we did. Consider that feast. The surroundings were drab—it was held on the grey sand of the compound outside our tent. An overcast day that stopped your vision at the wire; you couldn't even see the ricefields clearly. Mats rolled out on the dirt, a few branches of leaves, and food everywhere. Exotic fragrant food, coloured and varied. This was a men's-only meal, the women stood well back. We cracked a can each and there were no speeches, thank God. We just sat on the dirt and ate. I ended up seated on the left of the commandant because I liked the look of the food in that patch and because I couldn't tell the bastards apart, but he was a good host. He offered suggestions on sauces for various foods, laughing at my innovative Vietnamese. He suggested the shark next; it was hard by my right knee, a metre long and grey, steamed in wine and lifelike enough to make me start.

'Part skin with fingers, eat flesh' was commandant's recommendation. It was beautiful, the skin like gelatine, the flesh like crayfish. I wasn't going to shift for no bastard.

Some of the garrison had finished eating and were standing drinking one of the few second cans of beer. Dave noticed them for that reason—he'd miss out if he wasn't quick—and because they were horsing around behind his end of the spread. I looked up at their sound, then went back to the fish.

Shrieking and snarls were the next I heard, and I looked up to see one of the garrison pinned at on the ground by a knee in his back and a big revolver held at his head. He had a friend, but *he* was on his knees with a Colt 45 at his temple. These guys were playing Russian roulette a bit fierce and had a couple of mates to back them up. Dave knew how to handle crazies;

and he was crashing into them. The commandant hit the pack without treading on the rice, there was a brief, sharp melee and the nutters were carted off squealing and bucking beyond our view. Nothing much to be learnt from this little event; soldiers who are stressed by divisions within their ranks, divided loyalties, often overreact. Dave reckoned they couldn't handle their piss—which was probably just his way of saying, 'What the fuck brought all that on?'

Dave really grew attached to the local people here; couldn't wait to get involved in the daily issues of the village. He knew a bit of their language, courtesy of a three-week 'quickie' course—enough to say 'G'day, how much?'—and with his gestures and his actions he was able to communicate quite well while we were here. It was he who learned of the true economic plight of these people, because Dave understood money, and the game that surrounds it. He also understood how to survive in an uncertain environment: stay crazy.

I lacked Dave's skills and stayed aloof, content to watch, but I understood his fascination with these village people. They lived in chronic poverty, they were at war and they contended with crippling taxes that did nothing to improve their land, yet they were self-reliant and forthright in their dealings with us.

We'd rolled into this village wearing the uniform and bearing the weapons of an army not to be stirred up, unless you could fight. Daily we received 'Hey, chao Uc Dai Loi' from a straggling gang of the few village children of walking and talking age. And 'Chao anh'—G'day—from the women as you passed them in the street. The men shat in our toilet, listened to what we said, and disclosed to each of us a part of their system. I bought nothing here that I couldn't eat or drink. Nor was there any attempt to sell anything else. These people had integrity, and were determined to keep it.

Dave fitted in here instinctively. Big, wild-eyed, rough-edged, helpful whenever an opportunity presented itself; otherwise he minded his own business, had a beer, viewed the scenery, acted in his normal larrikin manner. Dave's intuitive appraisal of what we were dealing with here did most to make this mission a safe one for us. And, I guess, did the image of Australians in the eyes of the locals no harm either. One thing's fairly certain, if we'd rigidly followed the guidelines and attitudes of our high command, this garrison would have done for us. They'd done it before.

I felt as Dave felt. I also wanted to be like these people—we *were* like these people—but I wanted to live in a different land, my land, and to ensure that we weren't reduced to the level these people were: being manipulated by thugs. To me, at that time, this land of theirs seemed not worth stealing from them. The true jewel was in their soul. And that was the prize that warranted their extinction.

Chapter 14

We're back at the Dat and packing up—less than a fortnight to go. The advance party flies out tomorrow. Dave's supposed to be on the plane but someone gazumps him on family grounds. Jock, I think. Doesn't matter, because Dave's got some unfinished business. Packing up? I'm *packed*. Pick up the fags, quick piss if I remember in time, and I'm ready.

Lunch in the mess, mess in the lunch, whatever, and we're saying goodbye to OC in the boozer.

Every bastard's there. OC's looking jumpy. He's off to staff college at Queenscliff, the guillotine majors pass through, some to become colonels, even higher. Most get the chop at 43 or so and end up selling investment advice, insurance, real estate, mum's house, the kids' trust fund. The prospect of falling at that hurdle isn't on his mind, though. He's got to make a speech to us, one that counts. This is his last talk to a field command—no further chance. OC's not much of a speechmaker; he can't deal in bullshit, it makes him nervous.

Dave's little effort didn't help. Just as OC hauled up to deliver, Dave and Pigpen shoved a present at him, token of esteem and all that bullshit, from the company. First I'd heard of it. No one asked me to put in, and I wasn't that hard to find. It was mainly Dave's winnings that bought the present, which made it pretty universal I suppose. The choice wasn't—not from my standpoint. Dave and Pigpen had slipped off to

Vungers to select the present. And throw a quick leg over a slut, I'll bet. They gave OC a velvet box. When he opened it, there was a Cyma chronometer, solid gold, tiny diamonds littering its face. It looked like something you'd win at sideshow alley if you were a big enough mug. But I know it was genuine. At least, the price was.

That put OC off his swing for a moment but he was standing by then, so he started to talk. Gave us a bit of bullshit the CO had passed on for us, a bit of bullshit on what *he* thought of the situation. Then he said, 'But more importantly, this is about people,' and he started from his right side and gazed around the crowd just naming people, sometimes adding a remark. 'Peaches . . . and Mick . . . Sharkey, the epitome of a gunner, up for an MiD' and so on around the company. 'Jock, and Crowls . . .' That had him fucked. I could read his mind, it was in a spasm—what did I name that little pest for?—but he got going again when I answered to him. And in the thirty or so he named at random he never mentioned Pete. I looked across at Pete standing among the crowd, smiling at the proceedings the same as everyone else there, but I sensed disillusionment, confusion, behind his smile.

I didn't know if OC was being democratic or discreet, or if he just didn't know about Pete's actions that day. He was wrong about the MiD and anyway another bloke also got an award, whom he would have mentioned out of courtesy, if he'd known. At that stage no official list of awards for the company had been issued. And that was the last I saw of OC.

We got into the piss after that. Lovely hot sunny day. Big Mick left the bowler hat on his head—those toasts were for unity. No need now, we were going home and on our separate ways. Dave set up the crown and anchor game one last time and showed the bank could lose; he put the lot back. I put my first dollar on the mat and walked away with $30. I pissed it up against the wall of course, it wasn't mine anyway. At ten cents a beer it got quite a few drunk. The feeling was euphoric, we were going *home*!

The company was about to be systematically dismantled. Big Mick was a warrior; wars were to be fought out as long as your government was involved. He was accepted into the AATTV unit. For him it was a quick R&R in Bangkok, then straight back here again for another year or so. We Regs were being posted back home to soldier on. The Nasho's were looking at freedom. For many that was enough. People like Sharkey, Tank, Les, Pigpen, Ronnie, Fuzz, Makka—it was the end of a war they didn't like. They had opinions which they kept to themselves unless they knew you. They were going home to get on with life. Peaches was under no illusions. In his mind he'd failed miserably. He hated war and just wanted to hide, to stay out of the limelight.

Dave and Woofer had signed on as Regs. Must have been pissed. Neither of them consulted me on that either, the stupid pricks, so they kept their opinions to themselves. The whingers had a very different view. For much of the tour it had been: 'This cunt of a war, fucked my life, shouldn't be here, brainfucked army.' Now it was hero time—triumphant return home—let my country bestow great honour on *me*. Don't get me wrong, these guys did as well as anyone. In the field there was no difference, they were good. It was the sharp turnaround, the sudden expectations that had me grasping for supporting walls. I didn't think it was a just war, I didn't think it was right that they be here; the difference was that I kept to the same view because I believed it. To me these guys smelt opportunity and were looking to cash in. And they hadn't read their own wind correctly.

We'd been in a time-warp here, didn't know the feeling being produced back home. We had no papers, no TV. News from home was news from home. 'Dear darling, I'm three months pregnant.' 'Dear son, Dad stacked up your car, is it insured? How're things with you?' No one got: 'Dear son, you psychopathic maniac, how the fuck are ya?'

We didn't know that people all over the world were glued to their TV sets watching a hundred marines standing behind a wall, firing at some little Nog racing back and forth along a riverbank trying to surrender, while some colour sergeant's bellowing out, 'There he goes, shoot him! Shoot him!' Or seeing a little girl running naked down a dirt road with napalm still burning into her flesh. Or reading about US troops under the leadership of Lieutenant William Calley paying a visit to a village called My Lai and killing over a hundred of the occupants—men, women and children.

We were soldiers. We killed, sure. When someone shot at us, or was about to. That's what we were sent over here for. OK, we fucked up now and again. Some people liked it a bit too much, sometimes. That happens, considering the mix of the company. But how could we know the rest of our generation were marching through city streets, freaked out of their minds with fear at having to go next, or joining in for the fun of having a clout at a few coppers and getting on TV. What's that? Think I'm being cynical, bitter? We'll come back to that later. We didn't know much about all that at this time. Some of our blokes took it hard when they got home, none more than the whingers.

The last two weeks are a blur. The advance party of the incoming company had arrived and we were getting them acquainted with the place and the systems, giving them a warm-up look at the outside. Our remaining officers and senior NCOs were organising our return and briefing the new lot. I had nothing to do and did it without a fuss, I'm a professional.

One sunny morning I'm sitting on a truck and waving goodbye to the forlorn Diggers who joined us too late to go home with us. They'll be here until May, I guess. It is 26 November 1969. Leaving is a terrible wrench.

'Hey, Pete,' Dave shouts, 'there's a swimming pool here. Did you know that?'

'Nuh.'

'And what's that fucking thing over there?'

'That? That's the theatre shell, where they held that concert. Bazz and I went to it—you came too, didn't you?'

'Nuh.'

'You wouldn't have liked it anyway, Dave. Cunt of a show. Some black American five-piece with a fat sheila singer wearing funny hats. Weak as piss.'

'See ya Dat!!'

Then we're out the gate, cocking the rifles for the last time, and we're off down the track. Nothing's changed on the way; the villages look the same, a few more potholes in the road, the fishermen still casting their nets in the distance, Vungers still squalid. Only the company has changed. Just over thirty of the original hundred or so have gone the distance.

We're on the beach, standing in the shale, packs full of dutyfree items, sea bags and trunks crammed with R&R crap. There's the *Sydney* waiting out in the bay, pulling at our eyes like a beautiful woman. The landing barges are ferrying the new battalion in, then going back with a load of us. I'm shipping back with the company. BHQ have flicked me; I'm to be a section commander when we regroup in Brisbane, the battalion's new home. One barge has landed, my barge is coming in.

'Barrie! Barrie! How are you, how are you going?'

It's a tall, skinny, long-faced Pommy bastard of about 30. It's Britt, coming ashore leading his section. One of my touchstones from the early days, Corps training, when at times it got a bit tough.

Britt had been in the British army before joining us, an MP. He'd flown pretty high for a while, crack bodyguard, security to the mighty and the privileged. Always looked a bag of shit, even standing before me now, his giggle hat looking like a huge limp cabbage leaf held up by his big flapping ears.

Don't let looks fool you. This prick can go, and he can lead. Got psyched out of the British army after a tour of Malaya. Went into his room one day, tore his uniform off, lay on the bed with a machete and warned that if any cunt came near him he'd 'chop their fucking head off!'.

I've no idea what he did that for—he never explained. But if Britt was crazy we should all be like that. He was as intelligent, sensitive and compassionate a man as I've ever met.

'Britt . . . for fuck's sake! How was Malaya?'

'Much better this time. Bit soft. How did you go?'

'I'm looking over your shoulder at that fucking ship, mate . . . Look after yourself, OK?'

'Sure. Take care, Bazz. Gotta go too.'

With that he leads his section up towards the truck and we step on the ramp. And our part in that war officially ends.

The battalion was way under strength for the trip home, so space was no problem. I had a similar berth for the trip back except that Pete was with me this time, and some other members of CHQ. I can't remember any of the sights, or what we did—too diverted.

'What's with these cunts?' asked Dave, catching up with us

two days out. He was referring to the sailors. 'These cunts are pestering the fucking life out of me. Give me, give me, sell me. I thought these arseholes were supposed to be in this war too. They're all fucking grab.'

'Yeah. I'm down two bottles of brandy.'

Pete was down a whole lot more. The day before, he and I were looking for Dave in the holds and came across a little Healey Sprite sports car, dark red. Pete fell in love with it. It was for sale, of course, the ship's officer had it on board expressly for that purpose. Pete bought it. The outside world was starting to encroach.

The battalion was headed back to Adelaide for a march through the city centre to celebrate its homecoming, before disbanding for leave. Those due for discharge would then head to their local personnel depot to be processed out. This included all Dave's intake: Les, Tank, Makka, Pigpen, Peaches, most of the remaining original company. The group going to Brisbane to re-form were few: Dave and Woofer, Patto, Banjo, Jock, Brian, me—among the Regs—and Pete, which was a great shock. I thought he'd be transferred back to a hospital base. One tour with the grunts for a medic should be enough. But several of them stayed with the battalion, in fact. Once in, hard to get out, it seemed. Not too many volunteers queuing to have a go.

The *Sydney* stopped at Fremantle on the way through and Western Australian members could start leave from there. Bugger the march through Adelaide, I'm off! We lined the flight deck during the approach. I could see my family on the dock searching for my face. Pete picked me up and shook me at them till they noticed me. I was standing at the gangway, luggage beside me, as we pulled alongside.

'What's the rush, Barrie, aren't you going to say goodbye?'

'Pete, I'll see you in Brisbane, I'm fucking gone. Say goodbye to everyone for me.' And I was down the gangplank, through the barrier and back with my family for a month or so. Gave the boys a wave; spotted Pete waving like a maniac.

Now for some normalcy, for a moment. I stayed with Mum and Dad. They were living up in Kalamunda then, a lovely spot in the hills, village-type atmosphere, surrounded by forest. Nice

old ramshackle pub. I was driving there with Dad a day or two into my leave. He mentioned some bloke at work who'd just had his son return from Vietnam. 'Says the son keeps flushing the toilet and turning lights and the TV on and off all the time. Ever feel like doing that?'
'Nah.'
'Didn't think so. That cunt's probably pining for the three harlots he kept in his Saigon lovenest on the five hour's work a week he had to do.'
I didn't need it but it was confirmation. Dad knew about war from close up too. And that was the good side, being at home. Mum also understood—she knew about bombings and death in the street from the blitzes she'd experienced in her youth. But war does strange things to you. You're always looking, seeing, evaluating, judging—you can't switch off. You can't just see something and say, 'Hey, that's cool'. You look at it and say, 'What's that doing there? Who owns it? Who benefits? Why did you let it happen?'
That's what shocked me about coming home. It was another country, another country entirely. But it wasn't evolving, it was being occupied: the people, the places, the very structure of our society were being eroded. Not from ideal to bad—from bad to worse. I'd gone away, presumably to defend my country, and someone stole it while I was away. I'd been away a year but I'd been out of touch for twice that, with intensive training and very little leave beforehand.
There were fun things happening in Perth for the young now, sure. Plenty of nightclubs with pretty good bands sometimes; pub life was livelier, restaurants were more common; icecream parlours, coffee shops, clothes boutiques, the first fast-food outlets and shopping centres were making their appearance. There were more multinational companies in town—the mining boom was just getting under way.
Then there were the people. Let me look at only my generation, because I know them well. I couldn't believe the change. Heard of the flower children, the hippies, the children of peace? Yeah, Beatles, Doors, Mamas and the Papas, love, love, hate ya fascist parents, Easy Rider, love the world. The movement was a T-shirt, a hairstyle, lasting thirty seconds, like

all the other fads of my generation. And they didn't give a fuck, except for themselves.

Schoolmates were telling me what stocks and shares they wanted to get into, what bank loans they had out to finance properties they'd invested in, about transfers in their government work into computer departments because that's where the quick advancement was. Money, me, money, me. Sense of vocation? 'Bullshit! Loser's talk.' Money, me, money, me.

And meanwhile the invaders continued to come and set up their tents, and our leaders talked prosperity and greatness ahead—and for them it was true. And they opened the halls of justice and our seats of learning and our offices of sacred trust to the invaders, for sale, for commission. And the people saw it was true and lined up for their share. And those who had no soul and no vision proved adept at bleeding the new system; they flourished and built a proud society around themselves. Based on money. Fix your kid's future—good school—twelve hundred bucks, make you look good, worth twice as much. Want ya kids to succeed? Don't question, pay our fee. It's gunna be ugly for them otherwise. Got any life cover? Wanna drive a car a boong drives? Nah? Come this way.

But those who were hesitant, slowed by dilemmas of nationhood and a need to serve, and those who by birthright needed to be led, were falling away and becoming part of a growing and despised subsociety. And the invaders grew stronger, fed and encouraged by the new structure, which they had built at no cost to themselves.

I wasn't being paranoid, I knew invaders well. I'd just left them, still at play in a once green land. I knew how they operated: any way they chose.

As much as hippiedom was a myth, so was the focus in the reporting of Vietnam. See if you can get old clips of the coverage—I know what I'm talking about. The slant was all emotion: big *bangs*; burning kids; brave soldiers, Yanks of course; journalists indulging in what they do best, having a wank and a good cry at the same time. That's what they're paid to do. None focused on the *war*.

That was done in diplomatic circles, in closed sessions of political meetings, in editors' offices, Madison Avenue dreamtanks, corporate board rooms. And that wasn't covered at all, though it was going on in our own country as much as anywhere. We had Moratorium marches here—probably well-meaning people organised them—many marched. But they didn't march so much to stop the war as to make sure that they or those close to them were not dragged into it. Bullshit, you say? Then why are they not marching still? The war goes on today, more than ever, even if not many appear to be dying.

If I can distil what I saw and felt of my country on coming home into one word it has to be . . . superficial. And it *could* be paradise.

Going back to the battalion was a brutal reminder that I was no longer a soldier, simply a public servant. We were based at Enoggera, a suburb of Brisbane. Unlike Woodside, which was a battalion base only, set in beautiful forest above Adelaide in the hills, this was a large, modern Task Force-size base with all necessary support units living side by side. MPs, RPs, clerks, quacks and cunts all over the place. A few sappers. Tankies? Don't think so. Modern drab cream brick buildings, grey gravel parade grounds, sparse lawns intended to brighten the place. One boozer serving the whole camp—otherwise, the battalion had its own essential services, which it ran with an understrength unit. Plenty of duties coming up. Most of our former officers and senior NCOs had been scattered to the four winds—hopefully gale force in most cases—and replaced with new ones. Mainly career survivors who'd been overseas on holidays but never found time to serve, or young officers fresh out of college. The latter were the pick of the crop; they were at least still green, and interested. The ranks were filled out with new Nasho's coming from Corps training, most still wondering what had fucking hit them. They had more shocks in store yet, just observing us.

Then there were the Diggers, who knew exactly what had hit them but didn't know what to do about it. I was posted to a different company as a section commander, and had first-hand experience of controlling men after a slathering lunatic had led them for a year in the field, got his medal and moved on.

What a mess! I adopted various neurotic behaviours just in order to get through the confidence of the outer circle. But let's be cunning and move on too, for now. I reported in to CHQ and got my orders. Mess duty, guard duty, weekend orderly NCO, mess duty, guard duty, guard duty, weekend orderly NCO, 'Fucking hang on!', 'Shortstaffed!', mess duty, guard duty . . . that's the first month fucked.

I rolled up mid-morning the first Saturday to take over the company office as orderly NCO. You sit in an office for two days answering phone calls and sending messages, manning the fort. You have a Digger with you to run errands and polish the floors, to push around and be a cunt to, if you're of that mentality. The new, bald, dud CSM met me in reception and said, 'There's someone here to see you. Make it quick, you're due on duty.'

A kid of about 18, my height and dressed in greens, was waiting. He started to cry when he saw me. For a minute I thought I was being dumped with a bedwetter, but then I saw he was from another Corps and relaxed a bit.

'Corporal Crowley?'

'Yeah, come over here.'

'I believe you're a friend of Peter Bun.'

'Sure am.'

'He's dead, Corporal.'

Pete had run his little sports car off the road one night and had hit a tree or a pylon. He was alone when he died. The young soldier was from Pete's neighbourhood, one of the kids who used to tag along in Pete's circle, as long as he wasn't under notice too much. He knew the family.

'I don't think he should have been driving, he was upset. His girlfriend had dropped him for one of his mates while he was away.'

I thanked the young medic for coming out of his way to tell me personally, and dismissed him.

Sudden death. Of course it shattered me. I remember so clearly coming back from the Horseshoe with a back full of blisters and Pete ruling me unfit for the field. And OC saying, 'He'll *have* to go, we're short of numbers, CSM's already told you'. And Pete saying, 'He's not fucking going!' And I didn't, until the blisters had dried.

I remember a morning in a red clay shell scrape, hidden under our hootchies, silver rain gushing down, another muddy

night ahead. Pete and I were brewing tea, Dave skidded in boots first, saying, 'I'll have one of those'.
Then Dave dropped the grenade. 'I've signed for three more.'
'You've fucking *what*?'
'Barrie, shut up! I know what I'm doing, got it?'
I did get it, of course, one way or another. Dave had signed up so his term of service was within months of Pete's and mine. Dave had officially become the third peg. Not that we hadn't guessed. So that was Dave in camp. What about Pete?
'Any thoughts on what you'll do when you get out?'
'What can you do with a name like Bun? Bun's bakery, Bun's buns, that's me fucked. Any ideas? Nah, I'm where I am . . . Got any toilet paper, Pete?'
'What am I, ya fuckin' mother?'
'Would you like to die in agony Barrie?' Pete had asked me that. I never mourned Pete. I missed him, but even that's faded a bit over time. Ever since my Dad died I've yearned to see him walk round the corner and startle me like he enjoyed doing. But not with Pete. I knew he was gone. Even though I'd knelt alone at my father's side to comfort him in death and had then gone through the funeral arrangements—the whole disaster—and yet had only heard of Pete's death from a young stranger. There was a difference, and I understand it.

Pete was what, 21? His girlfriend had left him, OK. For his best friend? *There's* a mutual exclusion right in your lap. Pissed? Could have been. Went to sleep at the wheel? How important is any of this? In Pete's case it isn't. I thought back to the day on top of the APC with Pete. The funeral gongs, the monks in saffron, the flowers, and that solved Pete for me. He'd ascended. No big headlines, no medals, very few even knowing what he'd dared, and achieved. Never experienced the love of a wife and children, career advancement, the ageing process. But he'd gone as high as he could go, doing what he did. Blew it all at 21; learnt the answer, carried it out, then got careless and a lot unlucky.

Before we go back into picture, remember I'm a callous jungle loonie. I've cut a dead friend cold. Dead right. Pete's dead. But I do remember. How could I forget him? I've never met his like since, and I'll never stop looking.

The first of the old gang I saw was Brian. I was taking a break from mess duty, having a fag outside. I didn't have to do any of the shit work, just had to be there passing on the cooks' orders to the Diggers. Fuck the cooks, let them use their own powers on this bunch—kick 'em in the arse like they told *me* to, if they have the guts. Bet I made those pricks work at a less lofty level.

Brian was marching along the path like a palace guard, immaculate. Clipboard under the left arm, snapping a whippy at every officer cruising past, he was headed for the carpark.

'Where are you going, ya fucking arselicker?'

'Hi Bazz. Don't knock it, son. I've been back a fortnight, haven't turned a tap. These cunts wouldn't know if their arse was on fire.'

It was true alright: Brian all dressed up as the model soldier, quick trip round the camp, get mugged by the right people, 'Must get over to admin—shit, I'm behind to buggery', and out the gate in the MG for a cruise. Brian did nothing for three months or more, fucking nothing. Everyone thought he was tied up elsewhere. Now that's a civil servant for you.

I saw a fair bit of Woofer. He was getting a lot of therapy for his leg wounds. Lots of physio and gym work, so he had it fairly easy otherwise. Not before time. I mixed quite often with Woofer. I found him a straightforward moral type, and fun in a wild way, but he hadn't switched off at all. He could make you very tense sometimes. Not an easy friend to sell. I didn't introduce him to many of the new boys in my company—they weren't ready for Woofer.

He had a Lotus Super Seven, one of those little open racing shells that went like a rocket, about three inches off the ground. The first time he drove me through the boomgate he drove me through the boomgate. Straight under the fucking thing at about eighty miles an hour. He loved giving the MPs the shits. How could you not like a bloke like that? He took me down to Surfers Paradise, a bastard of a trip, the traffic was bumper to bumper all the way. We had to turn off the ignition and paddle the Lotus half the 60 or so clicks with our hands. Bloody thing had a radiator the capacity of my bladder and boiled if the car idled.

Banjo was good fun. He'd taken up mind-fucking as a hobby.

He used to plant words in people's minds so they would adopt them as buzzwords. 'What was that, Crowls . . . propensity? Fuck, I can use that one . . . Who gives a fuck what it means, you're missing the point.' Within a day or two, wherever you went on base you'd hear, 'The precise propensity of the issue is . . .' or 'Don't bullshit me, I'm no sagacious idiot . . .'

'Fuckin' cattle, Crowls. Just round 'em up and point 'em. Gimme another one a them big words, I'm in the mood.'

I saw a golden future for Banjo when his stint was up. A copper picked him up for a minor traffic offence. He wound the copper up so tight that the next item on the charge sheet was going to be attempted murder.

'Are you gunna lodge that? . . . Think about it.' I'd have paid the ten bucks fine, but Banjo beat the rap completely—the copper tore it up. 'You're only as good as you think you are, Crowls.'

There's something in that, but ain't it a bastard when wisdom is given too cryptically. Banjo was fun, and either highly intelligent or crazy.

Dave was trying out the married man bit, so I saw little of him for a while. He was in another company, playing with mortars. Met the wife briefly, fucking stupid bitch. Reminded me of Dave, physically.

All the changes meant I was forced to break new ground, meet new people. The new Nashos were good enough types but not my scene, they were just marking time. The war would pass them by unseen. The nation's mood was set on withdrawing from Vietnam, even though our government held out for another eighteen months. They knew they'd be back in office soon if they honoured cunning allies. The Vets within my new company were good blokes, but most were just hanging out for discharge. And of course they were still tightknit, and wound right up from the tour. They were a tough bunch of bastards.

I'd attend orders groups, at platoon level, sometimes higher, and be told the training routine or duty roster for the week; then be told to motivate the troops and keep their morale up. I'd have burst out laughing but these men were utter morons. Simply didn't know—or want to. We'd march out to company parade of a morning and report rollcall by platoon. The platoon sergeant would bellow to the CSM on the office steps, holding the clipboard. 'Present, thirteen; sick parade, ten; absent, two; AWOL, two—*Sarr*!' That was a good turnout. A bad one, you shonkey'd the roll and spaced out your ranks.

One case that remains vivid was a Digger called Snowy. He looked about 25, average height, solid build, bit of a gut, beer drinker's face and sparse, prematurely greying blond hair. On a good day he looked like he'd slept in the culvert last night. Sometimes he shaved. He'd got three months to go. Snowy passed the time going down to the Gold Coast, or sometimes just into the city, to a pub. He'd stay there until the MPs found him, usually when the publican tipped them off to come and pick the troublesome bastard up. He'd deck a couple of them and get brought back and put in the base slammer. He'd goad the RPs for the week or so he was in there, then he'd go out on sick parade for a week until he got enough money to hit the piss again.

He was just trying to enjoy himself. He meant no one any harm, he'd simply had enough of killing and listening to bullshit. Fucking good bloke. Intelligent, witty, typical hard-doing Aussie.

Here's another. A big bastard, a gunner, a Nasho who was due out soon. He was a communicator—most nights he could be heard from the top balcony of his barrack block keeping anybody who cared to hear informed of his progress towards normality. This is what you might hear: 'Went out with Stretch tonight, to a party. He conned on to a chick about ten o'clock. I snivelled around for a bit, but no luck. Got pissed and felt silly standing by the keg with every cunt ignoring me, so I caught the bus home. The driver reckoned I was too pissed to be on it and kicked me off halfway here. Walked fucking miles. Didja know they can chuck you off a bus for fucking sleeping? They fucking can, ya know. I've got a lot more on my mind I'd like to share with you . . . but I think I'm gunna herk. So good luck for now, keep ya head down till next I come on the air, and thanks for listening.'

He was a very placid man, did no harm, just wouldn't soldier anymore.

It was men like these I'd been told to motivate. My superiors were insensitive cretins, right up the line.

Which is why there was a change in the promotion criteria

about this time. There was opportunity for the NCOs to get ahead—for those who could follow the management style, who could become a *Yes Sarr!* Stamp, two three . . . turn, two three. Come here, you horrid little man! We were now a garrison battalion, twinkly medals, shiny boots. We guarded openings of parliament, provided the pomp at funerals, transformed ourselves into performing robots. Big Mick turned up around now, a sergeant, a legacy from his AATTV appointment. Got the clap in Bangkok on R&R before he joined them, and got the arse as soon as it was diagnosed. Did about two weeks with them. He toed the official line to some extent, maintained the discipline in his platoon, focused on the kids. He was a warrior still.

We had a new CO also. A man from Canberra. Fragile old bastard. Mid-fifties, vertical shoulders, flabby arse, watery blue eyes, high weak voice. Had a medal. A WTFT—a 'What The Fuck's That?' It came in handy: at least he didn't look an utter coward to the general public when we were honoured with the task of providing a ceremonial guard for the opening of parliament in Brisbane. That's how our intrepid leader described the event. An *honour*. The front rank of the battalion heard it at our parade and it filtered back in due course. This was big news; he thought we'd shit ourselves with excitement. He was very honoured to receive the order, it appeared. This was soldiering at its best, in his terms.

Parliament was due to be opened at one pm by the Queen, so we got there around nine am; there was a *lot* to do. We had to get to the spot across the road from the parliament house doors and line up in a single file some 600 men long. Then we had to fuck around with the line so that we got an even spread of medals along it. That took an hour or so. Then we had the dress inspection.

We'd had one at base but this was a ceremonial one, so that some wanker from the Air Force could cruise along our line checking for specks and smuts, and show off his sword and *his* WTFT. Half a dozen lesser lights sidled after him hoping to pick a fault worth highlighting. Got through that OK—getting a bit hot, though, being stood at attention for an hour, rifles at the salute, while these clowns had their look. Stood at attention for another hour while the crowd built up and started pressing at our backs, scrabbling through bags, smoking cigarettes, smacking irritating kids.

Then the weapon inspection, a real cunt. Held the rifle up at the port, motionless, with the left arm, with the thumb of the right hand stuck into the cocked breach to reflect light up the barrel so the inspector could inspect.

God Almighty! Look who's coming. A raddled geriatric in a nineteenth-century naval suit and a feather-plumed Napoleon hat creaking towards our line. One rheumy eye can distinguish night from day, the other is there to plug a hole. Complexion like a turkey's wattle, breath like a discarded bag of prawnheads, one paralysed leg dragging along behind, the spur screeching and sparking on the paving.

This old relic has six hundred rifles to inspect. This is when some of the weak and the lazy start fainting. About fifty hit the deck in succession. I hope they charge the cunning bastards. It isn't that fucking hot; even old Dragleg makes it right through to the last in line. Eventually.

One pm. Two pm. Two-forty pm and up drives the Rolls Royce. An almighty 'God Bless You' from the blue rinses hard at my back. The World's First Family has arrived. Betty gets out first, blinks like a goanna at the glare, ignores the crash of arms as we salute, collars some flunkey standing by the door and starts organising things. I nearly honk with laughter. She looks so like my Mum I can imagine her conversation: 'Get me inside, it's too hot out here. Is the kettle on? Better be!' Phil steps out and stands there. Charlie gets out and looks around, interested. Annie slides out with a face like thunder—there's a nice glimpse of thighs, strong—yanks the pink miniskirt back down over her arse, and goes to stand by Mum. Some comedian down the line from me farts like a thunderclap and the Windsors are shooed into the closeted auction house just as the straight line starts to bob up and down, as though they've just heard something funny.

Good day out, that one. I could look forward to many more of those.

We nearly had another one a week or so later. The State Premier asked the Army to deploy our battalion for street control while a Moratorium march went through the city. The brigadier told him to get fucked. This brigadier must have been a soldier at some stage. Imagine the scene—twenty thousand hyped-up young people who see soldiers as the main cause of a war they're terrified of becoming involved in. Sure, they're going to be shouting at parliament, but it's us they hate. We were to carry baseball bats. Might as well have been issued with machine guns. Who *is* this premier?

We did have to man military installations in case the marchers decided to do some damage. Dave took a party of ten to guard some backwater depot or other. There was a pub across the road, so Dave set the boys up there and asked the barman if his kelpie dog could keep an eye out for trouble.

Then there were the funerals—military funerals for the bodies being flown back from Vietnam. Done properly, a military funeral is an ornate, tightly choreographed performance, involving weapon drills and coffin drills and firing a rifle salvo at the end. A nightmare to perform, and I'm sure a worse nightmare to endure if you're some mum from nowhere in the suburbs seeing your son go under. I didn't do one; just drilled for hour after hour to master the procedure. But Dave did one. He dragged me up the boozer straight after.

'Didn't go well, eh?' I asked. Dave was on his third beer without uttering a word, and starting to titter.

'Nah, went great . . . fucking *laugh*. The drill went off OK, the kids did that pretty well, no fuckups that anyone'd pick. One of the coffin bearers was a shortarse, though. The coffin started towards the hole and it got a bounce up. The poor bastard in it must be in two bits. The head or some fucking thing started knocking on the side, the medals were rattling on the lid. Mum went fucking mental. "Let him out! Let him out! He's alive!" I had to drag her out the hole, then the rels got the fear, girlfriend got hysterical. Fuck, I thought I was through with all this shit.'

We now went on a shakedown exercise with a battalion who were due to head up to Vietnam. Our brief was to add realism to the experience so that the Diggers got as much advice as possible. It was a good idea. My role was to act as a Vietnamese national attached to BHQ as an interpreter. This unit didn't have any of their own with them on the exercise, so it was a bit of a waste of time for me. But most of the other guys, Dave,

Woofer, Banjo and so on, were out with the companies as observers, picking faults, suggesting solutions.

It was held up at Shoalwater Bay in the north of Queensland, hot country. BHQ didn't use me. They were concerned with their own systems, so I stayed out of their hair. Acted like a real interpreter—strung up the hammock, took a snooze, read a book, made myself available if any of the Diggers had any questions, otherwise doing it easy. Their RSM was a hawknosed, leather-hided cunt of about 50. Typical lifer, shouting the odds at every prick beneath his rank, hustling people about, organising chaos into the simplest tasks. Thought Diggers were morons. I had a couple of scrapes with him over my role and advised him that you don't treat Vietnamese nationals like Diggers—you take it easy, they do their own thing.

He had cottonwool in his ears—I thought he was spending time at the firing range and leaving it in his ears for convenience. He heard perfectly; just didn't hear what people said. He approached me on the second day and said, 'Get off that hammock, soldier, and dig your pit!'

'It's dug.'

Well it was, like the Nogs would, nine inches deep. I said it in Vietnamese. He eyeballed me and started threatening all sorts of shit, and I lost it completely and flew at the cunt.

We crashed into my pit, and this old prick knew how to fight, infantry-style. We didn't get too far—there were a couple of RPs near us and we got leapt on and torn apart. He started to shout charges at me and throw orders around but the RPs spotted a signal from an umpire and hauled us over to his tent. The umpire was a colonel, a shrink, and he called us in and got our stories. The RSM and I had another quick lunge over some fine point concerning the event and the umpire ruled we should be separated. I got packed off in a Landrover and driven out to a rifle company, to clomp around in the bush with them, while the tears of murderous rage abated.

'Crowls! Up here!' There was Woofer standing on top of an APC, taking it real easy. That's where I ended up for the duration. Woofer got off the APC now and again and gave the troops a few answers, a few suggestions. I said, 'Listen to Woofer!' One of the troops asked about my clash with their

RSM. Word had got around. 'Nah, didn't hurt him, only got to wrestling. Got me too shitty to think.'

'Pity. You know he's not going with us? Ear trouble. Never been overseas—Koala Bear Club, fully paid up. Glad to be rid of the cunt.' Koala Bear Club? Not to be exported or shot at.

This was at the very heart of my troubles with the army. So many men like this RSM. Thirty years service, thirty years of continual conflict. The Second World War, Korea, Borneo, Malaya, Vietnam—and never heard the call. Served only themselves, took no risk, and blocked up the system from the top. Sound familiar to you? I'll bet it does. I'd started to pester the administration for transfers by now, to other Corps, to something productive, something different, anything but copper's work. Nothing doing. OK, let me out then. Nothing doing.

My next task was with Dave, at a camp for school cadets. We turned up at the training complex, out in the bush somewhere, about 9.30 in the morning. There was the potbelly brigade—sergeants, staff sergeants, couple of warrant officers. CMF idiots, drinking piss in their little mess. Don't know what we were supposed to be training the kids in; we didn't get that far. One of this bunch sauntered out, gave us a list of jobs, pointed to the shovels, told us there were half a dozen Diggers to help; said, 'Get to it'.

'Fuck you!' Dave and I got back in his car and we were gone, back to base. I packed up, Dave went home for some stuff. I sat on the bed and went insane looking at the wall.

Then Dave honked the horn outside. I got up off the bed and we left. Dave later turned back. I did not.

And in the intervening years what has happened? We've gone backwards even further, as people. The tested are not heard from. True women and soldiers are denied voice, because they tend to preach compassion, continuity, a sense of duty. Too hard, too long term. So the harlots, swindlers, prancing academics, crawlers and salesmen hold sway. Over what? You may well ask. Very little, the way things are going. There must be one word to describe these people, the ones who now hold sway. There is. Cunts. Funny, that! Backed up by the cruisers, and the time-servers.

Does this offend you? It's virtually all I've been talking about since you sat down. The killing, the rooting, the boozing, the bravery, the cowardice and the yarns are all true. But why are you seeing *them*?

Turn away from these images now, and look back along the track that has led us to here. Look all the way back to where the track begins. Try to ensure that you notice everyone who has halted at a point along the way—what they're doing, what they're thinking, what they're getting out of all this. Can you see it all? If you can, you've just viewed life from the front.

And if a clique of cunts can run our system, why can't we all?

Chapter 15

Time to tell you the ending, or the middle . . . whatever. Anyway, we're back—back in country. One last look. One last lesson? No . . . I know you now. Let's call it affirmation.

This Op wasn't going anywhere. Too late for Tet, terrain no one could hide in, particularly by day. We'd been dragging arse around in company formation for days, through hot, barren, featureless grassland studded with copses of low stunted trees, with scraggly scrub beneath. Depressing country. Good ground for techno-warfare, but that wasn't our trade, not ours or theirs. At best, a trickle of ones or twos could pass unnoticed at night. But no trace remained of their passing for us to find—the enemy weren't here. There were many well-defined tracks, which indicated we were working off aerial reconnaissance intelligence; very interesting to desk observers but usually futile exercises for us on the ground.

Late in the afternoon of a mongrel of a day, the order was passed to prepare for a hot insurgency. Evidence of the formation of a battalion-strength VC or NVA unit had been detected some miles from our position. 'Hot insurgency' was a term not many of us were familiar with, but the general view at ground level was that it meant a quick chopper drop within shooting range of a known enemy. This proved correct. Funnily enough, we were going into just the type of incident the SAS would automatically be coming out of. About an hour was needed to call in all our search patrols, count heads and then secure a landing zone.

There were just enough choppers to take us in two flights, which was great for me because it meant I could go in the second flight. It also meant that the pilots risked two landings. They were Yanks; only the best, they were up to it. I flew in with the rearguard, sitting on the ledge close to the gunner—watch where the barrel goes and you see everything. We were flying into the dusk.

Our first sight of the general destination was heartening. Undulating golden hills with streams tracing the gullies, trees concealing the water. Our destination was the rapidly approaching flat grassland ending in thick scrub merging into pockets of tall forest. The blackened, still smouldering patches here and there on the plain confirmed recent bombing or shelling.

As we dropped I could see CSM's burly frame in the swirling dry grass of the landing zone, directing choppers, pointing men in various directions. The scene was fluid: men melted into the grass; choppers touched earth and then rose, nose down, tail up, and disappeared.

'There you are, Crowls!' CSM yelled above the clatter. 'We must all be here, then!'

He never tired of that joke. I did, but as he organised my order of flight, I privately approved of it nonetheless.

As I jumped clear and ran crouching to where he'd pointed, the company moved out and into the scrub for a kilometre or more. Just as we reached the treeline, darkness threatened. We set about harbouring for the night. At last light we were still standing, quietly sorting out positions for eighty or so men, when Spooky turned up with two of its mates. Spooky was a US helicopter gunship equipped with rockets, miniguns, a searing searchlight and a PA system that loosened your teeth from a thousand feet up. The mates were simpler machines with rudimentary searchlights, miniguns, possibly rockets.

Their role in relation to night-harbouring infantry units is worth describing. They'd been sent in in response to OC's final radioed location report for the night. That had been intended to tell command where we were, not get us put to bed US-style. Spooky hovered about twelve metres above our heads, its PA blaring out 'Don't move while the light is shining on you!'

The light pierced the canopy, transforming the night into an X-ray film. Jungle green uniforms and webbing turned grey, suntanned faces, necks and arms glowed corpse-white, lips were blue, veins stood out blue-black and knotted. Nobody moved. Who would? Even the enemy only had to stand still to be safe—no one was recognisable. Spooky slyly moved around our harbour area, snuffling for something to shoot at.

Meanwhile its mates were giving the surrounding area a savage strafing with miniguns. These were multi-barrelled machine guns, 7.62 mm, capable of thousands of rounds a minute. In action, they barked a cougar's cough right in your ear and cut a line through the sky metres wide with solid, unbroken, red tracer. We endured this for ten minutes or so, then they shoved off.

It was our only contact with this crude lunacy, so I guess it was the only time we worked directly under US dictates. It occurred to me then that my growing suspicions were well founded. Any ground troops needing this sort of mindless support to protect them were not well trained, or not listened to. The money was going on toys for the US elite. 'Fuck the rabble, no point in investing in them! They serve their purpose.'

We were different; effectively trained. We all saw to it. We quietly regrouped, moved clear of this area and set up secure harbour elsewhere, unaided. Some time after midnight one of our perimeter guns barked out, then quiet reigned for the rest of the night. After first light clearing-patrol we were off on the bearing of the previous night. Ten metres from our harbour perimeter we passed the body of a soldier killed by the gun picquet during the night. He was a solid bastard, quite tall, mid to late forties, square, heavy-featured face, more Chinese than Vietnamese. He lay on his back, legs and arms splayed out, relaxed. He was barefoot; his tyre-rubber sandals were discarded nearby. He was dressed in black trousers and a grey, collarless flannelette shirt. His face, hands and feet were the light chalk-grey of potter's clay, his hair greying. He'd been shot in the back; no wound was visible. No weapon or personal effects remained. He still bore the aura of authority.

The company pursued its directed course until late morning, flanking patrols out, making good distance. We entered a tall green forest copse with slender silver trunks and slanting bars of sunlight shimmering with life. Our lead scouts immediately encountered the perimeter shell scrapes of what proved to be a battalion-size enemy harbour. The red soil was still damp. We entered and spread out through the area to confirm our suspicions.

This was the camp of an enemy on the move, not a preparation for a permanent system. Small patrols were sent to find the exiting direction of the battalion so we could start the chase. In the meantime we hit the deck to wait. Some of us were searching the position for other useful clues. I was sitting on my pack yapping to Pete, keeping a quiet eye out over the grass field.

Crack! Enemy here! Where? Visibility was not good, the trees closely spaced, scrub everywhere. *Crack!* From somewhere else! Rifle shots. Fucking sniper. A number of men were caught away from their sections. Radio contact is noisy in this sort of situation, it gives position on sender and receiver. *Crack!* A new location. The sound was muted and bent by the whispering canopy above. The sniper was well hidden. *Crack!* He'd moved again. This time a section got a direction, swept the area— nothing. *Crack!*

Close to three hours later the position hadn't changed. Then Griffo was shot in the leg. Pete sprinted over to tend him, and Big Mick's roar went out. He'd got a bead on the bastard. His section swept the tangled growth. A short fusillade thumped into the canopy above. Big Mick ripped through the scrub chasing a wounded sniper and then yelled out, 'Grennaaade!' so we could take cover. *Crummpp!*

'It's OK . . . got him!'

I made my way to where Griffo was lying, surrounded by a group of Diggers waiting for a role to play, while one or two others got in Pete's way. Griffo's trousers were down by now, and he didn't look too bad: a nice neat hole through the upper right thigh, his underpants passable. He was kicking up a stink about the pain—a good sign. He was also quick to point out that he was in no mood to hear any fucking RTA jokes from any of us dickheads. Pete packed the wound despite Makka's help and they got the remains of his trousers back up. Griffo became his usual caustic self. Reminded us that he was going ta-tas, accused Dave of shooting him to gain promotion, then started grizzling about how long the chopper was taking. Wanted a beer.

Meanwhile his evacuation was being organised, so while the chopper was getting in to us we went back to our positions. Pete was heading for the landing zone with Griffo, so I went back alone. Makka insisted on carrying Griffo out and fucked his back up again, so *he* didn't last much longer either. As I returned, all was quiet and the tension was easing. There was just Big Mick's muted growl at the back of me telling some of his men, new boys, how the burial of a brave soldier is conducted. I wasn't about to be the one to try and tear Mick off them if they didn't comply. Fuck 'em, they shouldn't have had to be told.

I got back to where my pack lay, and noticed a low bough on the tree near it. Good seat height. I was on the edge of the treeline, overlooking a wide, oval clearing of thigh-height grass. Across the clearing, perhaps 150 metres away, the forest began again. I saw one of the platoons deploy directly in front of me in the grass. Beaut, I thought, let's have a sit down on that bough, rifle on the lap—roll a fag, take in the view of the trees.

The other sniper, the invisible one, rose up before me from the grass, thirty metres away. Almost among the platoon hidden in the grass at my front. I caught a glimpse of his face as he turned once to check for danger before running away toward the far treeline. A young version of the body on the track this morning. Tall, with broad shoulders and powerful limbs. He wore jungle greens still with the sheen of newness, black boots and a green webbing belt, and he carried an M1 carbine or similar.

How he could run! Straight across the clearing, hair shimmering, tearing his path to freedom, driven by the sheer will to live. I watched him until he made the cover of the far trees and disappeared. Without a doubt he was watched by others, but in these situations you either respond or shut up. Perhaps, like me, they decided that bodycount mentality had no place in a soldier's philosophy. I snapped out of it and lit the fag. Shortly afterwards I heard the dustoff chopper hover and then take off, bearing Griffo away on the first leg of the journey returning him home to Australia.

Later that evening, after we'd harboured and settled for the night, I was returning to my position after a cautious social roam around when I was hissed at by Big Mick. His bowler-hatted head was peering at me over the high thick scrub. 'Hey Crowls, over here!' I walked over and he led me into the thicket he was camped in. In a small sandy patch were Patto and another member of Mick's section, sitting around a deeply dug hole in its centre. A brew mug was heating up on the little tin stove at the bottom, too low to betray much light at ground level, even now in the full dark.

'Making coffee—do with some?' offered Mick. I sat down. Mick added five sachets of coffee, six sugars and half a tube of sweetened condensed milk to the pint metal mug. I was tempted to reverse my decision. Then he pulled a seven ounce bottle of rum from his pack and poured that in, which cheered me beyond caring.

We sat quietly and passed the cup around. It was superb. Mick reminisced in muted tones about a London dockside pub built into the underside of a Thames bridge. They served lethal scrumpy cider in pint mugs and the fights that it provoked were entertaining. Mick chuckled at the memory. We looked up at the stars and unwound. Nothing of consequence was said. I was honoured to be in the company of true soldiers, and the moment will last in my heart to my dying breath.

Next morning, at first light, we were off again, searching out the enemy. Perhaps it has to be done. But not here; not anywhere but at home.

What's that? . . . Soldier? Definition? OK, fair enough.

Soldier: member of an army, especially a private or an NCO; usually a person of military skill or experience who perseveres doggedly, carries on loyally, regardless of orders, to help safeguard equity for all.

But what's in a name?

CHAPTER 16

WELL, WE'RE BACK IN THE PINK ROOM. Wasn't so tough, was it? Not much of a ride maybe; you'd probably get better at the movies, or on the late news. Or at the Disneyland of your choice—if you had the imagination, the money, the connections. But on this ride, hopefully, you were thinking about things.

Let's do a bit of a rollcall. Just a few, in random order. I won't include everyone—certainly not the cunts. Who knows, they may have changed, and might be offended to have the past dragged up into the present. I'll give them the chance to seethe in anonymity. So, are you clear about this? Just because I don't mention somebody you know, that doesn't make them a cunt or mean they were no good.

Tizzy. Tizzy, or his wife, or perhaps both of them, fell in love with the woodlands around Woodside. Probably reminded them of England, only better—it was in Australia. Huge fires go through there now and then, lit by crazy, worthless shitheads. Tizzy died saving the family home. Whether it was the safety of their kids or the marital memories that drove him to his untimely end, I don't know. But that sort of action about sums up this little bloke—branded an administrator, always a soldier. He never did get my existence sorted out on paper, but he led us well and truly out of a place of certain death. And he taught many people to be *soldiers*, for which he should be remembered.

Woofer. Woofer is still switched on, and walking among you. The purest *soldier* I've ever met. He still scouts, still sees everything, still communicates in hand signals. Woofer has been described in other books, because his war exploits went on for years, and under more than one flag. Woofer believed armed conflict could solve a nation's problems, and it's only fair to say he is a master of his craft. His own book, if he ever gets it down, I will buy and keep, even though and perhaps because I will not feature in it.

Fuzz. I saw Fuzz in the Hay Street mall in the centre of Perth two years or so after I beat the court martial I'd copped for going on the run. He was working for Telecom again and he seemed lost. I'd never seen that in him. Compassion, craziness, companionship, leadership, yes. But never lost. I was in a hurry at the time, and there's heaps of his surname in the phone book. Fuzz didn't just look lost, he *was* lost, to me at least. He isn't now. I saw him the other day. Makka dragged him in and he looks years younger than me. Still the same, warm and honest. He's a college lecturer; seems he's found his vocation. Good to see.

Tank. I know I set Tank up as a central character near the beginning of the story, and then didn't really go on with him. That's because at first sight I saw him as a person of consequence—which he was—but he never confided in me and I never saw him in action. He ranked physically in the top three of the company. A judo champion. Let Big Mick miss with the first telling punch and Tank would have been a fair bet. But Tank was a true wrestler; a persuader, a debater. Otherwise I'd have been fucking crippled years ago, considering the way I used to wind the big bastard up. Tank saw and did it all and just shut up. A true soldier. He went back to teaching and at last call was a headmaster. I'm told he is now a very quiet man. He said very little when I knew him, but I'd never have described him as quiet. I wonder sometimes what he makes of it all now.

Pigpen. I last saw Pigpen when we went out on the town with a mate of his, in Brisbane, just before I walked out on it all.

He'd taken me out several times—usually class acts. One night we saw a forty-year-old stripper hide a plastic banana. The poodle never appeared, but it was a rugby show at a big city hotel, so maybe that had just been a come-on. But this last time was better than all that. We were standing at the counter eating a pie and peas at Harry's Stand In The Gutter caravan cafe. Pigpen's hefty mate picked a fight with some big bearded prick up the counter from us and smacked him unconscious with one almighty blow. I was enjoying the pie up to then and so, I suspect, was the bearded bloke. Pigpen's mate had to go then, he was due to go on duty—he was a copper. Pigpen also fell out with Dave a few years ago, over some stupid tribal issue. I worry about the company he's keeping, but he's still alive, and running his own business. What a soldier he was! Christ, I wouldn't be on the other side for anything.

Duntroon. Yes, well, Duntroon. Born to the breed—didn't need guts, just breeding and training. He was a good soldier at heart, but his training taught him to grab the edge. He threw his pips on the cashier's table and went off to study law, I believe. Whatever it was, it's brought him a degree of wealth and privilege but not enduring renown. He just didn't have it in him to think about leadership objectively. The single-minded pursuit of facile reward at the expense of the truly worthy is central to our leadership crisis today, as it has been through all eternity.

Staff. This old bastard's still alive, I believe. Bet he's waiting for the next ship. If we stay at peace he'll live forever.

CSM. I once thought he'd lost his dreams. It turns out he didn't. He stayed on, ending up a Major, dealing in personnel and administrative matters in Perth. It must have driven him crazy at times, but I was pleased to hear he'd stayed on. He was far too good to deliver softdrinks, even though he wasn't the friendliest of bastards at times—typical ex-SAS.

OC. OC suspended all disbelief by reaching the rank of brigadier. Suspended mine, anyway. Very few of his great calibre get so high. Peaches said to me recently, 'You know, if we hadn't had OC our company would've been fucked'. I had to agree with him. I've seen few, if any, better. It's a pity OC didn't find it easier to speak his mind in front of crowds—there's no knowing where he might have ended up. Literally. I had him picked for a teacher after he got the arse from the army, but he didn't get the arse from the army. And now, with soldiering behind him, he manages a retirement home. He'd be good at that too.

Peaches. Peaches lives on the other side of Perth from me and is a wharfie; has been virtually since he got out. It's still a tough way of life to hang on to, they're well-paid manual workers, a situation that seems to infuriate many people. His current wife is his third. She is big, intelligent, attractive and, in my opinion, long suffering. They have three young children. He has a grown-up son from an earlier marriage living somewhere nearby. Peaches served only six months in the field on the tour and still ranked second or third on our unofficial company-kill board at the end. And he served six months as a conscientious objector. Some bastards are never happy—Peaches is one of them. Remorse cripples him still.

Peaches was the finest fighting platform I've ever seen. It's no wonder the army exploited him. I would have done the same in their position. It's a pity neither of us know how to repair the spiritual damage done to all concerned. I suspect Peaches is fighting bad health—one of many from the company—but it's hard to say. Peaches is no whinger.

He decked a provoking young security guard a year or so back, then a month later the gutless cunt snivelled to the courts, determined to gain his own twisted form of justice. Peaches won the verdict on the grounds of reasonable provocation and a more forthright defence, so he hadn't lost any of his old skills. Bravery, loyalty, integrity and a funny sense of cunning. Maybe I just worry too much about him.

Did I mention that Peaches demonstrated he was the worst form of dickhead? Don't believe I did. He was already in the CMF when his year went into the barrel. He was exempt. He volunteered. Serves him right.

Big Mick. Big Mick got married. You should have seen her! Six foot and bloody good-looking too. Must have liked warriors. If they breed, we're covered for the next generation. Mick made regimental sergeant major—who was there to stop him?

Banjo. Fucking Banjo, the big lazy prick. Ended up in CMF, a weekend warrior, only on permanent staff. Sergeant major was enough to see him through to retirement. What a waste of grassroots leadership. He is a broken promise.

Jock. Jock made it to regimental sergeant major. He died of cancer before retiring. To me, Jock was another OC in terms of leadership and judgement—except that he was an accomplished speaker who didn't set his sights high enough. RSM isn't *that* high. I have been told his vision narrowed in peacetime, that he became insular, self-centred. If that did happen to Jock then it can happen to anyone, and it saddens me.

Ex-Corporal Bob. Bob made it to RSM also—might still be serving. I hope so. If you're a subordinate of his, ask him about the trip to Vungers. Peaches told me a fair bit of what happened and it's fucking hilarious. Yes, Bob had his wild side, which just makes his serious side all the more commendable.

Brian. I saw Brian on TV about 1986. It was a group discussion show, explaining how Vets had had a mongrel of a deal with marriage. Brian was having a bleat about how cruel the world was, marriagewise anyway. He wore a beard, which looked good on him—more than I can say for Peaches' Ho Chi Minh effort. Brian sat with a few other downtrodden howlers all telling much the same story. Now, this would have been Brian's second marriage. Hang on, sixteen years—could have been his thirteenth. It seemed to me, and to Peaches, who saw the same show—and he only watches telly when he's going to the fridge for a beer—that Brian ought to pick the right woman and stick with her. Brian . . . you're fine! A public servant who made the first grade without killing anyone.

Dave. After we drove out of the base that day, Dave went on the run with me for about three weeks, but his wife contacted us and told him she was near death's door and that the army wanted him back. He went back, knowing it was all bullshit, stuck it for thirty minutes, got the fighting spirit again and started punching the exit button. Two and a half years later the army admitted defeat and discharged him psychologically unsound. He'd fought his way right through the line. Dave's fucking crazy. I knew that the instant I first saw him.

The army had tried to straighten him out by employing counselling officers, psychologists, psychiatrists, and MPs. Smart move, that one! All these people were safe only when they stood quietly before Dave while he carefully and concisely explained to them what stupid, pumped up, worthless cunts they were.

Dave went into pubs. Drinking in them and hustling pool until money got tight. Then mopping floors, rolling barrels, chucking mugs out. A pause for a bit of mining, prospecting, going native in the Daintree, then right on up the ladder to publican. He shed the wife along the way, but women still like him—not his first wife, of course. What sort of pub? Switch on! An early opener for drains, cunts and lunatics.

Once he beats this rap for grievous bodily harm against a now one-eyed idiot who's fortunate to still be alive, Dave'll be back in the swing of things again. That's Dave's problem. His particular craziness. He has a rough and ready compassion for anyone, anyone on earth. But don't ever be a cunt to anyone in his presence, or show him less than basic courtesy, it insults his intelligence. He still wins at cards but won't live off it; still sees ahead but won't capitalise. He enjoys a good lifestyle and is as well liked as ever—loved even, in some quarters, for his unsurpassed sense of control and his fine sense of justice.

Makka. In some ways, Makka's the most special person in this rollcall—special because he is the most representative member of the group. He did the hard early part of the tour with us. During that time he almost certainly killed, and he saw a lot of shit he didn't want to see. That's what motivated his move out of the company. A job as RP was going and, in fairness, he'd have made a pretty good copper. He had something of that Aussie cum Scots 'straight down the line' approach to justice and fair play. Like Hipslops. Makka stuck it out with the RPs for several months then, after Lenny chucked it in, he put his hand up and rejoined the company and became a section commander. He went back to Lenny's old platoon, and stayed with it until the end of the tour.

Makka's is a common story in that he saw what was right, saw what was wrong, and tried everything he could to find a place in this organisation where he could do no harm but not have to renounce his country's government's actions. He wanted to stay a citizen of his country and he succeeded at every level.

Homecoming hit the Makkas of this war the hardest. Despised by most of you for being killers. He was accepted, but not always warmly, by his company. Left for dead by everyone, it must have seemed to him. Makka has coped with life, he's a gutsy bastard—a far from common characteristic in today's world—but I wouldn't envy him what he has got from life. I wouldn't describe him as crazy, but he has lived with despair all his adult life, and his despair is not a delusion of his own making. It is a very real affliction, a physical affliction, which few are prepared to see.

There are several thousand Makkas in this country. People who truly strived, to no worthy end, believing that those who led us were good. People like Makka will never know peace. I wish this were not true. They hold great value, once they think for themselves.

Lenny. Lenny disappeared from my view down Barrack Street one night in 1971, and went back to being a blackfella. He must have influenced many of his people, because around '75 or '76 he started to get on the TV, usually standing silently by the right shoulder of the talker, sometimes making a statement himself, about his people's issues. At one point he was interviewed when leaving for Libya with a contingent of other Aboriginal leaders, to attend a liberation seminar sponsored by Colonel Gaddafi. Lenny said, 'Well, it doesn't cost anybody anything to look'. The local press was taking the line that these black bastards might learn to kill from this crazy Arab. They didn't know Lenny. What could anyone tell Lenny about killing that we hadn't taught him?

I recently renewed my relationship with Lenny. I got his address through the electoral roll, after tracking him unsuccessfully everywhere from Telecom to Registrar for Births and

Deaths, and then wrote to him. (Did you know you can't trace a friend through these agencies? I'll bet if I was a fucking debt collector they'd talk to me.)

Lenny phoned me back, said he'd catch up with me, gave me his unlisted phone number. It was a bodgie number of course; all manner of cranks dogged his every step. We repeated the exercise several times—letter, phone call—and finally his wife dropped him at my home late one afternoon while she continued on to visit her mother in the next suburb. We sat out under the pergola watching the last of the sun shining down on our back garden and reminisced as old soldiers do, our minds jumping around like fleas from old memory to old memory, interspersed with glimpses of the present, some chilled white cask wine and a couple of cigarettes.

He talked in snatches about contacts we had both been involved in. 'Remember when Yabbie shot one of that patrol that walked right past ya? Pritch and me were cut off from you lot, down at the creek filling water bottles. I was holding the gun, Pritch was doing the filling. Fuck that, I wasn't gunna shoot. They'd of got past.' That was the time CSM had held his fire. 'Remember the night we had that blanket bombing drop right by our harbour. Fuck, that was big.' Dave had also mentioned that night. I was there too but I simply cannot remember it. It will not come back. Nor the desolated forest with napalm hanging like ghostly stalactites from limbs and shrubs. Some things I find too ridiculous to remember—it's a failing of mine. Dave can even remember boiling a brew on a particular day.

Lenny remarked out of the blue, 'I met that cunt Ban, up Geraldton way, a while back.'

'Ban?'

'Our interpreter. That was his fuckin' name, wasn't it?'

'Ah, you mean *Bé*. Don't worry, Dave calls him Bic.'

'Bé, eh. Sure it was him. That cunt had no sense of country. Didn't give a fuck about his people.'

Sandy came home from work then and joined us. Sandy's a welfare worker, so they had a fair bit to talk about: hopes, common goals. I left them to it and started rattling around in the kitchen. Then Sandy relieved me, cooked the food I'd prepared and we had a meal, talking about Lenny's current activities. He was too ill now to hold high office, like the Aboriginal Legal Service, but mentioned he still ran a community settlement and had an involvement with the Aboriginal and Torres Strait Islander Commission—still stirred the shit where he could. A veteran's pension provided his income.

Lenny's wife, Maureen, collected him just as we finished dinner, worst luck. Lenny was physically a shadow of his former self—ravaged by a mysterious ailment that was attacking his vital organs, killing them one by one. His proud face and graceful hands were the only reminders of what had once been.

I didn't see him for a week or so, then he phoned suggesting that we meet for another yap. Could I collect him, take him to his community's settlement to sort out a funding problem, then go to my place for a while? His house was small, and located in a poor suburb not far from my own. It had weathered the rigours of five now mostly grown-up children, and was bracing itself against the onslaught of the first four grandchildren, all now toddlers. Lenny and Clive, a young relative, joined me in my old Fiat and we headed north to visit the community.

It was a place more than a community. There were few people there. Lenny, I knew, had wanted me to see it, and I did. And I saw more—I saw Lenny the man. He was not a high-profile leader. He was a prime-mover. He had started the movement for justice that ultimately ran under the banner of Black Deaths in Custody. He had served his time in this State's harsh interior, supporting and defending Aboriginals in court. He was no lawyer, but a drink or two in the pub at day's end with the circuit judge would often affect the sentence, if not the verdict at the end of the trial.

Lenny later headed that legal service but I doubt that he was popular with the staff. He had a habit of reminding lawyers and council elders that they had a job to do, that they were servants, not gods. Land claims, civil rights, calls for justice—Lenny spent his adult life out in the heat, the dust, the flies, defending the people, looking just like any other busted-down blackfella, and suffering the abuse and incarceration that naturally followed on. Others among his people grabbed the microphones and the cameras, and the benefits. Lenny was not a showman. When first I met him he was a soldier, and he is still.

Your guide. I stayed out of reach of the army for nine months. Devised a foolproof way to beat the MPs. Lived at home, got a job and a car, paid taxes. They came to my home four or five times but my six-year-old brother Dave told them I didn't live there. I handed myself in eventually. I was getting promotions in my work and wanted to settle my future. The MPs were shat off with me when I walked in alone. They said they'd been staking out my home for nights and nights and were bound to catch me. I'll take their word for it, but I was usually at home. I got an honourable discharge—after they'd relieved me of my hooks and my pension fund. Well, let them shove it all up their arses! They didn't get *me*.

That'll have to do for the rollcall. I want to get back to the real war for a moment. To do that, I need to tell you about two days and a night in Melbourne, at a wet and wintery time in 1988. I was there attending a course, a company information course at the national head office of the Pommy international firm I worked for. I'd been there a day, along with other junior managers, learning what the company was now doing and where it was going. Most of the others were much younger than me, which was a drag because this particular course was widely considered to be both a load of empty bullshit and a ripper, drink till you drop, event. I hadn't found it so. Each division chief had come to the auditorium and given a speech. The messages were veiled, almost impenetrable. That night I woke at 3 am in my hotel room on the ninth floor, and looked down on the glittering-wet Melbourne street. It was drizzling; the street lights glowed orange, subdued with chilly mist. The tram tracks were shining and silent at this hour. Across the road stood a granite cenotaph, one I'd seen several times before on other trips—particularly once, as a small child, from my father's car. I'd asked Dad what it was and he'd said it was a war memorial, but wouldn't stop to show me over it. From the ninth floor of the hotel I took in the austere, eerie architecture for a moment, then went back to bed.

On the second day at the course the word 'matrix' appeared on the overhead screen, again and again, sometimes with a graphic looking much like a diagram of an atom. Now I knew what they were talking about, even though their talks were no clearer. 'Matrix' is not a commercial word. It means a womb or mould, or a small body of ore in which the most gems are contained. The executives were talking about exclusion, the deliberate pruning of staff to increase some people's personal share of the wealth.

Well, that was me fucked. At morning coffee time I thought, let's do something different. I crossed the road, darting between the cars, the trams and their concrete barriers, and went up to the cenotaph. It was very large, with steps leading everywhere, and suitably imposing battlements—the inevitable granite dick thrusting skywards, with the bullshit badge etched on it. The Rising Sun of the Defence Forces. Not many people were there. I had a walk around and saw a stairway going down into the structure, much like the entrance to the tunnel I'd hesitated at so long ago. I went down the steps and found the door ajar, a big, steel-strapped, studded door. Then through the door, down three more steps and I was in a dim, echoing stone crypt. It had an ornate vaulted ceiling, discreet stained-glass windows passing filtered light down, and a flagstone floor. High up on the walls there were battle standards, the real things, powdering slowly into dust, bearing the names of past battalions and the battles they'd been in. There were honour boards too, lists of the dead.

It was a grave for those who hadn't returned. In the centre of the crypt, mounted on a low plinth, dwarfing any man, towered the figure of a soldier cast in bronze. Hatless, unarmed, wearing field dress, bandoliers across the chest, arms extended as if to embrace. It reminded me starkly of the dream that had haunted me for the first ten years after my return from Vietnam.

I am standing on a rocky outcrop facing a low mountain range, purple-black now as the sun sets behind it. I am hatless, unarmed, with no insignia, just greens and boots. The rocky outcrop is not high. I can jump from it to the floor of the dark, featureless plain. The sunset is beautiful, briefly scribing the mountains in a line of searing gold light.

Then the full moon emerges, masked by phosphorescent bands of silver-red cloud. As I look, a temple appears in the middle distance, chalk-white, glowing faintly in the moon's first misleading rays. It's a temple surrounded by high-tiered battlements—only the ornate, twisting, conspiring towers thrusting heavenward above them reveal the structure's true purpose.

    I decide to take a look, bending my knees as I hop off the outcrop on to the mute, lifeless ground. Progress is easy; nothing but distance stands between me and the temple. When I reach it the structure is a puzzle. The battlements have wide, inviting stairs leading up them, right up to the top, tier by tier. Then they pass down and through to the temple proper, presumably. But this I cannot see, so I attempt to. I ascend the wide staircase, which feels slightly spongy underfoot. I look down and see that it's made of large, chalk-white sandbags, not marble blocks as I'd supposed. I reach the top of the first tier and sense a movement, over by the parapet. I look that way, not moving from where I stand. It's a young American, beckoning. It is his expression that beckons—his swaddling has rotted and gapes open to reveal his face and one arm. His bagged body forms part of the structure; his face is a question. I don't know the answer to his question and it grieves me. It becomes mine also. Why is he here? I start to move on, to learn more, and I realise that he and I are not alone. The whole structure is alive: all the blocks are bags, they're all swaddling bags, they're all bodies, they are all people. They are underfoot and all around me, seething now and finding voice.

    They are not enemy; they are everyone.